FOUR MAJOR PLAYS
OF CHIKAMATSU

Translated by DONALD KEENE

D0979972

COLUMBIA UNIVERSITY PRESS

New York

These translations are dedicated to

TSUNEARI FUKUDA

translator of Shakespeare

All the material published in this volume
appears in MAJOR PLAYS OF
CHIKAMATSU, which, as Number LXVI
of the Records of Civilization Sources and
Studies, was translated with the help of funds
granted by Carnegie Corporation of New York.
That Corporation is not, however, the author,
owner, publisher, or proprietor of this
publication, and is not to be understood as
approving by virtue of its grant any of the
statements made or views expressed therein.

Prepared for the Columbia College
Program of Translations from the Oriental Classics
Wm. Theodore de Bary, Editor

UNESCO COLLECTION OF REPRESENTATIVE WORKS—
JAPANESE SERIES
This work has been accepted in the Japanese Translations
Series of the UNESCO Collection of Representative Works,
jointly sponsored by the United Nations Educational,
Scientific, and Cultural Organization (UNESCO) and the
Government of Japan

CONTENTS

PREFACE

The plays of Chikamatsu Monzaemon were the most difficult works I have translated. *Any* work in Japanese is likely to be difficult to translate into English, but these plays presented exceptional problems. The language, especially the parts sung by the narrator in his own voice (as opposed to the parts recited in the persona of one or another character), abounds in complicated word play. But even when I thought I had at last unraveled the allusions, puns, and other complexities, it was by no means easy conveying in English what they meant in context. The problem of translating Chikamatsu had a further ramification: because his works are plays, I hoped that they might be staged by English-speaking actors; the translation therefore had to be not only accurate (and, I hoped, poetic) but natural, so that it would not sound stilted in performance.

In the years since the translations were first published, I have been fortunate enough to have heard several on the radio and to have seen one performed on a New York stage. I confess that I winced more than once as I listened to my English versions, wishing that the wording had been somewhat more felicitous, but (recognizing my limitations) my predominant feeling was joy that I had had the good fortune to introduce these plays of Chikamatsu to Western audiences.

Of course, problems must be overcome before the plays can be successfully staged in translation. The puppet theater, for which Chikamatsu wrote his major works, is strikingly unlike the Western theaters where realistic plays are customarily presented. Not only are all the roles taken by puppets operated by men who appear in full view of the audience, but one or more chanters, visible at the side of the stage, declaim and sing the texts to samisen accompaniment. A person who knows the theater of Chikamatsu only from photographs of puppet performances may well wonder how it is possible to sustain dramatic illusion when the audience can see, all too plainly, that the movements and voices of the puppets are produced by external agents. In performance, however, one really does forget the operators, and if from time to time one looks at them rather than at the puppets, it is for the pleasure of seeing these somehow tragic witnesses as they follow the puppets around the stage.

Chikamatsu is believed to have written his plays for performances by puppets because he was dissatisfied with the liberties taken with the texts by Kabuki actors; the puppets, having no personalities of their own or special fortes to display, performed the texts as written. In contrast, the Kabuki actors took greater and greater liberties over the years. In some cases they went so far as to transform the nature of the roles in the attempt to bring out histrionic possibilities they supposed they had detected. In recent years, however, other actors, repudiating the changes and accretions that had become traditional, have returned to Chikamatsu's original texts. Their successes demonstrate that no one knew better than Chikamatsu himself how to move audiences.

The plays chosen for this volume include some of Chikamatsu's best-known works. Three of the four are *sewamono,* tragedies based on real incidents known to contemporary audiences. They are likely at times to strike Western readers as being startlingly close to our own twentieth-century dramas, which have for their heroes not the kings and generals of Elizabethan tragedy but ordinary, socially humble men who are driven by overpowering emotions to risk and suffer death. The *jidaimono,* or historical works, represented here by *The Battles of Coxinga,* are filled with larger-than-life demonstrations of loyalty, courage, resolution, and other virtues. The continued popularity of these plays, even in times that seem to allow little possibility for heroics, is testimony to Chikamatsu's mastery of language and dramatic effectiveness.

Chikamatsu was for long burdened with the unfortunate sobriquet "the Japanese Shakespeare." Comparisons of this kind are rarely germane, but probably no more was meant than that Chikamatsu was the greatest Japanese dramatist, a distinction that few today would deny him.

INTRODUCTION

In the late nineteenth century, when Japanese first became aware of the glories of Western literature, they felt impelled to discover a "Japanese Shakespeare." Their unanimous choice for this honor was Chikamatsu Monzaemon (1653–1725), an unfortunate identification from which Chikamatsu's reputation in the West has suffered since. Western readers who hope that Chikamatsu will prove a second Shakespeare are bound to be disappointed: there never lived a second Shakespeare. Chikamatsu's plays offer instead a vivid picture of a unique age in Japan, and have a special importance among the dramas of the world in that they constitute the first mature tragedies written about the common man.

One reason why comparisons between Chikamatsu and the dramatists of Europe are meaningful only intermittently is that he lived in a society virtually sealed off from the rest of the world. During the period of his career Japanese subjects were forbidden by law to journey abroad, and the only visitors to Japan were a handful of Chinese and Dutch traders carefully isolated at the port of Nagasaki. Chikamatsu never read a foreign play, and he knew nothing of the theater outside his country. Because, unlike most European dramatists, he shared no traditions with writers abroad, his plays sometimes astonish us by a modernity not encountered in the West for another century or more, and sometimes equally by a violence or an uncontrolled fantasy which we associate with a more primitive theater. But this seeming modernity or primitivity is misleading, and really means only that Chikamatsu's development in isolation did not follow the course of the drama in Europe.

Another important difference dividing Chikamatsu from European playwrights was that he wrote his major works for the puppet theater. The special demands of this theater obliged Chikamatsu to conceive his plays in a manner which sometimes weakens their literary value: spectacular scenes of mayhem or superhuman feats may be intensely exciting when seen in a puppet performance, but when read as one reads a Western play they often seem absurdly exaggerated.

Chikamatsu, however, was not merely a skillful craftsman of the puppet theater. In his domestic tragedies especially he proved that he was an artist of subtlety and imagination. But here again we are faced with a difficulty in attempting to compare his characters with those of Shakespeare, Racine, or other European dramatists. Unlike classic tragedy with its princes and princesses, Chikamatsu's domestic plays have for their heroes merchants or petty samurai whose sweethearts are apt to be prostitutes. The griefs of Jihei, the paper dealer, lack the dignity of Hamlet's; he is inevitably less a hero determining his own fate than a creature of circumstances. Though we cannot doubt the sincerity and strength of his emotions, their range is limited. Jihei's closest counterparts in the Western theater are probably found in the twentieth-century dramas of the little man whose dreams and aspirations are doomed to frustration.

The expression of Chikamatsu's plays offers similar problems. The dialogue is usually straightforward and marked by the flavor of actual speech. We might conclude from it that Chikamatsu belonged to an age of prose, but his descriptive passages, particularly the accounts of the suicide journeys of the unhappy lovers, have a complexity and intricacy of texture which equal the achievement of any Western age of poetry.

Finally, the morality in Chikamatsu's plays is often disconcertingly unlike that of Shakespeare (though perhaps not so dissimilar to certain French and Spanish dramatists). Considerations of honor may override all other sentiments; when one husband decides to kill his wife as a punishment for adultery he is encouraged by her father and brother. We may even be expected to sympathize with a man who deserts his loving wife and children to commit suicide with a prostitute.

The differences between Chikamatsu's society and that of Shakespeare's (or modern) Europe account for many features of his plays puzzling to readers hitherto familiar only with Western drama. The usages of the puppet theater, where a narrator recites not only lines for the mute puppets but also connecting descriptions, and where a certain exaggeration is necessary to impart the sentiments of living people to wooden creatures, may also be unfamiliar. I have attempted in the following pages to sketch some of the background of the plays, in the hope of clarifying points which may be troublesome to Western readers. At the same time, however, I do not wish to suggest that the plays require elaborate explanation. They should be immediately intelligible despite their occasional unfamiliarities. The matters I hope to elucidate in this introduction are of less importance to an understanding of Chikamatsu than a sensitivity to the themes of love and death which are the heart of his writings.

Chikamatsu's Career

Chikamatsu Monzaemon was born in 1653 in the province of Echizen, the second son of a minor samurai family named Sugimori.[1] In a brief account of himself written shortly before his death Chikamatsu stated, "I was born into a hereditary family of samurai but left the martial profession. I served in personal attendance on the nobility but never obtained the least court rank. I drifted in the market place but learned nothing of trade." This modest confession of failure as a samurai, noble, and merchant does not suggest how important a knowledge of these three classes was to prove in the composition of his plays.

We know little about Chikamatsu's youth. Apparently his family moved to Kyoto when he was still in his teens, and the boy served some years as a page to a noble family. At the time the nobility included patrons of the puppet theater, and Chikamatsu may have had a first meeting with some celebrated chanter in a princely mansion. His own family had literary talents, as we know from a family collection of *haiku* compiled in 1671 in which Chikamatsu's first published work appears:

Shirakumo ya	White clouds
Hana naki yama no	Cover the shame
Haji kakushi	Of the flowerless mountain.

Soon afterwards he left the household where he had been serving, and apparently stayed for a while at the Chikamatsu Temple in Ōmi

[1] See Mori Shū, *Chikamatsu Monzaemon*, pp. 12–15. Genealogical tables are reproduced in *Chikamatsu no Kenkyū to Shiryō*, pp. 57–72. Some scholars read Chikamatsu's surname as Suginomori.

Province. The sojourn may have led young Sugimori Nobumori (as he was then called) to take the stage name Chikamatsu, but this remains conjectural.[2]

Chikamatsu's career as a dramatist probably began in 1683 when, at the age of thirty, he wrote the puppet play *The Soga Successors* for the chanter Uji Kaga-no-jō. Some scholars, however, credit more than fifteen earlier, unsigned works to Chikamatsu. *The Soga Successors* was highly acclaimed, and the great chanter Takemoto Gidayū (1651–1714) used it to open his theater in Osaka in 1684. Two years later Chikamatsu wrote for Gidayū *Kagekiyo Victorious*,[3] so important a work that it is considered the first "new" puppet play.

Puppet plays of a sort go back in Japan at least as far as the twelfth century. The puppeteers, a gypsy-like people, wandered about the country, performing at festivals and wherever else there was a demand. The plays put on were probably elementary skits, perhaps incorporating legends of the shrines where they were performed. By the seventeenth century, when the puppet theater assumed much of its modern form, moralistic plays on Buddhist themes constituted the bulk of the repertory. Most puppet plays (or *jōruri*, as they were called) before *Kagekiyo Victorious* were crudely constructed and filled with stereotyped expressions. *Kagekiyo Victorious*, from its first unconventional phrases, proclaimed the appearance of a new star in the puppet theater.

Between 1684 and 1695 Chikamatsu also wrote many Kabuki plays, chiefly for Sakata Tōjūrō (1647–1709), the outstanding actor of the day. This collaboration proved so fruitful that in the next decade (1695–1705) Chikamatsu devoted his major efforts to Kabuki. From 1705 until his death in 1725, however, he wrote almost exclusively for the puppet theater. Various reasons have been suggested for Chikamatsu's final preference for the *jōruri*. In 1705 Sakata Tōjūrō was fifty-eight years old and soon to retire from Kabuki; Chikamatsu may have felt that Tōjūrō's successors were unlikely to interpret his plays as

[2] Shuzui Kenji (*Chikamatsu*, p. 29) seems disposed to accept this theory, but Mori (*Chikamatsu Monzaemon*, pp. 53–55) offers evidence that Chikamatsu's pen name was derived from his real name by plays on the Chinese characters.

[3] Translated into German by Johannes Barth in *Jubiläumsband* (Deutsche Gesellschaft für Natur- und Völkerkunde Ostasiens, 1933). *Shusse Kagekiyo* is generally believed to have been written in 1686, but Shinoda Jun'ichi argues (in "Shusse Kagekiyo no Seiritsu ni tsuite") that 1685 is correct.

skillfully. Or he may have decided that the puppet theater under Gidayū promised to be more popular in the growing city of Osaka than the Kabuki was in Kyoto. Or, as frequently has been stated, Chikamatsu may have felt dissatisfied with the liberties taken with his texts by temperamental actors and may therefore have decided to write instead for the more obedient puppets. In any case, the huge success of the puppet play *The Love Suicides at Sonezaki* in 1703 determined his future career. The announcement of his *jōruri The Mirror of Craftsmen of the Emperor Yōmei* (1705) bears the inscription "By Our Staff Playwright, Chikamatsu Monzaemon," indicating his new status. Chikamatsu moved early in 1706 from Kyoto to Osaka, the stronghold of the puppet theater.[4]

During the remainder of his career Chikamatsu devoted himself to writing two kinds of puppet plays, those treating the heroes of the distant or recent past, known as history plays (*jidaimono*), and those about the ordinary people of his own day, known as domestic plays (*sewamono*).

Chikamatsu's most successful work, the history play *The Battles of Coxinga* (1715) demonstrates his mastery of the unique possibilities of a theater of puppets. In the first act occur two moments which would be intolerable if performed realistically by actors: the first when the villain Ri Tōten gouges out his eye and offers it on a ceremonial baton to the Tartar envoy as a pledge of fealty, the second when Go Sankei performs a Caesarean operation on the dead empress in order to deliver the heir to the throne. The stylization of puppets, by making such scenes endurable, touches springs of pity and terror forbidden to actors. The second act of the same play presents a desperate encounter between the hero and a tiger. The scene when performed by actors is inevitably amusing, as the audience detects the movements of the man inside the tiger skin, but on the puppet stage a tiger is no less real than a human being, and the combat produces real excitement. The fourth act of *The Battles of Coxinga* affords a series of fantastic scenes which exploit the resources of the puppets. There are distant battles seen in visions; characters who age seven years before one's eyes; ghostly figures who vanish deliberately; and, finally, a rainbow bridge which mysteriously spans a gorge only to evaporate suddenly, sending those on it plummetting down into the abyss. These dramatic

[4] Mori, pp. 36–37.

effects do not necessarily contribute to the literary value of *The Battles of Coxinga,* but they account for its stunning success as entertainment The puppet theater under the guidance of Takeda Izumo (d. 1747), who became the director of Gidayū's Takemoto Theater in 1705, was to feature in the history plays a marked increase in stage machinery (*karakuri*). Takeda Izumo's influence in this direction is so noticeable at times that many of Chikamatsu's plays must be considered as collaborative efforts.

Yet, despite their craving for spectacle, Chikamatsu's audiences responded with enthusiasm to his domestic plays. *The Love Suicides at Sonezaki,* in fact, set Gidayū's theater on its feet after a shaky financial start. This play marked Chikamatsu's first attempt to use themes from daily life as the subject of a play, though other men had occasionally experimented with such materials in Kabuki. The greetings to the public by Tatsumatsu Hachirobei (d. 1734), chief puppet operator at the first performance of *The Love Suicides at Sonezaki,* explained the circumstances of composition. "The play we are about to present, *The Love Suicides at Sonezaki,* was written as the result of a chance visit by Chikamatsu Monzaemon of Kyoto to this city. Learning of the events described in the play, and thinking that they might prove entertaining on the stage, he composed a *jōruri* on the subject for your approval. The story has already been performed in Kabuki at various theaters and has lost its novelty, but this is the first time that it is offered as a *jōruri*." [5]

The hero of *The Love Suicides at Sonezaki* is a clerk in an oil shop, and its heroine is a prostitute. Aristotle clearly would not have considered persons of such humble station to be fit subjects for tragedy, and not for some years in Europe was a work written in which "for the first time, everyday commercial life is made the theme of a tragedy." [6] But the beauty of Chikamatsu's writing lifted his account of the love suicide of these little people from the gossip of a scandal sheet to the level of tragedy. Chikamatsu showed that their unhappy love was as worthy of our tears as the griefs of mighty princes. His audiences, given to applauding the superhuman feats celebrated in the

[5] *Ibid.,* p. 89.
[6] *The Oxford Companion to English Literature,* p. 316. The work referred to is *The History of George Barnwell, or The London Merchant,* a domestic tragedy in prose by George Lillo, produced in 1731.

history plays, responded to this new work because its closeness to their own lives gave the events special poignancy.

Chikamatsu continued to write both history plays and domestic plays until his death. Sections of certain history plays have remained popular favorites and are still presented as written. His domestic plays, on the other hand, have survived on the stage only in the adaptations of later men. The contemporaneity which attracted audiences to *The Love Suicides at Sonezaki* and to Chikamatsu's subsequent domestic plays lost its appeal for audiences of a later day, and the taste for the spectacular scene and the bold dramatic gesture grew ever more pronounced. Chikamatsu's domestic plays seemed pallid beside the works of such men as the second Takeda Izumo (1691–1756), each containing a scene in which a child or an adult is put to death as a substitute for another person. The audience apparently delighted especially in this moving but often inhuman theatrical device.[7]

The declining fortunes of Chikamatsu's plays on the puppet stage should not, however, be attributed solely to their overly literary qualities. Because the texts and music were coordinated with the movements of puppets operated by one man, the adoption of the three-man puppet in 1734, nine years after Chikamatsu's death, produced a disequilibrium. Chikamatsu's lines did not leave the cumbersome new puppets sufficient time to manoeuvre. Moreover, the invention of the three-man puppet whetted the appetite of the audiences for spectacular demonstrations of technique, and they were bored by plays which failed to show in a virtuoso manner the capabilities of the new puppets for both delicate and bold movements.

The same preference for the overstated and florid spread to the style of chanting. Chikamatsu had adapted his style to the demands of the successive chanters for whom he wrote, but he could not anticipate the changes after his death. The ability to utter a hysterical burst of laughter or a prolonged bout of sobbing came to be prized more highly than any subtlety of delivery. The chanters themselves neglected Chikamatsu's plays in favor of showier vehicles for their talents. As a result the music for virtually all the plays was lost and revivals today are at best an approximation of Chikamatsu's intent.

After Chikamatsu's death the distinction between history play and

7 See Shuzui Kenji, *Giri*, p. 56. For a discussion of later adaptations of Chikamatsu's works, see Wakatsuki, *Chikamatsu Ningyō Jōruri no Kenkyū*, pp. 816–26.

domestic play tended to disappear. Combined historico-domestic works, in which scenes of martial action alternate with quieter moments in the home or brothel, became the typical form. The loose structure discernible behind a history play by Chikamatsu broke down into two or three virtually unconnected stories joined under one title. Many later puppet plays were the product of several men's efforts not always controlled by a single guiding hand. The puppet theater lost rapidly in popularity to the Kabuki at the end of the eighteenth century, and has continued to dwindle since. Puppet plays, including some by Chikamatsu, were adapted for the Kabuki stage, but here too the preference for exaggerated action was so strong that only drastically altered versions which afford moments of bravura display have remained in the repertory. Despite his high reputation, Chikamatsu's works are imperfectly known to theatergoers today.

Chikamatsu's Age

The name Genroku strictly applies only to the years between 1688 and 1703, but it is commonly used today to designate the period stretching roughly from 1680 to 1730, the most brilliant flowering of Japanese culture during the Tokugawa period. The age could boast of Ihara Saikaku (1642–93), the first great novelist since the eleventh-century Lady Murasaki; Matsuo Bashō (1644–94), the master of haiku poetry; and Chikamatsu Monzaemon. It was also the age of the painter Ogata Kōrin (1658–1716), of the mathematician Seki Kōwa (1642–1708), of the philosopher and statesman Arai Hakuseki (1657–1725), and of the Kabuki actor the first Ichikawa Danjūrō (1660–1704), all outstanding figures in their respective fields. The ruler of Japan through most of this period was Tsunayoshi (1646–1709), the fifth Tokugawa shogun, a man of culture and learning who turned late in life to extravagance and eccentricity. Tsunayoshi's prodigality resulted in mounting indebtedness which he attempted to relieve by devaluing the currency. After four devaluations between 1704 and 1711, silver coins were 80 percent copper. Something of the confusion and grief that such economic measures caused among the common people is reflected in the domestic plays of Chikamatsu.

The political structure of Japan during the Genroku period was a military dictatorship, the shogunate established by Tokugawa Ieyasu at the beginning of the seventeenth century. The nominal ruler of Japan, the emperor, was a recluse in Kyoto occupied chiefly with ceremonials and poetry. Chikamatsu wrote a number of history plays about ancient and medieval emperors, but apart from one mysterious reference to an amnesty in honor of the accession of a new sovereign, he never alludes to the reigning emperor in his domestic plays.[8] The real ruler of Japan was the shogun in Edo. His government, despite its military structure, was devoted to peaceful pursuits and the maintenance of the existing order.

Society was divided into four classes: the samurai, the farmers, the artisans, and the merchants. The samurai princes (or daimyo) were in absolute control of the political life in the parts of the country they held in fief from the shogun, but their subservience to the central authority was assured by compulsory residence in Edo during alternate years. Several of Chikamatsu's plays tell of the loneliness of wives left behind in their provinces while their samurai husbands are serving in Edo. Chikamatsu depicted mainly the lesser ranks of samurai who suffered the cramping restrictions of a feudalistic society without sufficient income to enjoy their privileged status as samurai.

The farmers, as the sustainers of the nation, officially ranked next below the samurai. In fact, however, their living conditions were by far the worst of the four classes, and any material improvement in their lives was frowned on by the samurai. Many left the land for work in the cities, though this practice was not sanctioned. Farmers figure rather infrequently in Chikamatsu's plays. Chūbei's father in *The Courier for Hell* is a farmer, but nothing distinguishes his sentiments from those of Chikamatsu's benevolent old men of other classes. Chūbei remarks somewhat condescendingly of an old friend that he "has an unusually chivalrous nature for a farmer." Actually, however, the morality expressed in Chikamatsu's plays is essentially that expected of the farmer class.[9] Though Chikamatsu treated mainly the merchant class in his domestic plays, he is far less interested than, say, Saikaku in describing ways of amassing a fortune or business ethics. Nor does he glorify prudence and calculation, the merchant virtues. Instead, his plays accept the unquestioning obedience and selflessness

[8] See Kitani Hōgin, *Chikamatsu no Tennō Geki*, pp. 168–72.
[9] See the stimulating article by Seo Fukiko, "Chikamatsu ni okeru Nōminteki naru mono," in *Bungaku*, June, 1951.

demanded of the farmers no less than of the samurai. One book of maxims for farmers published in 1721 declared, "Cleverness and resourcefulness are aberrations of the intellect," [10] a sentiment in which Chikamatsu, though not Saikaku, would concur. Chikamatsu's heroes are not notable for their cleverness, but in their purity of heart unencumbered by thought they closely resemble the ideal farmer.

The artisans and merchants, though officially distinguished, were usually lumped together as townsmen (*chōnin*). Their status was low, but they set the tone of Genroku culture. Some merchants amassed huge fortunes and even had daimyo for their debtors. They lived in opulence quite unlike the hard-pressed samurai or the downtrodden farmers. But the samurai on occasion demonstrated that political power remained in their hands: in 1705 the richest and most respected of the Osaka merchants, the house of Yodoya, accused of ostentatious luxury not befitting the merchant class, had its entire fortune confiscated. The apparent reason behind this action was to free certain daimyo of western Japan from their hopeless indebtedness to Yodoya, but the central government at the same time received a windfall from the fabled Yodoya wealth. The action emphasized that despite the merchants' prosperity they would be kept in their place.[11]

Nevertheless, Genroku culture belonged to the merchants. Saikaku's best novels were written about and for merchants; the *haiku* of Bashō found widest favor among the merchants; Chikamatsu's domestic plays are mainly concerned with their lives. The gay quarters, the center of town culture at the time, were intended for the merchants' pleasure, and samurai visiting them forfeited their special privileges. The rich merchants could buy the favors of the most beautiful women of the day, and a host of lesser courtesans awaited the call of less affluent men.

The theaters, associated directly or indirectly with the licensed quarters since the birth of Kabuki early in the seventeenth century, were similarly swayed by the tastes of the merchants. Though samurai and even nobles attended the theater, the chief source of income was derived from the merchant class, and ultimately their preferences prevailed. *Ukiyoe* paintings of both gay quarters and the theaters are still another example of the dominance of the arts by the townsmen.

[10] Seo, p. 61. The sentence is quoted from *Hyakushō Bunryōki*, a work of 1721.
[11] See Sheldon, *The Rise of the Merchant Class in Tokugawa Japan*, pp. 102–4.

The classes, though distinct in their functions and pleasures, were not castes. The daughters of rich merchants attracted samurai husbands, and prosperous merchants might themselves become samurai through adoption. On the other hand, samurai and farmers not infrequently became merchants, and there was a good deal more mixing of the classes than the government thought desirable. In *The Uprooted Pine* Okiku, a samurai's daughter, has married the merchant Yojibei. The failure of the marriage is blamed on the difference in class by Okiku's mother. Her father says, "My wife tried to stop the marriage when they were first engaged. She insisted that Okiku would do better to marry a samurai, even a poor one, and that if she married a businessman, no matter how rich he might be, they would never get along together." She now sees her fears justified. To this Jōkan, Yojibei's father, answers, "A samurai's child is reared by samurai parents and becomes a samurai himself because they teach him the warriors' code. A merchant's child is reared by merchant parents and becomes a merchant because they teach him the ways of commerce. A samurai seeks a fair name in disregard of profit, but a merchant, with no thought to his reputation, gathers profits and amasses a fortune. This is the way of life proper for each." In *The Love Suicides in the Women's Temple* a merchant father is against marrying his daughter to a samurai. "A horse goes with a horse, an ox with an ox, a merchant's daughter with a merchant."

Chikamatsu in these and other examples seems to be supporting the class divisions. His lack of criticism of the social hierarchy has exposed him to condemnation as "feudal" by certain modern critics, but they miss Chikamatsu's intent. He was absorbed with the problems of different kinds of men and women within each class; their particular griefs, rather than a class struggle, became the subjects of his plays.[12] This does not mean that Chikamatsu was incapable of criticism; his thinly disguised satire of the excesses of the shogun Tsunayoshi must have found a ready response in his audiences.[13] However, he chose to write in terms of both arrogant and benevolent rulers, noble and depraved samurai, rather than to deal in black-and-white characterizations of an entire class. He describes with compassion the

[12] Mori, p. 205.
[13] See Shively, "Chikamatsu's Satire on the Dog Shogun," *Harvard Journal of Asian Studies*, XVIII, 159–80.

sufferings of his ill-starred heroes and heroines, but he traces the causes to their own mistakes rather than to the ills of the age.

The Plays

Chikamatsu's first important work, *Kagekiyo Victorious* (1686), was the direct descendant of earlier plays on the same theme and is not typical of the mature Chikamatsu. It nevertheless affords a tantalizing glimpse of the kind of dramatist he might have become if he had been writing for a different theater.

Kagekiyo Victorious opens unpromisingly (save for the language) with a disjointed and ineptly written first act, hardly superior to the discredited old *jōruri*. The defeated warrior Kagekiyo first appears as he takes leave of his new wife, Lady Ono. In the next scene he attempts in the guise of a workman to kill his mortal enemy Minamoto no Yoritomo at the Tōdaiji in Nara. His plot is foiled by Yoritomo's omniscient adviser Shigetada, and the act concludes as Kagekiyo, pursued by innumerable soldiers, escapes by flying off (literally!), taking advantage of his supernatural powers. So far little suggests the dramatist that Chikamatsu was to become. In the second act, however, we are suddenly confronted with a genuine human being, Kagekiyo's rejected mistress Akoya. Kagekiyo, retreating from Nara, visits Akoya in Kyoto and asks her to shelter him. She upbraids him for his alliance with Lady Ono, but Kagekiyo, lying, swears that Lady Ono means nothing to him. "How could you suppose that I would love anyone else in the world but you?" he asks. Akoya, at length convinced, answers in womanly tones, "I love you too much. That's why we have these quarrels. At least this one has been harmless." Her flare-up of jealousy, her quick assent to what she wants to believe, and the naturalness of her speech after so much bombast, create a startling impression of reality.

The following day Kagekiyo leaves for the Kiyomizu Temple, intending to spend a week in prayer before the statue of Kwannon, a deity he has always worshiped with special devotion. During Kagekiyo's absence Akoya's brother Jūzō arrives and attempts to persuade her to disclose Kagekiyo's whereabouts. Jūzō hopes for a reward if he can turn in Kagekiyo. Akoya spurns him, declaring that betrayal would be dishonorable. Jūzō counters sarcastically, "Such concern over your reputation! Such a high-minded refusal to take profit! You sound like an old-fashioned samurai! But those ways have gone quite out of fashion these days." [14] He insinuates that Kagekiyo is in love with Lady Ono. Akoya refuses to listen, but at that moment a courier delivers a tender note from Lady Ono for Kakekiyo. Akoya is stung into fury. She betrays Kagekiyo, though she regrets it the next instant. Kagekiyo's enemies at once attack him at Kiyomizu Temple, but he repulses them and escapes, again over the treetops.

In the third act Lady Ono travels to Kyoto in search of her husband. She is captured by the enemy and subjected to terrible tortures in the hope of forcing her to reveal her husband's whereabouts. But Ono, unlike the courtesan Akoya, cannot be coerced into betrayal. The cruel soldiers, having dangled her in vain from a tree, now propose to torture her by fire, when Kagekiyo appears. He allows himself to be bound, rather than cause Ono further pain.

The fourth act shows us Kagekiyo's prison. He is kept under extraordinarily severe bonds in his stoutly built cell. His hair is braided in seven strands fastened down in seven directions. His legs are pinioned by huge logs dragged down from the mountains by seventy-five men, his knees are clamped in iron chains. Kagekiyo, unperturbed, prays to Kwannon. Akoya appears with their two children and begs his forgiveness. Kagekiyo, scorning her, asserts that he would kill her if he had even a single finger free. Akoya tries to explain how jealousy drove her to her act, but Kagekiyo will not hear her. He announces that he no longer recognizes the two little boys as his own children. Akoya in an amazing speech declares that she intends to kill her sons and herself before Kagekiyo's eyes. She quickly stabs one boy, but the other one, terrified, runs to Kagekiyo and begs to be saved. Akoya urges the boy to let her kill him, and he reluctantly consents. Akoya stabs her son and then herself.

Soon afterwards Jūzō returns to taunt the captive, but Kagekiyo with a mighty effort bursts his bonds and slays his tormentor. He starts off, only to remember that Lady Ono and her father will suffer if he escapes. He returns to his cell and takes up his chains.

In the fifth act we are informed that Kagekiyo has been beheaded by his enemies. Shigetada, however, insists that Kagekiyo is still alive.

[14] This passage is of course anachronistic; for someone in Chikamatsu's day these virtues might be "old-fashioned," but in Kagekiyo's day the samurai code had hardly yet evolved.

The others investigate and discover that the severed head of Kagekiyo, publicly displayed at a Kyoto street corner, has been mysteriously replaced by a head of the goddess Kwannon. Priests from the Kiyomizu Temple rush up to report that the head of the statue of Kwannon is missing and the body covered with blood. Kagekiyo's enemies realize that a miracle has occurred: the deity Kwannon, whom Kagekiyo so faithfully worshiped, has substituted her head for his. Yoritomo, impressed by the miracle, spares Kagekiyo's life and grants him a province. Kagekiyo gracefully accepts. The play ends with rejoicing over the reconciliation of the two enemies, praise for Kagekiyo, and prayers for the prosperity of the country.

Kagekiyo Victorious contains many elements inherited by Chikamatsu from his predecessors, but also shows the germs of the future development of his art. The crudities are all too obvious. A concession to popular tastes or a desire to demonstrate the superhuman talents of the puppets may have inspired the scenes of Kagekiyo flying or the horrible tortures of Lady Ono. The miraculous substitution of Kwannon for the condemned man is a variation on a familiar theme of the old *jōruri* which survived long after Chikamatsu. The happy ending (in complete disregard of history) again reflects old *jōruri* traditions. *Kagekiyo Victorious* outstrips its predecessors, however, in the character of Akoya. She figures only briefly in the play, but her actions have a tragic intensity. The scene in which she betrays Kagekiyo is crudely set: it is highly improbable that Kagekiyo would have informed his present wife of plans to stay in Kyoto with his old mistress, and the arrival of the fatal message at the critical moment strains credulity. But Akoya's fury has genuine accents, and the weakness which led to betrayal is entirely plausible.[15] In her next encounter with Kagekiyo she rises to Medea-like emotions. The moment when her second son tries to escape his mother's knife is almost unbearably moving. After this superb scene the rest of the play is anticlimax.

If Chikamatsu had been writing for a different theater and audience *Kagekiyo Victorious* might have served as the first sketch for a true *Medea,* the study of a woman driven by jealous love to betray her husband and kill her children. But though *Kagekiyo Victorious* estab-

[15] In earlier plays on the subject Akoya betrays Kagekiyo in the hope of advancing the fortunes of her sons, and Kagekiyo kills the children. (See Watsuji Tetsurō, *Nihon Geijutsu Shi Kenkyū,* I, 511–18.)

lished Chikamatsu's reputation, it did not accord with prevalent tastes. The puppet theater was not intended to represent characters with life-blood in their veins. The various personages on the stage and their sentiments were normally no more than instruments of the plot and the stage machinery.[16] Akoya killing her children gives vent to individual passions; she might have been more easily intelligible to Chikamatsu's audiences if her actions had been inspired by feudal loyalty rather than by a desire to expiate her guilt. Chikamatsu created many figures who died for love, but none asserts individuality as strikingly as Akoya in her few short scenes. Her violence has a Western intensity which was out of place in the puppet theater.

The oldest play by Chikamatsu still read and performed today is *The Love Suicides at Sonezaki* (1703). The story is simple. A shop clerk, Tokubei, in love with a prostitute, Ohatsu, refuses to marry the girl chosen for him by his uncle. He must therefore return to his uncle the dowry money which his mother has already accepted. He obtains it with difficulty, but is at once persuaded by his friend Kuheiji to lend it for a few days. Kuheiji tricks Tokubei out of the money. In despair over the consequences Tokubei and Ohatsu commit suicide.

The Love Suicides at Sonezaki, at first so acclaimed, came to seem insufficiently engrossing to audiences accustomed to Chikamatsu's later domestic plays; when it was revived in 1717 Chikamatsu was obliged to add a few scenes to increase the complexity. The characters at first blush also seem to lack distinction. Tokubei is an ineffectual, excessively naïve young man, as little like a hero as Kagekiyo is like a human being. Ohatsu, unlike the passionate Akoya, seems little more than a warm-hearted prostitute. Kuheiji is a paper-thin villain. What is most striking in these characters is the contrast with their predecessors. Chikamatsu deliberately created a weakling hero, an insignificant young man who foolishly trusts a wicked acquaintance. Even Tokubei's decision to share in a lovers' suicide is guided by the stronger will of his sweetheart. Ohatsu too is by no means the stereotyped courtesan of earlier plays. A more normal treatment of the prostitute—the faithless woman who sells her favors to any man—was the heroine of Saikaku's *The Woman Who Spent Her Life in Love* (1686).[17] Sai-

[16] Katō Junzō, *Chikamatsu Shishō no Kenkyū*, p. 36.
[17] Partial translation by Howard Hibbett in *The Floating World in Japanese Fiction,* pp. 154–217.

kaku's heroine, devoted to her career, would never have dreamt of committing a lover's suicide with one of her customers. Ohatsu is not only devoted to Tokubei but urges him to the death in which she joins him. Chikamatsu showed in *The Love Suicides at Sonezaki* that a courtesan, even one of low rank, is capable of true feelings. By the magic of his poetry, particularly in the *michiyuki* (or lovers' journey), he managed to transform most unpromising figures into the hero and heroine of tragedy.

Most of Chikamatsu's subsequent love-suicide plays conformed to the general scheme of this early work. Lesser characters were strengthened; the motivation of the suicides (so inadequate at Sonezaki) was made more compelling, particularly for the women; and the role of the villain was given greater depth by lending ambiguity to his motives or imparting a comic interest. But the general outline of the story—the young man of the townsman class who falls in love with a prostitute, is unable to "ransom" her (buy her contract from the owner), and eventually joins her in death—remained the same.

This similarity in plot structure of the love-suicide plays, though modified by the enrichments of Chikamatsu as his art matured, inevitably makes his literary production seem less varied than that of other important dramatists. In general, variety in the Japanese drama is more likely to occur in details—minor twists of the plot—than in over-all structure. Chikamatsu did not expect to surprise his audiences; the titles "The Love Suicides at—" if nothing else give away the conclusions. The developments in the plots of his play were often known in advance from the scandal sheets sold in the wake of interesting double suicides, and Chikamatsu was not even averse to borrowing his material from another man's play.[18] His desire was to create affecting characters from the scraps of information gleanable in the accounts of their suicides, and to transform the pathetic or sometimes sordid details into literature. We know from more factual descriptions of the love suicides treated in his plays that Chikamatsu invented characters and motivations, made fickle courtesans into paragons of fidelity, and otherwise altered at will his materials. His audiences, for whom the love-suicide plays were merely an interlude in a full day's entertainment at the theater, did not demand that they be

---

[18] His last domestic play, *Shinjū Yoigōshin* (1722), is generally believed to have been much influenced by a rival work by Ki no Kaion, produced a few weeks earlier.

of entirely new conception, but welcomed such changes as Chikamatsu imparted to the familiar stories. Within the established framework of his suicide-plays Chikamatsu was able to achieve the kind of variety he sought, as a reading of *The Love Suicides at Sonezaki* and *The Love Suicides at Amijima,* works of roughly similar plots, will show.

The Love Suicides at Sonezaki not only reflected its time but actually started a vogue for love suicides, as we may gather from a publication of the following year, *The Great Mirror of Love Suicides.* In the succeeding years the number of such suicides, both in life and on the stage, rapidly multiplied, until in 1722 the government banned plays with the word *shinjū* (love suicides) in the title. It has been suggested that the unsettling effect of the devaluation of the currency in 1706 contributed to this grim craze, and various natural disasters during the next few years (earthquakes, volcanic eruptions, conflagrations) undoubtedly drove many people to despair.[19] The brilliance of the gay quarters did not flicker, and the theater was better attended than ever, but society could poorly afford these luxuries. The inadequate motivation of the suicides of Tokubei and Ohatsu becomes more convincing in the later love-suicide plays, where financial difficulties play the largest part.

The Love Suicides at Sonezaki was so popular that Chikamatsu refers back to this success in four later domestic plays. *Two Picture-Books of Love Suicides* (1706) bears the subtitle "The Third Anniversary of Sonezaki: Another Dream at the Temma House," and otherwise assumes a knowledge of the earlier work. *Two Picture-Books* is interesting also because of its first paragraphs, a description of the opening of the 1706 season at the Takemoto Theater in Osaka with Chikamatsu's play *The Mirror of Craftsmen of the Emperor Yōmei.*

The Year of the Bird, 1705, will soon be a memory—the 1706 season is about to begin. Long before dawn today the wooden portals were thrown open, and while lamplight still glittered on the first frost, lively shouts of "The show is about to start!" drew eager customers young and old into the theatre. The morning sun has peeped out now, and soon the puppet show, sprung from the seeds of poetry, the age-old art of the ageless Land of the Rising Sun, will move Heaven and Earth, stir the gods and demons, and make the ties between husband and wife or the heart of the fierce

[19] See Yokoyama Tadashi, "Chikamatsu Shinjū Jōruri no Tenkai," *Kokugo to Kokubungaku,* May, 1958, pp. 58–59.

warrior soft as—"Jam buns!" "Cakes!" "Matches!" "Programs!": even the vendors' cries have a lilt at the puppet theatre. "Get your authorized libretto!" "Check your hats and umbrellas!" "Cushions! Cushions!" [20]

The Mirror of Craftsmen, a history play with spectacular effects, marked the first collaboration of Chikamatsu (the staff playwright), Takeda Izumo (the director of the company), and the chanter Gidayū. It has been called the dividing line between Chikamatsu's early and mature work.[21]

Chikamatsu's next important domestic play, *The Drum of the Waves at Horikawa*, introduced new themes. Here he deals not with merchants but with members of the samurai class. Otane, the wife of a samurai serving in Edo with his master, consoles her loneliness with drink. One night, under the influence of liquor (and provoked by another man), she has an affair with her stepson's teacher. The guilty pair, once sober again, are thoroughly ashamed of their transgression, but powerless to change what has happened. When Otane's husband returns from Edo he learns that his wife is pregnant. He forces her to commit suicide. Later the husband and members of the family track down the teacher and kill him.

In the background of this play and two others which Chikamatsu wrote on similar themes was the law that a wife guilty of adultery was to be executed. The severity of this law reflected the double standard which permitted men openly to indulge in the pleasures of the licensed quarters while relegating their wives to neglected homes. The wife was helpless: jealousy itself was grounds for divorce, and the divorced woman was disgraced. The wife who endured without complaint the indignities inflicted by her husband was generally praised. Yet, as Chikamatsu realized, the wife who like Otane was left for a year at a time while her husband served in Edo, or who like Osan in *The Love Suicides at Amijima* waited in a lonely house for her husband to return from nights in the gay quarters, could not be satisfied merely with people's praises for her chastity. She missed her husband sexually, as Chikamatsu tells us with a directness unusual in Western tragedies.

[20] The play in which this passage appears was produced in the third moon of 1706. It describes the opening of a play in the eleventh moon of 1705, which marked the first performances of the 1706 season, as it was considered.

[21] Takano Masami, "Chikamatsu Sakuhin no Bunruihō," *Kokugo to Kokubungaku*, March, 1948, p. 21.

The wife in all three plays dealing with adultery is portrayed as an unwitting victim of circumstances. Otane is horrified to discover what she has done while intoxicated; Osai in *Gonza the Lancer* is unjustly accused of improper relations with her intended son-in-law; Osan in *The Almanac of Love* [22] sleeps with Mohei because she thinks he is her husband. Nevertheless, a twentieth-century reader may wonder if Chikamatsu has not drawn these characters in such a manner as to suggest that the three wives subconsciously desired the guilty relations in which they became so unhappily embroiled. Otane, so lonely that she plays games with herself pretending that her husband has returned, is attracted to the polite drum teacher from the capital. She yields to her weakness for saké, perhaps dimly aware that drunkenness will permit a lapse in conduct. Or so it would seem, though it may be dangerous to attempt to analyze Chikamatsu's characters in such terms.

The case of Osai is even more intriguing. Her extravagant praise for Gonza's qualities, her joking remark that she would take him if her daughter did not (an incredible joke, considering the penalties if anything improper were suspected of her!), her impatience at Gonza's hesitation, and her excessive jealousy at the news of Gonza's engagement to another woman, all indicate an interest in the young man which goes beyond a mother-in-law's solicitude. Then, when the two are falsely accused by the villainous Bannojō, Osai proposes to Gonza that they become lovers in fact, ostensibly so that her husband Ichinoshin will have grounds for killing them. Her reasoning is so tortuous that we can only suspect that she is the prey of emotions not fully understood even by herself: she wants to sleep with Gonza before she dies. The complexity of Otane and Osai makes the "adultery plays" among Chikamatsu's most affecting works.

Chikamatsu's other domestic plays have been divided by Japanese scholars into various categories. In some the hero (Chūbei in *The Courier for Hell* or Sōshichi in *The Girl from Hakata*) commits a crime for which he and his sweetheart will be punished; in some the leading character (like Yojibei in *The Uprooted Pine*) is driven out of his mind by grief. Chikamatsu wrote only one murder play (*The Woman-Killer*), fewer than we would expect, considering the popularity of this subject in the Kabuki of the time.

[22] Translated by Asataro Miyamori in *Masterpieces of Chikamatsu*, pp. 65–106.

The later history plays treat events ranging in time from the legendary Age of the Gods to a year-old rebellion in Formosa. The characters include gods, emperors, generals, priests, and commoners. They would thus seem to possess a wider range than the domestic plays, but our enjoyment of them is marred by their extravagances and the inconsistent characterization of the different personages.

Subjects, Characters, and Performances of the Domestic Plays

The domestic plays all share one feature, their contemporary setting. Most of them depict incidents which occurred only a month or two before, and they are made vivid by the use of the actual names of persons involved. Sometimes delicacy obliged Chikamatsu to alter slightly the names and occupations of the chief figures in the different tragedies, a practice to which he openly alludes ("I hear that Kōzaemon's done a play on the murder of the oil merchant's wife, except he's changed it to a saké merchant").[23] Few in the audience can have been deceived by such thin disguises. References are frequently made also to well-known entertainers of the day, to theaters, teahouses, and brothels. Chikamatsu quotes snatches from popular songs, and even inserts what appear to be advertisements for familiar products.[24] In contrast to the improbable activities of the history plays, the allusions in these dramas must have brought smiles of recognition to the spectators.

Chikamatsu's domestic plays have been called "living newspapers." Like newspapers they reflect society,[25] but only a small part of it. There were happy and prosperous merchants in the Genroku era, as we know from other sources, but in Chikamatsu's plays they do not figure prominently. On the other hand, he did not choose to depict hard-working men, devotedly pursuing their trades, who go bankrupt nevertheless because of economic conditions which they are

---

[23] From "The Woman Killer," Keene, *Major Plays of Chikamatsu.*

[24] In "The Girl from Hakata," *ibid.,* for example, he mentions the brand name of a kind of *geta* which Kojorō was especially requested to buy.

[25] In *Ikudama Shinjū,* the hero goes to see Chikamatsu's earlier work, *The Love Suicides at Sonezaki,* performed on the Kabuki stage, and remarks, "Kabuki plays and *jōruri* are the mirrors of good and evil men" (Tadami Keizō, *Chikamatsu Jōruri-Shū* [*Yūhōdō Bunko* edition], III, 70).

powerless to control. Jihei (in *The Love Suicides at Amijima*) has trouble meeting his monthly bills because he neglects his business in order to frequent the gay quarters. Yojibei (in *The Uprooted Pine*) is equally remiss in his affairs. Presumably they would have both been prosperous if they had applied themselves to their work. Chikamatsu does not moralistically hold these men up as dreadful examples. They were the men he chose for his "headlines," and the virtuous, prudent merchants of the day were dismissed with scant mention.

The heroes of the domestic plays are mainly young men of undiluted emotions but weak characters. Tokubei in *The Love Suicides at Sonezaki* is the model for the rest. We can only marvel at his guilelessness in trusting so obvious a villain as Kuheiji. He cuts a pathetic figure when, battered by Kuheiji and his henchmen, he tearfully assures the bystanders of his innocence or when he furtively creeps up to Ohatsu for comfort. Only at the end of the play does he acquire the stature of a tragic figure.

Jihei, the hero of *The Love Suicides at Amijima,* is another Tokubei, but with two women in his life, one of the first tragic heroes to be caught in this predicament. He loves and needs both the prostitute Koharu and his wife Osan. Desperate at the thought of losing either, he can think of no solution. The tragedy develops in terms of the relations between the two women while Jihei lies in a stupor of self-pity. His problem is hopeless. Even if he somehow managed to ransom Koharu, how could he keep her and Osan under one roof? Threatened with the loss of Osan, he implores his father-in-law not to take her away. He promises to reform. But his assurances, though sincere, do not convince us; he lacks the moral courage to renounce his past and become a worthy husband and father. Only in death can the purity and strength of his emotions find adequate expression.

Chūbei in *The Courier for Hell,* like Tokubei a young man in love with a courtesan, is more striking if only for his foolishness. He breaks the seal on a packet of three hundred pieces of gold, though he knows that it will bring disaster to everyone involved. His only justification is the necessity he feels to assert his honor before half a dozen prostitutes. In this total disregard of reason he may stir us more than either Tokubei or Jihei. The audience sympathizes with Chūbei because his emotions are untainted by considerations of personal advantage: this is the indispensable characteristic of a hero of one of Chikamatsu's domestic plays. Hachiemon, Chūbei's friend, though reasonable and solicitous for his friend's welfare, exerts little appeal on the audience if only because his emotions are less direct than Chūbei's. Characters in other domestic plays are redeemed by emotional purity even if guilty of contemptible actions (like Yosaku in *Yosaku from Tamba*). Excessively powerful and conflicting emotions drive Yojibei in *The Uprooted Pine* to madness, without his forfeiting the audience's admiration and respect.

Chikamatsu neither praises nor condemns his heroes for their hopeless involvement with prostitutes (even when they have wives and children), nor for the other follies of which they are guilty. The deplorable circumstances he describes are necessary for the flower within them—an expression of emotional purity—to bloom.[26] If Jihei had never met Koharu, if he had remained a devoted husband and hard-working businessman, the world would never have known of his capacity for deep emotion, nor of the nobility of spirit that Osan and Koharu display out of love for him. The failings of Jihei not only move us to tears, but enable us to see that these humble people—a paper dealer, his wife, and a prostitute—possess true grandeur. Jihei is clearly no Aristotelian hero inspiring our pity and terror by a flaw in his otherwise superior nature; he is weakness itself, but his emotional intensity, which leads him to abandon his wife and children, kill his beloved, and finally commit suicide himself, somehow wins our hearts if not our minds.

The heroes of some other domestic plays are so ambivalent that we may even dislike them until their final display of emotional integrity. Yosaku is a samurai reduced to working as a horse driver because of his offenses in the past. He has betrayed his wife, failed to repay his master's kindness, and abandoned his child. We learn that he gambles and has recently lost at a game in which the stake was a horse belonging to another man. In order to raise some money, Yosaku persuades the boy Sankichi to steal. When Koman, the courtesan who is Yosaku's sweetheart, protests, Yosaku answers, "You're too timid. If the kid is caught, the worst he'll get is a spanking." Sankichi is in fact caught, and eventually condemned to be executed. Yosaku and Koman, overcome with remorse, decide they must kill themselves. On their journey

<hr>

[26] Compare the remarks by Motoori Norinaga on *The Tale of Genji* (in Tsunoda, *et al.*, *Sources of the Japanese Tradition*).

to death Yosaku emerges as a tragic figure, and his transgressions, though not forgiven, seem to have made possible at last the flowering of his true nature.

Gonza (of *Gonza the Lancer*) is an even less likely hero. In the opening scene we learn of his affair with the girl Oyuki and his promise to marry her. He swears that he will live up to this obligation: "If ever I am untrue to what I say, may I fall that instant headfirst from my horse and be trampled to death!" But in the very next scene Gonza, discovering that the secret traditions of the True Table tea ceremony can only be transmitted within the tea master's family, agrees to marry his master's daughter. Again he swears: "If I should violate this oath, may I never again wear armor on my back, may I be slashed to bits by Ichinoshin's sword, and may my dead body be exposed on the public highway!" This time his vow is to be granted. Later in the play, much against his desires, he becomes involved in an adulterous relationship with Osai. He has no reason to die with her, but he generously sacrifices himself, and in the end is slashed to bits by the sword of her husband, Ichinoshin. The calculating, deceitful Gonza, more like the villains of *The Love Suicides at Sonezaki* or *The Love Suicides at Amijima* than like Tokubei or Jihei, is redeemed by his most wicked act.

One of Chikamatsu's most unusual heroes is Kumenosuke in *The Love Suicides at the Women's Temple*. At the outset of the play he is a novice at the Buddhist monastery on Mount Kōya. His love affair with Oume, a girl who lives in a nearby town, is accidentally discovered, bringing the violent rebuke of the High Priest and Yūben, a senior priest with whom Kumenosuke has apparently had intimate relations. Kumenosuke, appalled by their censure, asks Yūben, "If I break with Oume, will you be as kind and loving as before?" "Of course," answers Yūben. Kumenosuke shows himself—for the moment at least—willing to give up his sweetheart in favor of his "brother," but on second thought he bursts into tears. "What's the matter now?" Yūben asks. "What shall I do if Oume refuses to break with me?" Surely there could be no less heroic figure.

Kumenosuke is driven from Mount Kōya. In the second act he joins Oume at her father's house. Oume, unlike her lover, is high-spirited and sharp-tongued. In a movingly erotic scene the two beautiful, foolish young people express their physical longing for each other. The act ends in farce as they escape under cover of darkness, thwarting the suitor Oume was supposed to marry. In the third act the same young man who was so abjectly willing to yield his sweetheart and the same harum-scarum girl who nearly got caught in bed with her lover while her fiancé grumbled downstairs develop mysteriously but convincingly into the hero and heroine of tragedy. They journey together to the Women's Temple, where Kumenosuke kills Oume and soon afterwards commits suicide. The action of the entire play occurs in about ten hours, but there is infinitely more character development than, say, in *The Battles of Coxinga,* which extends over seven years. As we read *The Love Suicides in the Women's Temple* we are persuaded that the miracle of their transformation is possible. We are even prepared to believe that heroes compounded of such fragile materials are more affecting than the Aristotelian hero with a solitary tragic flaw.

Chikamatsu's style enabled him to arouse our sympathy for heroes whose faults he did not conceal. One literary device he employed in this process was the *michiyuki,* or lovers' journey, a typical feature of puppet plays (and, in briefer form, of Nō plays before them). The *michiyuki* has often been dismissed as mere ornamentation, a pretext afforded Chikamatsu to demonstrate his virtuosity in elaborating puns on the names of places passed by the lovers on their journey. The *michiyuki* certainly displays Chikamatsu's verbal dexterity, but it was also indispensable in creating the tragic atmosphere of his final scenes. Tokubei and Ohatsu, a shop clerk and a prostitute when they creep out from the Temma House, acquire in the *michiyuki* the dignity of a man and woman about to meet death. As they travel, the narrator magically describes their emotions in one of the loveliest passages of Japanese literature. "Farewell to this world, and to the night farewell. We who walk the road to death, to what should we be likened? To the frost by the road that leads to the graveyard, vanishing with each step we take ahead: how sad is this dream of a dream!" Any lovers described in such language must command our sympathy.

Yosaku, the dissolute samurai, stirs us when he tells Koman during their *michiyuki,* "Three years ago, companions on a secret journey to Ise, we first exchanged vows. In the middle of Kushida Town I confessed my deep love—I can still see the purple hat you wore. I won your heart and we swore by the Jizō of Seki to be true. Though

I bore the heavy burden of love, my feet went lightly as I drove my horse; my heart was buoyant, expansive as Toyoku Plain. How heartbreaking that now, while yet I delight in you, have not had my fill, this autumn frost has overtaken us. Tonight will be our last. We shall bury our fame in Sunken Fields." This passage, true to the traditions of the *michiyuki,* is imbedded with puns on the places passed (some of which are translated above), but it was obviously not meant merely to satisfy a craving for fancy language. It transmits to us the belief that despite Yosaku's failings the strength of his love is worthy of our sympathy and respect.

Our understanding of the characters, then, at times results less from their words or actions than from the manner in which Chikamatsu describes them in the *michiyuki.* Tokubei, hitherto portrayed as a weakling, has found the strength to kill his beloved by the time he reaches the wood of Sonezaki. Kumenosuke becomes an adult on his journey and is ready for the man's business awaiting him at the end. Yosaku, remembering his past, recovers his lost dignity.

Chikamatsu's ability to create complex, evolving characters was no asset in the puppet theater, and the domestic plays, though popular at their first showings, did not long remain in the repertory. In the puppet theater only a limited number of heads was available to represent the different parts. There was a definite head for a male, middle-aged, good character and another for a male, middle-aged, bad character. As soon as the puppet came on stage the audience knew (as clearly as from the mustache on the villain in an old-fashioned Western) whether he was a good or a bad man. One may imagine the audience's uneasiness, then, when despite the handsome features of a "male, young, good" puppet head, Gonza acts in a decidedly ambiguous manner. Yosaku and Hachiemon must also have puzzled Chikamatsu's audiences, as we can gather from the revised versions of the plays (the work of later men). In these versions, the ones still performed today, the ambiguous characters are made clearly bad or clearly good, or else they are omitted altogether. Neither the puppet theater with its fixed categories of heads, nor the Kabuki with its traditional stylized gestures allowed for subtlety. It was possible for good characters to pretend to be wicked and later to reveal their true natures, or for evil characters to repent at the end, but there was no room for characters whose natures were not immediately apparent.

The present repertory of the puppet theater is largely from the century
after Chikamatsu's death. With the exception of *The Battles of Cox-*
inga, a work whose swift action and varied stage effects have always
been popular, no play by Chikamatsu is regularly performed as written,
though there is a movement to return to the original texts.

The Plays as Literature

Chikamatsu did not intend his plays as armchair dramas, but each
of them was printed in many different editions during his lifetime, both
for amateur chanters who wished to practice the parts and for readers
who enjoyed Chikamatsu as a poet.[27] Chikamatsu's valedictory verse,
written just before his death, seems to anticipate that his future fame
will rest with these printed texts rather than with stage performances of
his works.

Sore zo jisei	This will be my valediction:
Saru hodo ni sate mo	"In the meanwhile . . . Well, then,
Sono nochi ni	Afterwards . . ."
Nokoru sakura ga	If on the cherry tree left behind
Hana shi niowaba	The blossoms are fragrant.

This cryptic verse, which incorporates some of the stereotyped phrases
of the old *jōruri* ("In the meanwhile . . . Well, then, afterwards . . ."), has been interpreted as meaning, "If my works, marked
by the phrases of the old theatre, surviving in books printed from blocks
of cherry wood, are praised by later men [are fragrant], they will be
my valediction." [28] If this interpretation is correct, Chikamatsu hoped
that his plays, living on in books after his death, would express his
message to the world.

Chikamatsu clearly took great pains with his texts, not only to ensure
their success on the stage, but to give them literary distinction. He told
a friend, "From the time that I began to write *jōruri* . . . I have used
care in my writing, which was not true of the old *jōruri.* As a result
the medium has been raised one level." [29] Chikamatsu's care shows

[27] In *Shinjū Yoigōshin* one character offers another this choice of reading matter: *Essays*
in Idleness, The Love Suicides at Amijima, or *The Tale of the Heike* (Tadami,
Chikamatsu Jōruri-Shū, III, 542). See also the article by Yokoyama Tadashi "Chikamatsu
no Maruhon," *Kaishaku to Kanshō,* January, 1957.

[28] Watsuji, pp. 447–49.

[29] Tsunoda, *et al., Sources of the Japanese Tradition.*

itself in the extraordinarily varied language of the plays, which ranges from pungent colloquialisms to flights of obscure allusion. The dialogue is often close to the language that was actually spoken, but it is nevertheless a stage language marked by artificial and sometimes difficult constructions. The most beautiful passages, however, are not those of the dialogue but the descriptions narrated by the chanter. A narrator was needed in the puppet theater to supplement the circumstances of a speech or action for the puppets whose facial and bodily expression was necessarily limited, but he was otherwise called upon to announce the setting of an act, often a marvelously vivid evocation of the gay quarters or a festival; to race through such virtuoso passages as the *tsukushi,* a kind of catalogue (of plants, place names, shells, textiles, bridges, and even love suicides) in which puns on the items in the catalogue make up an independent meaning; and to intone the fantastically complicated tissues of puns, allusions, and half-finished phrases of the *michiyuki* and descriptive interludes. The spectators in Chikamatsu's day, though poorly educated, were able to grasp the general meaning of Chikamatsu's intricate passages. Familiarity with earlier plays and with the songs and stories of the day was assumed, and if the audience could not analyze precisely all the word plays in the *michiyuki,* they could at least relax in the stream of beautiful language, carried along by the musical accompaniment.

Chikamatsu's style is almost endlessly complex. We can only marvel that he could produce such astonishing textures of language in the few weeks that normally sufficed for writing an entire play. Perhaps the most characteristic feature of his style is the *engo,* or related word. Chikamatsu seems never to have chosen a word without considering its overtones and pursuing them. For example, the opening description of Tokubei in *The Love Suicides at Sonezaki* runs literally, "A handsome man who has piled up spring after spring can drink one cupful of peach wine and his willow hair is also loosened." In English this does not sound like much, but the original, a chain of *engo,* produces a delightful effect. Chikamatsu, having said "piled up spring after spring" (meaning, to spend a number of years), chooses for "handsome man" an *engo,* the word *hinaotoko,* "doll man," referring to a doll at the spring festival. This festival is known also as the peachblossom festival, thus occasioning the next *engo,* "peach wine". Willow twigs with fresh young leaves also decorate this festival; hence, the *engo* "willow" as an adjective for Tokubei's hair, long and elegant as willow shoots. Finally, the verb *toku,* used for "to loosen", is at the same time the shortened form of Tokubei's name. A translation obviously cannot do justice to this richness of language; one can merely suggest the central ideas.

Another verbal device employed by Chikamatsu was the *kakekotoba,* or "pivot word". The *kakekotoba* changes in meaning depending on the preceding and following words. Thus, *toku* with the preceding word "hair" means to "loosen the hair", but with the following verb "to be called" it means Toku, the hero's name. Chikamatsu's best pivot words (this is not one) add a complexity to the lines, as if a word set the author thinking of ideas related by sound rather than meaning.

Chikamatsu delighted also in head rhymes and end rhymes. Sometimes these are merely repetitions of the same syllables in successive phrases, as in *asamashiya asagizome.* Sometimes they are more extended, as in *fūfu ni furumino furugasa ya,* with its repetitions of the initial *fu.* End rhyme, though usually avoided in Japanese poetry, also contributes to the music of Chikamatsu's texts. *Kussame, kussame, murazame, murazame to* is a simple example; a more complicated one is *oyakata no mokkyaku ari, waga shinjō no mekkyaku ari, ikyaku mo majiri* (Some have parents or masters to pay for their pleasures, others destroy their own fortunes, and bankrupts mingle among them), where the repetition of the rhyme in *kyaku* heightens the rhythm and sense.

The basic rhythm of the plays is the alternating line of seven syllables and five syllables. Chikamatsu heaped scorn on playwrights who tried to cast their lines exactly into this pattern, resorting to meaningless particles to fill out the syllable-count.[30] Chikamatsu's dialogue is usually in prose, and he reserves the regular seven-five, seven-five beat for the descriptive passages.

The following excerpt from *Gonza the Lancer* illustrates many of Chikamatsu's stylistic devices:

Shinki shinki no/ sorarinki/ tsui ni wa ga mi no/ adashigusa/ yo no soshirigusa/ ukikusa ni/ Asaka no mizu no/ moresomete/ Sasano no tsuyu to/ okimadoi/ nemadoi ayumi/ madoite wa . . . (Her mind gave itself to the tortured, pointless jealousy that finally became the seed of her undoing and the slander of the world. The water of Asaka

---

[30] Keene, *The Battles of Coxinga,* p. 94.

trickled away from this rootless plant, to mingle confusedly with the dew of bamboo fields. Awake or in dreams or in aimless wandering . . .).

This excerpt is cast exactly in alternating lines of seven and five syllables. Internal rhyme is used extensively (*shinki* . . . *rinki;* adashi*gusa,* soshiri*gusa,* uki*kusa;* oki*madoi,* ne*madoi, madoi*te). The words in *kusa* (plant) suggest a brief *tsukushi,* or catalogue. *Ukikusa* (a rootless plant) leads to the *engo* of *mizu* (water), and this in turn to its *engo, tsuyu* (dew). The name Asaka (that of Osai's husband) refers also to the famous marsh of Asaka, another watery *engo,* while the dew settles on Sasano (bamboo field), which is Gonza's surname. *Okimadoi* (rising uncertainly) contains the pivot word *oki,* used with the preceding word "dew" to mean "to settle".

These complexities (and there are more) occur in about one line of printed text. Chikamatsu's virtuosity in such passages dazzles us. His dialogue, on the other hand, can be absolutely unadorned. The bareness of the dialogue reflects Chikamatsu's conviction that the social stations of characters must be revealed in their speech. He seems to have felt that a shop assistant would converse in straightforward prose, rather than in poetry, and we have such lines as these by Chūbei to his beloved: "You look a mess. Here, tighten your sash." Shakespeare was apparently less convinced of this point; the sergeant in *Macbeth,* presumably not an eloquent or cultured man, declares, "As whence the sun 'gins his reflection/ Shipwracking storms and direful thunders break . . .". We accept this language from a sergeant as a convention of Shakespeare's theater, but Chikamatsu, writing for a theater in which far greater demands were otherwise made of the audience's imaginative powers, preferred realism in the dialogue of his domestic plays. His sergeants, if any appeared, would have talked like sergeants.

Chikamatsu gave great care to the subtle differences in speech depending on the speaker's class in society and the person addressed.[31] He uses no less than thirteen different levels of politeness for the female characters. Because his plays have no stage directions, it is sometimes necessary to rely on the degree of honorifics to determine who is speaking to whom. In the following brief excerpt three levels of politeness reveal the person addressed: *To lady:* "I'm honored that you have come. Would you perchance be from Osaka?" *To lady's servant:* "Please come in and fan madame." *To her own servant:* "Bring some tea." [32]

Chikamatsu did not make much use of individual or regional peculiarities of speech. Almost all his characters use the same stage language of the Osaka-Kyoto area. Occasionally a man is marked by his localisms; the samurai Honda Yasazaemon in *Yosaku from Tamba* uses the familiar Edo exclamation *saa,* and Kezori in *The Girl from Hakata* introduces Nagasaki words into his long monologues. Chikamatsu, though familiar with all classes of society in Osaka and Kyoto, seems not to have known much else of Japan, and he failed to create local color for Matsue, Hamamatsu, or other parts of the country he treated. Chikamatsu's interest in relations tended to be vertical rather than horizontal; though he was at pains to distinguish the speech of a shop assistant from an owner, or a second rank courtesan from a great courtesan, his various Tokubeis, Jiheis and Yoheis talk much alike.[33]

Structure of the Plays

Most of Chikamatsu's history plays are in five acts, probably in keeping with the number of plays presented in a Nō program.[34] The history plays generally lack a sense of unity of time, scene, or even plot. Thirty or forty years may elapse in the course of a work; even a relatively well-knit play like *The Battles of Coxinga* extends over six or more years and requires nineteen different settings. The looseness of the times and places of the action favored diffuseness and complexity; subplots are almost independent of the main story, and each act tends to stand on its own. In *The Battles of Coxinga* only one character who appears in the first act is seen again until the fourth act. In *The Snow Maiden* (1705) several unrelated stories are arbitrarily joined; though the play contains only three acts, no character in the first act reappears in the second.

Each act of a history play was normally built around a familiar

---

[32] *Uzuki no Momiji* (Tadami, *Chikamatsu Jōruri-Shū,* II, 180).

[33] Compare what Gerald Brenan says of Lope de Vega: "It was typical of the popular nature of his genius that he showed little interest in the moral qualities that differentiate people: his characters are built on the way of life or profession" (*The Literature of the Spanish People,* p. 207).

[34] See Keene, *The Battles of Coxinga,* pp. 27, 86.

situation.[35] A self-sacrificing suicide, the killing by a father of his own child in place of his master's child, the inspection of the severed head of an enemy general, the separation of a mother and child, the appearance of a vengeful spirit or a madwoman—any one of these afforded the puppets or the Kabuki actors with superb moments. The audience, relaxed for a whole day at the theater, looked up from its food and drink for the highlights. Because unity of plot was not important, plays after Chikamatsu's death tended to be sprawling affairs in many acts, any one of which could be presented separately. Today at the puppet or Kabuki theater a program often consists of five acts from five different plays.

The spectacular *karakuri* effects in the puppet theater, or the magnificent posturing and resounding delivery in the Kabuki theater are provided by history plays rather than by the more sophisticated domestic tragedies. This may explain why Chikamatsu continued, even after his artistic triumphs with his domestic plays, to devote the major part of his efforts to the composition of implausible, disjointed histories. It is true that some of the later works in this form show insights that we recognize from the domestic plays, but their structure remains flawed, and the scenes of artistic merit are lost in a farrago of disparate elements. Presumably the history plays were what Chikamatsu's audiences really wanted despite the popularity of some of his domestic plays. Rather than marvel at Chikamatsu's attachment to the former, we might better admire his success with the somber themes of his true tragedies.

Credit for the development of the domestic play should probably be shared by Chikamatsu with Gidayū. Between 1703 and 1714 (the year of Gidayū's death) Chikamatsu wrote sixteen of his twenty-four tragedies. In the following decade, at the height of his powers, he wrote only half as many. We might like perhaps to imagine that Chikamatsu wrote the history plays only in order to give himself the leisure to compose works which meant more to him, but little evidence supports such a view. During 1716, while *The Battles of Coxinga* was enjoying its record-breaking run of seventeen months, he did not feel moved to write a single play. In 1718, a more normal year, he wrote four, including *The Uprooted Pine, The Girl from Hakata,* and two of his best

[35] Utsumi Shigetarō (in *Ningyō Jōruri to Bunraku*, p. 151) distinguishes twenty such situations.

history plays. Probably Chikamatsu did not consider one type of play more elevated than the other.

Nevertheless, as readers two hundred and fifty years later, we cannot fail to be impressed by the superior craftsmanship of the domestic plays. Unlike the amorphous histories, these tragedies approach unity in time, place, and action. Both *The Love Suicides at Sonezaki* and *The Love Suicides in the Women's Temple* take place in less than twenty-four hours. Usually only one setting is needed for each act in a domestic play. Above all, the action in the domestic plays is unified. If there is a subplot, as in *Yosaku from Tamba,* it is carefully joined to the main story. Unlike the all but independent acts of the history plays, those in the domestic plays are so closely linked that sometimes Chikamatsu seems to have intended them to be played without interruption. The last words of one act frequently tie directly to the opening words of the following act. Of course, we need not insist that all tragedies be fitted to the Procrustean bed of the three classical unities, but in a work so closely derived from daily life as the domestic play these unities increase the tension and the sense of tragedy.

The formal structure of the domestic play is simpler and more orderly than that of the history play. The first act presents a problem, the second sees its crisis, and the final act shows us the resolution in the death of the characters or their miraculous deliverance. The *michiyuki,* a purely ornamental feature of the history plays, acquires in the domestic plays a structural function. Not only does it lend tragic stature to the characters, in the manner already described, but its dreamlike atmosphere provides a welcome contrast to the realism of the other scenes.

Unlike that of the history plays, the conclusion of a domestic play is generally reached logically, perhaps because Chikamatsu worked backwards from the conclusions in writing these plays. When he learned, say, of a smuggler who committed suicide on apprehension by the police, it may have set him wondering, "But why did he become a smuggler in the first place?" and so on. In the history plays the requirement of a happy ending could easily lead the whole play into blatantly unhistorical conclusions; in the domestic plays the occasional implausible ending seems hastily tacked on in order to make the work performable at New Year or some other felicitous occasion. The fact that we find some endings in the domestic plays unconvincing is in itself a sign of their superior merit; in the history plays no ending is more or less convincing than another.

Chikamatsu's success in evolving the tight dramatic structure of such a work as *The Love Suicides at Amijima* was not to be matched in Japan for another two hundred and fifty years.

Morality of the Plays

The greatest obstacle to the enjoyment of Chikamatsu by a Western reader is undoubtedly his morality. The chief elements of this morality were *giri* (obligation) and *ninjō* (human feelings), generally depicted as warring with each other. The meanings of *giri* varied considerably according to the circumstances. It might mean obligation to members of one's own family, to fellow townsmen, to one's class, or to society at large, or refer to something closer to the abstract concept of honor. *Ninjō* represented the human sentiments balancing the austere ideals of *giri*.

In *The Love Suicides at Amijima* Koharu is obliged by her *giri* to Osan as a woman to give up Osan's husband. Later, Osan in turn is moved by *giri* to Koharu, and urges her husband to ransom Koharu, though she knows it can only lead to her own unhappiness. Jihei and Koharu in their final moments together talk not of their love but of their *giri* to Osan, and they make elaborate arrangements to die in separate places so as not to offend her.

These examples of *giri* may seem strained; other examples are positively exasperating. In the last scene of *The Courier for Hell*, for instance, Magoemon yearns for a glimpse of his son's face, but he decides that it is not possible. To look at his son, a criminal, would be shirking his *giri* to society. He starts away, only to turn back and ask Umegawa, "What do you think? Would there be any harm in my seeing him?" She answers, "Who will ever know? Please go to him." But Magoemon decides this time that *giri* to Chūbei's adopted family in Osaka does not permit him to look at a son with whom he has formally severed all ties.[36]

Giri among samurai takes even stronger forms. Shigenoi (in *Yosaku from Tamba*) must reject her long-lost son because of her *giri* to the

[36] See Shuzui Kenji, *Giri*, pp. 18–19.

princess she serves; if it is known that the princess's governess has a son who is a horse driver, the princess will be disgraced. A sense of *giri* leads Yura in *The Drum of the Waves of Horikawa* to taunt her brother for his failure to fulfill his obligations as a samurai by killing his wife. Her brother eventually meets the requirements of *giri* only to break down and reproach his family, "If you think so much of your mother, sister, or sister-in-law, why didn't you beg me to spare her life? Why didn't you suggest that she put on Buddhist robes and become a nun?"

In the history plays *giri* assumes its most extravagant forms. In the first act of *The Battles of Coxinga* Ri Tōten gouges out his eye, apparently out of *giri* to the Tartar benefactors of China. Go Sankei, though abused and trampled on by the foolish Ming emperor, retains such a strong sense of *giri* that he kills his own infant son and substitutes it for the imperial child whom he has safely delivered. In the third act Kanki is torn by conflicting kinds of *giri*, which are resolved only when his wife, equally sensitive to *giri*, commits suicide. *Giri* then compels Coxinga's mother to vindicate the honor of Japan by killing herself.

Even more extreme instances of *giri* occur in plays by Chikamatsu's successors. In Takeda Izumo's *Prince of the Great Pagoda* (1723), Saitō Tarozaemon causes the deaths of his son-in-law and his daughter, beheads his grandchild, and finally cuts off his own head, all out of *giri* to the Prince of the Great Pagoda.[37]

Giri, however, is frequently softened by *ninjō*, the tenderer feelings. In *The Woman-Killer* Yohei's mother, a woman of samurai origin, follows the dictates of *giri* in disinheriting her son, but we soon discover that *ninjō* has made her steal money to give her wayward child. Sōshichi's father in *The Girl from Hakata* is prevented by *giri* from looking at his son, a smuggler, but he breaks a hole in the wall big enough for his hand to pass through, and offers Kojorō a cup of water. In *The Almanac of Love* Osan's parents, happily unlike the parents of Osai in *Gonza the Lancer,* trust in their daughter's chastity, and with *ninjō* help her to escape.

Giri untouched by *ninjō* may seem inhuman. It suggests at times the sense of *gloire* in Racinian tragedies with its stern insistence on reason

[37] *Ibid.,* pp. 26–27.

and duty.[38] *Giri* denies the individual's right to be happy at the expense of society. In so doing it preserves society, as *ninjō* unchecked by *giri* must eventually destroy it.

Many Western readers find the manifestations of *ninjō* even harder to take than those of *giri*. Killing one's child to save the child of one's master makes a kind of sense, unspeakable though the act is, but abandoning one's children in order to commit suicide with the woman one loves somehow seems contemptible. Koharu abandons her old mother, doing piece work in a back alley, in order to die with Jihei; Koman gives Yosaku her money and runs away with him, though she knows this means the return of her father to a terrible dungeon. The human feelings which dictate such actions seem reprehensibly self-indulgent, and make us appreciate better the selflessness of *giri*.

But of course we are not meant to consider the actions of the characters in coldly rational terms. "All for Love, or the World Well Lost" might be the title of most of Chikamatsu's domestic plays, and his audiences agreed to this principle, though it meant shutting their eyes to the unfortunate consequences. The sniveling Jihei is, objectively, unmanly, yet we are expected to sympathize with this unfortunate creature, the prey of an overpowering love. Chikamatsu wanted us to feel that despite Jihei's sense of *giri*, which gives dimension to this display of *ninjō*, he is no match for his love. In the end, the strength of this love, which brings him to suicide, will assure him of salvation and Buddhahood.

Religion

Buddhism provides the religious background to the plays as Confucianism, with its insistence on *giri*, provides the ethical basis. The characters in most of the plays are believers in Amida Buddhism, the chief tenet of which is that faith in the bodhisattva Amida's saving grace will enable the believer to be reborn in paradise. The invocation *Namu Amida Butsu* is frequently on the lips of the characters, especially when faced with death. Other Buddhist doctrines which figure in the plays include the notion that causes from a previous existence have their effects in the present existence. Brief passages from the holy writings of

[38] See Francis Fergusson, *The Idea of a Theater*, p. 74.

Buddhism are quoted, and there are descriptions of such popular religious practices of the day as mass excursions to the temples of Kwannon. However, Chikamatsu's characters evince surprisingly little real piety. It does not occur to Tokubei and Ohatsu (or the other unfortunate lovers) to spend their lives in prayer instead of committing suicide. Organized religion is sometimes harshly portrayed, as in the account of the priests on Mount Kōya in *The Love Suicides in the Women's Temple*. In *The Courier for Hell* old Magoemon says, "Some people go to the temples for the sermons, but if they are cruel here, in their hearts, they might just as well not go." At the end of the play, when he thinks that his son has escaped, he cries out in joy, "I owe this to Amida's grace. I must go to the temple again immediately and offer my thanks to the Founder. How happy and grateful I am!" The next instant, however, a voice proclaims the news of the arrest of Chūbei and Umegawa, as if in denial of Magoemon's faith in prayer.

Only rarely is reference made to the specific religious beliefs of the characters. In *Kasane-izutsu* Tokubei and Ofusa are about to depart on their suicide journey. Ofusa suggests that they commit suicide before the gate of a temple belonging to the Lotus (Nichiren) sect. Tokubei agrees, but on reflection realizes that there is a difficulty.

TOKUBEI: You belong to the Lotus sect, and I to the Pure Land. I'm not sure that we'll be together after we die if our prayers are different. I'll change my sect so that we can stay together. Recite the Invocation of the Sutra Name for me. Hurry.

NARRATOR: He joins his hands in prayer. Ofusa is lost in tears that well up despite her.

OFUSA: Instead of asking me to join the Pure Land sect, you have been converted to the Lotus! How happy you make me! Forgive me for having forced you to it. Your conversion must have been brought about by my recitation of the Sutra Name a thousand times each day for the past five years.

The above passage makes clear that doctrinal differences did not unduly sway the characters. Regardless of the sect, the lovers who committed suicide hoped to be reunited after death. The present world, as texts of the Pure Land sect in particular insist, is a place of suffering, and only the future life—rebirth in Amida's paradise, the Pure Land—affords the possibility of happiness. Suicide was not condoned, but no canon against self-slaughter made the lovers hesitate on their final journey. Though their deaths are pathetic they are also filled with joy and confidence in eternal life together on one lotus in the garden of Amida.

Shintō, the Way of the Gods, the native Japanese religion, also figures in the plays, chiefly in the numerous mentions of the sacred dignity of the Grand Shrine of Ise. In *The Battles of Coxinga* the Shintō gods vouchsafe miracles to help the restoration of the Ming. Their importance in the play, however, is patriotic—emphasizing the mysterious strength of Japan—rather than religious.[39] Mediums, faith healers, and other persons connected with Shintō appear in some of the plays. Chikamatsu accepts their powers as he accepts ghosts, will-o'-the-wisps, and other evidences of the supernatural, though he paints some individuals in unflattering terms. Superstitions in Chikamatsu almost invariably turn out to be true, and bad luck is often presaged by violations of superstitious taboos.

Conclusion

A detailed examination of Chikamatsu's time, his language, his religious beliefs, and any other aspect of his work one might choose unfortunately tends to make his plays seem more remote and difficult than when approached without preparation. This, however, is largely true also of Shakespeare, or any other dramatist of the past. We accept the witches in *Macbeth* without worrying too much about Elizabethan demonology, but if we pursued this subject seriously we might become aware of a greater gap between our society and Shakespeare's than we had first supposed. Without research we may sometimes interpret words or sentiments incorrectly, lending them an excessively modern meaning, but in the end such mistakes may become our final truths. Careful study of the text seems to show that Hamlet should be portrayed by a portly, bearded gentleman, rather a dandy, but we no doubt will cling to the image of a thin, beardless, disheveled hero. In the case of Chikamatsu the danger is grave that some readers may be turned away from him by the fear that his society was too remote, his language untranslatable, and his morality alien. Years devoted to a

[39] In the sequel, *The Latter Days of Coxinga*, Kanki denounces Coxinga for his excessive fondness for Japanese ways (including Shintō), and Coxinga is finally obliged to leave the mainland of China for Formosa.

study of these problems would, of course, make Chikamatsu easier. Yet anyone who approaches his masterpieces with an open mind will discover that something important comes through the difficulties, a voice which speaks with human accents about human problems. Across the centuries and the barriers of language and custom we recognize our brothers and ourselves.

THE LOVE SUICIDES
AT SONEZAKI

First performed on June 20, 1703. The suicides described in this play took place on May 22, 1703. Chikamatsu was stirred by them to compose his first domestic tragedy. *The Love Suicides at Sonezaki* has sometimes been criticized for the excessive simplicity of its plot, but it remains one of Chikamatsu's finest works, if only for the poetry in the love journey. Chikamatsu in 1717 added a few scenes to lend the play greater complexity, and perhaps to satisfy a demand that the villain be punished, but the directness of the earlier version appeals more to modern readers and spectators. In the present translation the 1703 text has been used, except that the opening scene, consisting chiefly of an enumeration of the thirty-three temples of Kwannon in the Osaka area (with a pun on each name), is omitted. The scene, virtually unrelated to the remainder of the play, contains no dialogue.

The play, perhaps because Chikamatsu had not yet determined the form of the domestic tragedy, is not divided into acts.

Cast of Characters

TOKUBEI, aged 25, employee of a dealer in soy sauce
KUHEIJI, an oil merchant
HOST of Temma House
CHŌZŌ, an apprentice
CUSTOMER of Ohatsu
TOWNSMEN
OHATSU, aged 19, a courtesan
HOSTESS
COURTESANS
SERVANTS

Scene One: The grounds of the Ikudama Shrine in Osaka.
Time: May 21, 1703.

NARRATOR:

This graceful young man has served many springs
With the firm of Hirano in Uchihon Street;
He hides the passion that burns in his breast
Lest word escape and the scandal spread.
He drinks peach wine, a cup at a time,
And combs with care his elegant locks.
"Toku" he is called, and famed for his taste,
But now, his talents buried underground,
He works as a clerk, his sleeves stained with oil,
A slave to his sweet remembrances of love.
Today he makes the rounds of his clients
With a lad who carries a cask of soy:
They have reached the shrine of Ikudama.

A woman's voice calls from a bench inside a refreshment stand.

OHATSU: Tokubei—that's you, isn't it? [1]

NARRATOR: She claps her hands, and Tokubei [2] nods in recognition.

TOKUBEI: Chōzō, I'll be following later. Make the rounds of the temples in Tera Street and the uptown mansions, and then return to the shop. Tell them that I'll be back soon. Don't forget to call on the dyer's in Azuchi Street and collect the money he owes us. And stay away from Dōtombori. [3]

NARRATOR: He watches as long as the boy remains in sight, then lifts the bamboo blinds.

TOKUBEI: Ohatsu—what's the matter?

NARRATOR: He starts to remove his bamboo hat.

OHATSU: Please keep your hat on just now. I have a customer from the country today who's making a pilgrimage to all thirty-three temples of Kwannon. He's been boasting that he intends to spend the whole day drinking. At the moment he's gone off to hear the imper-

---

[1] His face is covered by a deep wicker hat, commonly worn by visitors to the gay quarters.

[2] The pronunciation of the name given in the text is Tokubyōe, but I have followed the more normal modern pronunciation.

[3] A street in Osaka famed for its theaters and houses of pleasure.

sonators' show,[4] but if he returns and finds us together, there might be trouble. All the chair-bearers know you. It's best you keep your face covered.

But to come back to us. Lately you haven't written me a word. I've been terribly worried but, not knowing what the situation might be in your shop, I couldn't very well write you. I must have called a hundred times at the Tamba House, but they hadn't any news of you either. Somebody—yes, it was Taichi, the blind musician—asked his friends, and they said you'd gone back to the country. I couldn't believe it was true. You've really been too cruel. Didn't you even want to ask about me? Perhaps you hoped things would end that way, but I've been sick with worry. If you think I'm lying, feel this swelling!

NARRATOR: She takes his hand and presses it to her breast, weeping reproachful and entreating tears, exactly as if they were husband and wife. Man though he is, he also weeps.

TOKUBEI: You're right, entirely right, but what good would it have done to tell you and make you suffer? I've been going through such misery that I couldn't be more distracted if Bon, New Year, the Ten Nights, and every other feast in the calendar came all at once. My mind's been in a turmoil, and my finances in chaos. To tell the truth, I went up to Kyoto to raise some money, among other things. It's a miracle I'm still alive. If they make my story into a three-act play, I'm sure the audiences will weep.

NARRATOR: Words fail and he can only sigh.

OHATSU: And is this the comic relief of your tragedy? Why couldn't you have trusted me with your worries when you tell me even trivial little things? You must've had some reason for hiding. Why don't you take me into your confidence?

NARRATOR: She leans over his knee. Bitter tears soak her handkerchief.

TOKUBEI: Please don't cry or be angry with me. I wasn't hiding anything, but it wouldn't have helped to involve you. At any rate, my troubles have largely been settled, and I can tell you the whole story now.

My master has always treated me with particular kindness because

[4] Within the precincts of the Ikudama Shrine were booths where various types of entertainment were presented. The impersonators mimicked the speech and posture of popular actors.

I'm his nephew. For my part, I've served him with absolute honesty. There's never been a penny's discrepancy in the accounts. It's true that recently I used his name when I bought on credit a bolt of Kaga silk to make into a summer kimono, but that's the one and only time, and if I have to raise the money on the spot, I can always sell back the kimono without taking a loss. My master has been so impressed by my honesty that he proposed I marry his wife's niece with a dowry of two *kamme*,[5] and promised to set me up in business. That happened last year, but how could I shift my affections when I have you? I didn't give his suggestion a second thought, but in the meantime my mother —she's really my stepmother—conferred with my master, keeping it a secret from me. She went back to the country with the two *kamme* in her clutches. Fool that I am, I never dreamt what had happened.

The trouble began last month when they tried to force me to marry. I got angry and said, "Master, you surprise me. You know how unwilling I am to get married, and yet you've inveigled my old mother into giving her consent. You've gone too far, master. I can't understand the mistress's attitude either. If I took as my wife this young lady whom I've always treated with the utmost deference and accepted her dowry in the bargain, I'd spend my whole life dancing attendance on my wife. How could I ever assert myself? I've refused once, and even if my father were to return from his grave, the answer would still be no."

The master was furious that I should have answered so bluntly. His voice shook with rage. "I know your real reasons. You've involved with Ohatsu, or whatever her name is, from the Temma House in Dōjima. That's why you seem so averse to my wife's niece. Very well—after what's been said, I'm no longer willing to give you the girl, and since there's to be no wedding, return the money. Settle without fail by the twenty-second of the month and clear your business accounts. I'll chase you from Osaka and never let you set foot here again!"

I too have my pride as a man. "Right you are!" I answered, and rushed off to my village. But my so-called mother wouldn't let the money from her grip, not if this world turned into the next. I went to Kyoto, hoping to borrow the money from the wholesale soy sauce dealers in the Fifth Ward. I've always been on good terms with them. But, as ill luck would have it, they had no money to spare. I retraced

[5] A measure of silver, worth about one thousand dollars.

my steps to the country, and this time, with the intercession of the whole village, I managed to extract the money from my mother. I intended to return the dowry immediately and settle things for once and for all. But if I can't remain in Osaka, how shall I be able to meet you?

My bones may be crushed to powder, my flesh be torn away, and I may sink, an empty shell, in the slime of Shijimi River. Let that happen if it must, but if I am parted from you, what shall I do?

NARRATOR: He weeps, suffocated by his grief. Ohatsu, holding back the welling tears of sympathy, strengthens and comforts him.

OHATSU: How you've suffered! And when I think that it's been because of me, I feel happy, sad, and most grateful all at once. But please, show more courage. Pull yourself together. Your uncle may have forbidden you to set foot in Osaka again, but you haven't committed robbery or arson. I'll think of some way to keep you here. And if a time should come when we can no longer meet, did our promises of love hold only for this world? Others before us have chosen reunion through death. To die is simple enough—none will hinder and none be hindered on the journey to the Mountain of Death and the River of Three Ways.[6]

NARRATOR: Ohatsu falters among these words of encouragement, choked by tears. She resumes.

OHATSU: The twenty-second is tomorrow. Return the money early, since you must return it anyway. Try to get in your master's good graces again.

TOKUBEI: I want to, and I'm impatient to return the money, but on the thirteenth of the month Kuheiji the oil merchant—I think you know him—begged me desperately for the money. He said he needed it only for one day, and promised to return it by the morning of the eighteenth. I decided to lend him the money since I didn't need it until the twenty-second, and it was for a friend close as a brother. He didn't get in touch with me on the eighteenth or nineteenth. Yesterday he was out and I couldn't see him. I intended to call on him this morning, but I've spent it making the rounds of my customers in order to wind up my business by tomorrow. I'll go to him this evening and settle everything. He's a man of honor and he knows my predicament. I'm sure nothing will go wrong. Don't worry. Oh—look there, Ohatsu!

[6] Places in the Japanese afterworld.

NARRATOR:

> "Hatsuse is far away,
> Far too is Naniwa-dera:
> So many temples are renowned
> For the sound of their bells,
> Voices of the Eternal Law.
> If, on an evening in spring,
> You visit a mountain temple
> You will see . . ." [7]

At the head of a band of revelers

TOKUBEI: Kuheiji! That's a poor performance! [8] You've no business running off on excursions when you haven't cleared up your debt with me. Today we'll settle our account.

NARRATOR: He grasps Kuheiji's arm and restrains him. Kuheiji's expression is dubious.

KUHEIJI: What are you talking about, Tokubei? These people with me are all residents of the ward. We've had a meeting in Ueshio Street to raise funds for a pilgrimage to Ise. We've drunk a little saké, but we're on our way home now. What do you mean by grabbing my arm? Don't be rowdy!

NARRATOR: He removes his wicker hat and glares at Tokubei.

TOKUBEI: I'm not being rowdy. All I ask is that you return the two *kamme* of silver I lent you on the thirteenth, which you were supposed to repay on the eighteenth.

NARRATOR: Before he can finish speaking, Kuheiji bursts out laughing.

KUHEIJI: Are you out of your mind, Tokubei? I can't remember having borrowed a penny from you in all the years I've known you. Don't make any accusations which you'll regret.

NARRATOR: He shakes himself free. His companions also remove their hats.[9] Tokubei pales with astonishment.

TOKUBEI: Don't say that, Kuheiji! You came to me in tears, saying

---

[7] A passage from the Nō play *Miidera*, here quoted mainly because the first word, "Hatsuse," echoes the name Ohatsu in the preceding line. The last words similarly point to the arrival of Kuheiji. Most of this passage would be sung not by a single chanter but by a chorus, as in a Nō play.

[8] Tokubei, relieved to see Kuheiji, at first teases him about his singing of the Nō passage, but his words have an undertone of criticism of Kuheiji's past behavior.

[9] Readying themselves to come to Kuheiji's defense.

that you couldn't survive your monthly bills,[10] and I thought that this was the kind of emergency for which we'd been friends all these years. I lent you the money as an act of generosity, though I needed it desperately myself. I told you that I didn't even require a receipt, but you insisted on putting your seal to one, for form's sake. You made me write out a promissory note and you sealed it. Don't try to deny it, Kuheiji!

NARRATOR: Tokubei rebukes him heatedly.

KUHEIJI: What's that? I'd like to see the seal.

TOKUBEI: Do you think I'm afraid to show you?

NARRATOR: He produces the paper from his wallet.

TOKUBEI: If these gentlemen are from the ward, I am sure that they will recognize your seal. Will you still dispute it?

NARRATOR: When he unfolds the paper and displays it, Kuheiji claps his hands in recollection.

KUHEIJI: Yes, it's my seal all right. Oh, Tokubei, I never thought you'd do such a thing, not even if you were starving and forced to eat dirt. On the tenth of the month I lost a wallet containing the seal. I advertised for it everywhere, but without success, so as of the sixteenth of this month, as I've informed these gentlemen, I've changed my seal. Could I have affixed the seal I lost on the tenth to a document on the thirteenth? No—what happened was that you found my wallet, wrote the promissory note, and affixed my seal. Now you're trying to extort money from me—that makes you a worse criminal than a forger. You'd do better, Tokubei, to commit out-and-out robbery. You deserve to have your head cut off, but for old times' sake, I'll forgive you. Let's see if you can make any money out of this!

NARRATOR: He throws the note in Tokubei's face and glares at him fiercely in an extraordinary display of feigned innocence. Tokubei, furious, cries aloud.

TOKUBEI: You've been damned clever. You've put one over on me. I'm dishonored. What am I to do? Must I let you take my money brazenly from me? You've planned everything so cleverly that even if I go to court, I'm sure to lose. I'll take back my money with my fists! See

[10] I have converted all dates to the Western calendar, but the dates in the lunar calendar correspond to the end of the third moon. Kuheiji needs the money to pay end-of-the-month bills.

here! I'm Tokubei of the Hirano-ya, a man of honor. Do you follow me? I'm not a man to trick a friend out of his money the way you have. Come on!

NARRATOR: He falls on Kuheiji.

KUHEIJI: You impudent little apprentice! I'll knock the insolence out of you!

NARRATOR: He seizes the front of Tokubei's kimono and they grapple, trading blows and shoves. Ohatsu rushes barefoot [11] to them.

OHATSU (to townsmen): Please everybody, stop the fight! He's a friend of mine. Where are the chair-bearers? Why don't they do something? Tokubei's being beaten!

NARRATOR: She writhes in anguish, but is helpless. Her customer, country bumpkin that he is, bundles her forcibly into a palanquin.

CUSTOMER: It won't do for you to get hurt.

OHATSU: Please wait just a moment! Oh, I'm so unhappy!

NARRATOR: The palanquin is rushed off, leaving only the echoes of her weeping voice.

Tokubei is alone; Kuheiji has five companions. Men rush out from the nearby booths and drive them all with sticks to the lotus pond.[12] Who tramples Tokubei? Who beats him? There is no way to tell. His hair is disheveled, his sash undone. He stumbles and falls to this side and that.

TOKUBEI: Kuheiji, you swine! Do you think I'll let you escape alive?

NARRATOR: He staggers about searching for Kuheiji, but he has fled and vanished. Tokubei falls heavily in his tracks and, weeping bitterly, he cries aloud.

TOKUBEI (to bystanders): I feel humiliated and ashamed that you've seen me this way. There was not a false word in my accusation. I've always treated Kuheiji like a brother, and when he begged me for the money, saying he'd never forget it as long as he lived, I lent it to him, sure that he'd do the same for me, though the money was precious as life, and I knew that without it tomorrow, the twenty-first, I'd have to kill myself. He made me write the note in my own hand, then put his seal to it. But it was a seal which he had already reported as lost, and now he's turned the accusations against me! It's mortifying, in-

---

[11] In her agitation she fails to slip on her *geta*. We must suppose that her country customer has returned during the dialogue between Tokubei and Kuheiji.

[12] This pond may still be seen today at the Ikudama Shrine.

furiating—to be kicked and beaten this way, dishonored and forced to my knees. It would've been better if I had died while smashing and biting him!

NARRATOR: He strikes the ground and gnashes his teeth, clenches his fists and moans, a sight to stir compassion.

TOKUBEI: There's no point in my talking this way. Before three days have passed I, Tokubei, will make amends by showing all Osaka the purity at the bottom of my heart.

NARRATOR: The meaning of these words is later known.

TOKUBEI: I'm sorry to have bothered you all. Please forgive me.

NARRATOR: He speaks his apologies, picks up his battered hat and puts it on. His face, downcast in the sinking rays of the sun, is clouded by tears that engulf him. Dejectedly he leaves, a sight too pitiful to behold.

Scene Two: Inside the Temma House.
Time: Evening of the same day.

NARRATOR:
The breezes of love are all-pervasive
By Shijimi River,[13] where love-drowned guests
Like empty shells, bereft of their senses,
Wander the dark ways of love
Lit each night by burning lanterns,
Fireflies that glow in the four seasons,
Stars that shine on rainy nights.
By Plum Bridge,[14] blossoms show even in summer.
Rustics on a visit, city connoisseurs,
All journey the varied roads of love,
Where adepts wander and novices play:
What a lively place this New Quarter is![15]

But alas for Ohatsu of the Temma House—even after she returns the day's events still weigh on her. She cannot swallow her saké, she feels on edge. As she sits weeping, some courtesans from the neighboring houses and other friends come for a little chat.

[13] The word *shijimi* means the corbicula, a kind of small shellfish, and the name of the river thus occasions mention of shells.

[14] Umeda Bridge, the name of which means literally "plum field".

[15] The Dōjima New Quarter in Osaka was opened about 1700.

FIRST COURTESAN: Have you heard, Ohatsu? They say that Toku was given a thrashing for something bad he did. Is it true?

SECOND COURTESAN: No, my customer told me that Toku was trampled to death.

NARRATOR: They say he was fettered for fraud or trussed for counterfeiting a seal. Not one decent thing have they to report: every expression of sympathy makes their visit the more painful.

OHATSU: No, please, not another word. The more I hear, the worse my breast pains me. I'm sure I'll be the first to die. I wish I were dead already.

NARRATOR: She can only weep. But amidst her tears she happens to look outside and catches a glimpse of Tokubei, a pathetic figure wearing a wicker hat, even at night.[16] Her heart leaps, and she wants to run to him, but in the sitting room are the master and his wife, and by the entrance stands the cook, while in the kitchen a maid is hovering: with so many sharp eyes watching, she cannot do as she pleases.

OHATSU: I feel terribly depressed. I think I'll step outside for a moment.

NARRATOR: She slips out softly.

OHATSU: What happened? I've heard rumors of every sort about you. They've driven me out of my mind with worry.

NARRATOR: She thrusts her face under the brim of his wicker hat and weeps in secret, soundless, painful tears. He too is lost in tears.

TOKUBEI: I've been made the victim of a clever plot, as no doubt you've heard, and the more I struggle, the worse off I am. Everything has turned against me now. I can't survive this night. I've made up my mind to it.

NARRATOR: As he whispers, voices are heard from within.

VOICES: Come inside, Ohatsu. There's enough gossip about you as it is.[17]

OHATSU: There—did you hear? We can't go on talking. Do as I show you.

NARRATOR: She hides him under the train of her mantle. He crawls behind her to the garden door, where he slips beneath the porch at the

[16] The wicker hat was worn for concealment, but at night this precaution was normally unnecessary.

[17] Standing in the street outside the teahouse was likely to occasion gossip about secret lovers.

step. Ohatsu sits by the entrance and, pulling the tobacco tray to her, lights her pipe. She assumes an air of unconcern.

At this moment Kuheiji and a couple of his loudmouthed friends burst in, accompanied by a blind musician.

KUHEIJI: Hello, girls. You're looking lonesome. Would you like me for a customer? Hello there, host. I haven't seen you in ages.

NARRATOR: He strides arrogantly into the room.

HOST: Bring a tobacco tray and some saké cups.

NARRATOR: He makes the customary fuss over the guests.

KUHEIJI: No, don't bother about saké. We were drinking before we came. I have something to tell you. Tokubei, the number one customer of your Ohatsu, found a seal I'd lost and tried to cheat me out of two *kamme* in silver with a forged note. The facts were too much for him, and he finally met with some unpleasantness from which he was lucky to escape alive. His reputation has been ruined. Be on your guard if he comes here again. Everybody will tell you that I speak the truth, so even if Tokubei tells you the exact opposite, don't believe him for a moment. You'd do best not to let him in at all. Sooner or later he's bound to end up on the gallows.[18]

NARRATOR: He pours out his words convincingly. Tokubei, underneath the porch, gnashes his teeth and trembles with rage. Ohatsu, afraid that he may reveal himself, calms him with her foot, calms him gently. The host is loath to answer yes or no, for Tokubei's a customer of long standing.

HOST: Well, then, how about some soup?

NARRATOR: Covering his confusion, he leaves the room. Ohatsu, weeping bitterly, exclaims.

OHATSU: You needn't try your clever words on me. Tokubei and I have been intimate for years. We've told each other our inmost secrets. He hasn't a particle of deceit in him, the poor boy. His generosity has been his undoing. He's been tricked, but he hasn't the evidence to prove it. After what has happened Tokubei has no choice but to kill himself. I wish I knew whether or not he was resolved to die.

NARRATOR: She pretends to be talking to herself, but with her foot she questions him. He nods, and taking her ankle, passes it across his throat, to let her know that he is bent on suicide.

---

[18] Literally, "he's bound to end up at Noe or Tobita." Noe and Tobita were execution grounds on the outskirts of Osaka.

OHATSU: I knew it. I knew it. No matter how long one lives, it comes to the same thing. Only death can wipe out the disgrace.

NARRATOR: Kuheiji is startled by her words.

KUHEIJI: What is Ohatsu talking about? Why should Tokubei kill himself? Well, if he kills himself, I'll take good care of you after he's gone! I think you've fallen for me too!

OHATSU: That's most generous of you, I'm sure. But would you object if, by way of thanks for your kindness, I killed you? Could I go on living even a moment if separated from Toku? Kuheiji, you dirty thief! Anyone hearing your silly lies can only suspect you. I'm sure that Toku intends to die with me, as I with him.

NARRATOR: She taps with her foot, and Tokubei, weeping, takes it in his hands and reverently touches it to his forehead. He embraces her knees and sheds tears of love. She too can hardly conceal her emotions. Though no word is spoken, answering each other heart to heart, they silently weep. That no one knows makes it sadder still.

Kuheiji feels uncomfortable.

KUHEIJI: The wind's against us today. Let's get out of here. The whores in this place are certainly peculiar—they seem to have an aversion for customers like ourselves with plenty of money to spend. Let's stop at the Asa House and have a drink there. We'll rattle around a couple of gold pieces, then go home to bed. Oh—my wallet is so heavy I can hardly walk.

NARRATOR: Spewing forth all manner of abuse, they noisily depart. The host and his wife call to the servants.

HOST: It's time to put out the lights for the night. Lay out beds for the guests who are staying on. Ohatsu, you sleep upstairs. Get to bed early.

OHATSU (to herself): Master, mistress, I shall probably never see you again. Farewell. Farewell to all the servants too.

NARRATOR: Thus inwardly taking leave, she goes to her bedchamber. Later they will learn that this was a parting for life; how pitiful the foolish hearts of men who do not realize the truth in time!

HOST: See that the fire is out under the kettle. Don't let the mice get at the relishes.

NARRATOR: They shut the place and bar the gate. Hardly have their heads touched their pillows than all are snoring merrily. So short is the night that before they've had a chance to dream, two o'clock in the morning has come. Ohatsu is dressed for death, a black cloak dark as the ways of love thrown over her kimono of spotless white. She tiptoes to the staircase and looks down. Tokubei shows his face from under the porch. He beckons, nods, points, communicating his intent without a word. Below the stairs a servant girl is sleeping. A hanging lantern brightly shines. Ohatsu in desperation attaches her fan to a palm-leaf broom, and from the second step of the staircase attempts in vain to extinguish the flame. At last, by stretching every inch, she puts it out, only to tumble suddenly down the stairs. The lamp is out, and in the darkness the servant girl turns in her sleep. Trembling, the lovers grope for each other—a fearful moment. The host awakens in his room to the back.

HOST: What was that noise just now? Servants! The night lamp has gone out. Get up and light it!

NARRATOR: The servant girl, aroused, sleepily rubs her eyes and gets up from bed stark naked.

SERVANT: I can't find the flint box.

NARRATOR: She wanders about the room searching, and Ohatsu, faint with terror, dodges this way and that to avoid her. At last she catches Tokubei's hand, and softly they creep to the entranceway. They unfasten the latch, but the hinges creak, and frightened by the noise, they hesitate. Just then the maid begins to strike the flints; they time their actions to the rasping sound, and with each rasp open the door farther until, huddled together and their sleeves twisted round them, they pass through the door one after the other, feeling as though they tread on a tiger's tail. They exchange glances and cry out for joy, happy that they are to die—a painful, heart-rending sight. The life left them now is as brief as sparks that fly from blocks of flint.

Scene Three: The journey from Dōjima to the Sonezaki Shrine.

NARRATOR:
Farewell to this world, and to the night farewell.
We who walk the road to death, to what should we be likened?
To the frost by the road that leads to the graveyard,
Vanishing with each step we take ahead:
How sad is this dream of a dream!

TOKUBEI:

> Ah, did you count the bell? Of the seven strokes
> That mark the dawn, six have sounded.
> The remaining one will be the last echo
> We shall hear in this life.

OHATSU:

> It will echo the bliss of nirvana.

NARRATOR:

> Farewell, and not to the bell alone—
> They look a last time on the grass, the trees, the sky.
> The clouds, the river go by unmindful of them;
> The Dipper's bright reflection shines in the water.

TOKUBEI:

> Let's pretend that Umeda Bridge
> Is the bridge the magpies built [19]
> Across the Milky Way, and make a vow
> To be husband and wife stars for eternity.

OHATSU:

> I promise. I'll be your wife forever.

NARRATOR:

> They cling together—the river waters
> Will surely swell with the tears they shed.
> Across the river, in a teahouse upstairs,
> Some revelers, still not gone to bed,
> Are loudly talking under blazing lamps—
> No doubt gossiping about the good or bad
> Of this year's crop of lovers' suicides;
> Their hearts sink to hear these voices.

TOKUBEI:

> How strange! but yesterday, even today,
> We spoke as if such things did not concern us.
> Tomorrow we shall figure in their gossip.
> If the world will sing about us, let it sing.

NARRATOR:

> This is the song that now they hear.
> "I'm sure you'll never have me for your wife,

[19] Allusion to the Chinese legend, familiar also in Japan, which tells of two stars (known as the Herd Boy and the Weaver Girl) that meet once a year, crossing over a bridge in the sky built by magpies.

I know my love means nothing to you . . ."
Yes, for all our love, for all our grieving,
Our lives, our lots, have not been as we wished.
Never, until this very day, have we known
A single night of heart's relaxation—
Instead, the tortures of an ill-starred love.
  "What is this bond between us?
  I cannot forget you.
  But you would shake me off and go—
  I'll never let you!
  Kill me with your hands, then go.
  I'll never release you!"
  So she said in tears.[20]

OHATSU:

Of all the many songs, that one, tonight!

TOKUBEI:

Who is it singing? We who listen

BOTH:

Suffer the ordeal of those before us.

NARRATOR:

They cling to each other, weeping bitterly.
Any other night would not matter
If tonight were only a little longer,
But the heartless summer night, as is its wont,
Breaks as cockcrows hasten their last hour.

TOKUBEI:

It will be worse if we wait for dawn.
Let us die in the wood of Tenjin.[21]

NARRATOR:

He leads her by the hand.
At Umeda Embankment, the night ravens.

TOKUBEI:

Tomorrow our bodies may be their meal.

OHATSU:

It's strange, this is your unlucky year [22]

[20] The song overheard by Ohatsu and Tokubei is derived from a popular ballad of the time which describes a love suicide.
[21] The shrine of Sonezaki, sacred to Tenjin (Sugawara no Michizane).
[22] According to yin-yang divination, a man's twenty-fifth, forty-second, and sixtieth years were dangerous; for a woman her nineteenth and thirty-third years.

Of twenty-five, and mine of nineteen.
It's surely proof how deep are our ties
That we who love each other are cursed alike.
All the prayers I have made for this world
To the gods and to the Buddha, I here and now
Direct to the future: in the world to come
May we be reborn on the same lotus!

NARRATOR:

One hundred eight the beads her fingers tell
On her rosary; [23] tears increase the sum.
No end to her grief, but the road has an end:
Their minds are numbed, the sky is dark, the wind still,
They have reached the thick wood of Sonezaki.

Shall it be here, shall it be there? When they brush the grass, the falling dew vanishes even quicker than their lives, in this uncertain world a lightning flash—or was it something else?

OHATSU: I'm afraid. What was that now?

TOKUBEI: That was a human spirit.[24] I thought we alone would die tonight, but someone else has preceded us. Whoever it may be, we'll have a companion on the journey to the Mountain of Death. *Namu Amida Butsu. Namu Amida Butsu.*[25]

NARRATOR: She weeps helplessly.

OHATSU: To think that others are dying tonight too! How heartbreaking!

NARRATOR: Man though he is, his tears fall freely.

TOKUBEI: Those two spirits flying together—do you suppose they belong to anyone else? They must be yours and mine!

OHATSU: Those two spirits? Then, are we dead already?

TOKUBEI: Normally, if we saw a spirit, we'd knot our clothes and murmur prayers to keep our souls with us,[26] but now we hurry towards our end, hoping instead our two souls will find the same dwelling. Do not mistake the way, do not lose me!

NARRATOR: They embrace, flesh to flesh, then fall to the ground and weep—how pitiful they are! Their strings of tears unite like en-

---

[23] The Buddhist rosary has 108 beads, one for each of the sufferings occasioned by the passions.

[24] *Hitodama*, a kind of will-o'-the-wisp believed to be a human soul.

[25] The invocation to Amida Buddha used in Pure Land Buddhism.

[26] Exorcism practiced to prevent the soul from leaving the body.

twining branches, or the pine and palm that grow from a single trunk,[27] a symbol of eternal love. Here the dew of their unhappy lives will at last settle.

TOKUBEI: Let this be the spot.

NARRATOR: He unfastens the sash of his cloak. Ohatsu removes her tear-stained outer robe, and throws it on the palm tree; the fronds might now serve as a broom to sweep away the sad world's dust. Ohatsu takes a razor from her sleeve.

OHATSU: I had this razor prepared in case we were overtaken on the way and separated. I was determined not to forfeit our name as lovers. How happy I am that we are to die together as we hoped!

TOKUBEI: How wonderful of you to have thought of that! I am so confident in our love that I have no fears even about death. And yet it would be unfortunate if because of the pain we are to suffer people said that we looked ugly in death. Let us secure our bodies to this twin-trunked tree and die immaculately! We will become an unparalleled example of a lovers' suicide.

OHATSU: Yes, let us do that.

NARRATOR: Alas! She little thought she thus would use her light blue undersash! She draws it taut, and with her razor slashes it through.

OHATSU: The sash is cut, but you and I will never be torn apart.

NARRATOR: She sits, and he binds her twice, thrice to the tree, firmly so that she will not stir.

TOKUBEI: Is it tight?

OHATSU: Very tight.

NARRATOR: She looks at her husband, and he at her—they burst into tears.

BOTH: This is the end of our unhappy lives!

TOKUBEI: No I mustn't give way to grief.

NARRATOR: He lifts his head and joins his hands in prayer.

TOKUBEI: My parents died when I was a boy, and I grew up thanks to the efforts of my uncle, who was my master. It disgraces me to die without repaying his kindness. Instead I shall cause him trouble which will last even after my death. Please forgive my sins.

Soon I shall see my parents in the other world. Father, Mother, welcome me there!

NARRATOR: He weeps. Ohatsu also joins her hands.

[27] Such a tree actually existed, as contemporary accounts of the Sonezaki Shrine show.

OHATSU: I envy you. You say you will meet your parents in the world of the dead. My father and mother are in this world and in good health. I wonder when I shall see them again. I heard from them this spring, but I haven't seen them since the beginning of last autumn. Tomorrow, when word reaches the village of our suicides, how unhappy they will be! Now I must bid farewell for this life to my parents, my brothers and sisters. If at least my thoughts can reach you, please appear before me, if only in dreams. Dear Mother, beloved Father!

NARRATOR: She sobs and wails aloud. Her husband also cries out and sheds incessant tears in all too understandable emotion.

OHATSU: We could talk forever, but it serves no purpose. Kill me, kill me quickly!

NARRATOR: She hastens the moment of death.

TOKUBEI: I'm ready.

NARRATOR: He swiftly draws his dagger.

TOKUBEI: The moment has come. *Namu Amida. Namu Amida.*

NARRATOR: But when he tries to bring the blade against the skin of the woman he's loved, and held and slept with so many months and years, his eyes cloud over, his hand shakes. He tries to steady his weakening resolve, but still he trembles, and when he thrusts, the point misses. Twice or thrice the flashing blade deflects this way and that until a cry tells it has struck her throat.

TOKUBEI: *Namu Amida. Namu Amida. Namu Amida Butsu.*

NARRATOR: He twists the blade deeper and deeper, but the strength has left his arm. When he sees her weaken, he stretches forth his hands. The last agonies of death are indescribable.

TOKUBEI: Must I lag behind you? Let's draw our last breaths together.

NARRATOR: He thrusts and twists the razor in his throat, until it seems the handle or the blade must snap. His eyes grow dim, and his last painful breath is drawn away at its appointed hour.[28] No one is there to tell the tale, but the wind that blows through Sonezaki Wood transmits it, and high and low alike gather to pray for these lovers who beyond a doubt will in the future attain Buddhahood. They have become models of true love.

[28] It was believed by practitioners of yin-yang divination that a person's hour of death was determined at his birth and could be foretold by an examination of the celestial stems governing his birth. Death normally occurred with the receding of the tide.

THE BATTLES
OF COXINGA

First performed on November 26, 1715. "The Battles of Coxinga" was Chikamatsu's most popular work. Its first run lasted seventeen months, and it was frequently revived thereafter. The popularity of the play has been attributed to the appeal it exerted on the Japanese during the period of Tokugawa seclusion, when they were prohibited by law from going abroad. The Chinese scenes undoubtedly had an exotic interest for the audience, but the quality of the writing was in the end responsible for the play's great success. It is Chikamatsu's finest history play (*jidaimono*), and the only one represented in this collection. Unlike his domestic tragedies, "The Battles of Coxinga" is filled with heroics and even bombast. The incessant surprises and shifts of mood may also bewilder some readers, but this variety, which exploits to the full the possibilities of the puppet stage, has delighted audiences for over two hundred years.

Cast of Characters

WATŌNAI, later known as Coxinga
IKKAN, also called Tei Shiryū Rōikkan, his father
EMPEROR of China
CROWN PRINCE, later Emperor Eiryaku
GO SANKEI, loyal minister of the emperor
KANKI, ally of Coxinga
KING of Tartary
BAIROKU, a Tartar prince
RI TŌTEN, Chinese confederate of the Tartars
RI KAIHŌ, his brother
AN TAIJIN, captain under Ri Tōten
GŌDATSU, his henchman
SARYŌKO, URYŌKO, Tartar generals

FIRST OLD MAN, ghost of first Ming emperor
SECOND OLD MAN, ghost of Liu Po-wen
BOY, god of Sumiyoshi
SOLDIERS, BEATERS
EMPRESS of China
SENDAN, a Chinese princess
RYŪKAKUN, wife of Go Sankei
KINSHŌJO, wife of Kanki, half sister of Coxinga
KOMUTSU, wife of Coxinga
MOTHER of Coxinga
LADIES, MAIDS

ACT ONE

*Scene One: The court of the Emperor Shisōretsu in Nanking.
Time: May, 1644.*

NARRATOR:
Blossoms scatter and butterflies take fright
At spring's departure, but men are not grieved:
In the Water Pavilion and Gallery of Clouds
Another spring has been created.
From dawn a thousand ladies in gay attire
Dazzle the eye with glossy brows and crimson lips.
The ground itself seems rich with plum flower scent;
The peach and cherry blossom eternally
In glorious Nanking where brilliance reigns.
Now, he who is styled the Emperor Shisōretsu, the seventeenth
sovereign of the great Ming, is the second son of the Emperor Kōsō.
The thread of succession has passed unbroken from generation to
generation; the lands to the four directions, bowing in submission like
a green willow in the wind, offer rich treasures in tribute. The emperor delights in song, dancing, and revels, and within his lovely palace
he keeps three consorts, nine spouses of the second rank, twenty-seven of
the third rank, and eighty-one concubines. Some three thousand maids
of honor delight him with their beauty. His ministers and nobles, vying
for his favors, present him with rare and precious gifts: in dead of
winter he is offered summer melons. Such is the luxury of his court.

Now, the Lady Kasei, most beloved by the emperor of his three thousand women, conceived in the autumn of last year, and in this month an imperial birth is expected. Great is the pleasure of the emperor and the joy of his subjects, for although he has reached his fortieth year there is no crown prince to carry on the succession. The previous prayers to Heaven and Earth have this time been granted. When the forthcoming birth of a royal child was confirmed, the lying-in chamber was decked with pearls and jade. Swaddling clothes have been sewn of Etsu silks and Shoku brocades, and everything is ready for the birth which may occur at any moment.

Among those at court Ryūkakun, the wife of Go Sankei, the president of the council of war, was safely delivered recently of her first child and, especially because her milk is for a boy, she has been designated as the wet nurse for the imperial child. Other wet nurses, serving maids, and palace ladies of every rank attend Kasei, and carefully watch over her, as though she were a precious jewel in their hands.

Early in May of the seventeenth year of Sōtei,[1] the Great King Junji, lord of Tartary, has sent an envoy to offer presents to the emperor— tiger skins, leopard skins, cloth from the South Seas washed in fire, horse-liver stones from Ceylon,[2] treasures from remote kingdoms and islands. The envoy, Prince Bairoku, respectfully addresses the throne.

BAIROKU: Tartary and China have vied for supremacy from ancient days. We have quarreled over territory, mobilized troops, fought with our weapons, and formed lasting enmities—a violation of the friendship expected of neighboring nations and a source of affliction to our peoples. Tartary is a big country and, I may say, we are not wanting in the Seven Precious Things[3] or the Ten Thousand Treasures, but our women are not as beautiful as those of other lands. Our great king, hearing that there is a peerless beauty named Lady Kasei at the court of the emperor of China, has become enamoured and deeply desires her. He asks that the emperor send the Lady Kasei to him so that he may honor her as the consort of the great king and thereby establish future relations like those of parent and child between China and Tartary. He has sent these tributary offerings in order to promote lasting peace. I,

---

[1] 1644. For a further explanation of the historical personages of this scene, see Keene, *The Battles of Coxinga*, p. 179.
[2] One of the magical properties of this stone was that it would turn white hairs black.
[3] Gold, silver, lapis lazuli, crystal, coral, agate, and pearls, according to one classification.

Prince Bairoku, though a person of no account, have come to this court
to welcome our new queen.

NARRATOR: The emperor and the nobles great and small are astonished
by this unprecedented and unreasonable Tartar demand, and the emperor wonders uneasily if it may lead to war. At this moment the
general of the right Ri Tōten, first of his vassals, steps forward and
reports to the throne.

RI TŌTEN: I have until now kept concealed what I felt was this country's shame. Several years ago, in the Year of the Serpent,[4] the five
grains did not ripen at Peking. When the people were reduced to starvation I secretly requested Tartary to aid us with some ten million
bushels of rice and millet. I thereby saved the people. I solemnly swore
in return that if ever the Tartars desired anything of us it would be
granted them on one occasion, no matter what their wish might be.
You, my lord, possess the Land within the Four Seas and rule the
people because of the generosity of Tartary at that time. He who
knows not gratitude is no better than a brute beast. It is natural that
you feel regret, but you would do well to send the Lady Kasei away
as soon as possible.

NARRATOR: Go Sankei, the president of the council of war, has been
listening attentively in an antechamber. He leaps up the stairs and over
the balustrade and seats himself abruptly beside Ri Tōten.

GO SANKEI: Alas! When did you become the slave of those animals?
In China the three emperors and the five rulers[5] invented the rites and
music; Confucius and Mencius transmitted their teachings; and since
then the way of the five constant virtues and five relationships has
flourished as it does today. In India the Buddha taught the doctrine of
cause and effect, and the way of renouncing evil and cultivating virtue
is practiced. In Japan there is the way of the eternal gods enjoining
honesty. In Tartary though they eat their fill and wear warm clothes,[6]
there is neither a way nor laws. The strong stand on top and the weak
are pushed below. They make no distinction between good and evil
nor between wise and foolish. These northern barbarians are no differ-

[4] 1641.
[5] Three emperors: Fu Hsi, Shên Nung, and Huang Ti. Five rulers: Shao Hao, Chuan
Hsü, Ti K'u, Yao, and Shun.
[6] A quotation from Mencius: "But men possess a moral nature; and if they are well
fed, warmly clad, and comfortably lodged, without being taught at the same time, they
become almost like the beast" (Legge, *Chinese Classics*, I, 251).

ent from beasts, and their country is therefore commonly spoken of as a beast-land.

It is most suspicious, however much you may have requested their aid, that the Tartars should have been willing to save this country by providing ten million bushels of grain. But why were the people reduced to the point of starvation? It was because you encouraged senseless extravagance at the court, expended the treasury in feasting, and exacted cruel levies from the people. If you had ceased these expenditures with which you indulged your taste for luxury, a great country like ours would not have lacked the strength to nourish its people for five or even ten years of lean harvests. Now, disregarding the wishes of the emperor, and without even consulting the nobles, you wish without further ado to deliver our empress, who is with child, into the hands of the barbarians. I do not in the least comprehend your intent.

The agreement was between you and the Tartars. The emperor was no party to it. The tribute offerings of a beast-land are a defilement to the palace. Officers! Take these objects and throw them away!

NARRATOR: His contempt for the northern barbarians and proud display of his country's might recall Kuan Chung who nine times summoned the feudal lords.[7] The Tartar envoy Prince Bairoku is enraged.

BAIROKU: Any country, whether large or small, which does not appreciate help it has received to feed its people and which breaks solemn promises should be termed a beast-land beneath human contempt. China has proved herself to be without a way and without laws. You have only to count the days until we attack with our troops, capture your emperor and empress both, and make them the shoe bearers to our great king!

NARRATOR: He kicks aside his seat and rises to depart, when Ri Tōten stays him.

RI TŌTEN: Just a moment! Just a moment! Your indignation is well merited. I acted as a loyal minister should when I accepted your country's help a few years ago and saved my country, without taking a grain of rice for myself. But now men would break promises, incite armed disturbance, trouble the emperor, and afflict the people, and worst of all, cause it to be said that China is a beast-land which knows no gratitude. This would be a disgrace to the dynasty and a disgrace to the country. It is now the task of a loyal minister to sacrifice himself, to

---

[7] Kuan Chung was the famous counselor of Duke Huan of Ch'i (d. 643 B.C.).

reassure the emperor, and to wipe out our country's shame. Behold what I do!

NARRATOR: Grasping his dagger with the point downwards, he thrusts it into his left eye, then turns it round along his eyelids. He draws out the crimsoned eyeball.

RI TŌTEN: Excellency! A man's eyes are his sun and moon. The left eye belonging to the yang principle is his sun.[8] I have become deformed without that eye. I offer it to the king of Tartary. This is the conduct expected of a loyal minister of the emperor of China, a man who preserves his integrity by respecting the way.

NARRATOR: He places his gouged-out eye on a ceremonial baton and offers it to Prince Bairoku, who reverently accepts it.

BAIROKU: What noble devotion! Go Sankei's words a moment ago all but plunged our countries against our wills into a contest of strength and even into warfare. But you have settled the issue by sacrificing yourself on behalf of your country. Magnificent! Words fail me when I realize what a loyal and wise minister you have proved. I feel as though I had already received the empress as my master's bride. The great king will be moved, and I who have served as his envoy could know no greater honor. I shall take my leave now.

NARRATOR: The Emperor is highly pleased.

EMPEROR: The way Ri Tōten gouged out his eye reminds me of Wu Tzu-hsü, and Go Sankei's far-reaching plans suggest those of Fan Li.[9] With these two ministers correcting our rule the country will endure unchanged for a thousand generations, for ten thousand generations. Let the Tartar envoy return to his country.

NARRATOR: With these words he goes into the banqueting hall. Indeed, wicked and loyal ministers look much alike on the surface and may easily be mistaken. The lord of Nanking, who cannot distinguish good from evil, devotes himself to a prodigality without example.

[8] The yang (male, positive, bright, left) principle and the yin (female, negative, dark, right) principle are elemental in Chinese conceptions of the universe.

[9] Wu Tzu-hsü was a counselor of the king of Wu. When the king of Wu defeated the king of Yüeh at Kuai-chi Mountain, and then made peace, Wu Tzu-hsü criticized him, declaring that he should instead crush Yüeh. Wu Tzu-hsü's plan was rejected by the king of Wu, who gave him a sword with which to commit suicide. Wu, in despair over the king's stupidity, gouged out his own eyes and placed them on the eastern gate, where they would see the Yüeh troops advancing on Wu. Fan Li was the counselor of the king of Yüeh at this time. His wisdom brought about the final victory of Yüeh.

Scene Two: The apartments of the Princess Sendan.

NARRATOR: The Princess Sendan, younger sister of the emperor, is a maiden barely sixteen, of such jewellike beauty that one might take her for the offspring of some dweller of the moon, fallen to earth with the dew. She excels at music, each word of her poems excites wide praise. In Japan they say that poetry makes sweet the ties between men and women.[10] Here in China too poetry serves as a go-between in love.

The princess, older than her years, shows her disapproval of the extravagance of her brother, the emperor, by conducting herself with the utmost decorum. Sometimes she summons her attendant ladies and they talk of love, but only in whispers. Her ears yearn for such tales, though her eyes reprove them. Her heart is versant in love, and her days are spent in smouldering dreams.

From the Pavilion of Long Life comes the cry, "His majesty the emperor!" and he enters, accompanied by two hundred ladies, none more than twenty years of age. They bear aloft artificial branches of plum and cherry, a hundred of each.

EMPEROR: My lady sister. Ever since first I ascended the throne the general of the right Ri Tōten has been the most faithful of my many subjects in obeying my commands. When I learned that this first of my loyal ministers, a man who brings me comfort day and night, had fallen in love with you, I was delighted to think that I might make him my sister's husband, but you have to this day refused absolutely to hear him. Today Tartary made us an outrageous proposal, and when it seemed that we had already reached the point of war and national calamity, Go Sankei, with the smug air of a loyal minister, reasoned with his tongue, as anyone might. But Ri Tōten gouged out his left eye and appeased the envoy, who at once returned to his country. For the sake of his country, for the sake of his emperor, he sacrificed himself and became deformed. This minister whose loyalty stands unrivaled throughout the ages must be rewarded. I promised him that I would without fail make him my sister's husband and yield to him the capital

---

[10] A reference to the preface of the *Kokinshū* (A.D. 905), written by Ki no Tsurayuki (883–946): "Poetry makes sweet the ties between men and women and comforts the heart of the brave warrior."

at Peking. Knowing, however, that you were unlikely to agree, I have ordered a tournament of flowers. The plum blossoms will be your side—they suggest your airs of the learned lady and your unfeeling heart.[11] My side will be the cherry blossoms. I shall ask the ladies to join in battle. If the cherry blossoms scatter and the plum triumphs, you may have your way, but if the cherry wins and the plum blossoms fall, your defeat is decided, and you will become Ri Tōten's wife. Let the marriage be determined as Heaven wills it! Whoever wins, whoever loses, we shall have a battle of elegance! Lay on! Lay on!

NARRATOR: The plum and cherry branches, obedient to his command, divide into two ranks and stand ready. The princess, powerless to resist the imperial edict, has no choice but to oppose a match that goes against her heart. Her flowering branch and her person are to the fore.

SENDAN: I shall be the general in the contest to decide the marriage of the Princess Sendan, younger sister to the emperor.

NARRATOR: Hardly has she proclaimed herself than the bough of plum she bears aloft brushes someone's sleeve, and a fluttering as from the wings of a cluster of song thrushes scatters the blossoms. The air is heavy with the fragrance of plum. They do battle, thrusting and parrying. The princess gives commands.

SENDAN: You can tell that there must be a wind underneath the willow whose leaves are twisted round. Against their weak branches lean your budding twigs. Against their strong branches make the blossoms of your achievements burst into bloom! Change your faded boughs for fresh ones, and join your efforts with the others!

NARRATOR: They attack with a cry of battle, obeying her flower-wise commands. Some regret the blossoms trampled underfoot, but they charge boldly forward, branches held horizontally over their heads, scattering blossoms like snow in February. Blossoms tumble pell-mell from the branches; the battle sends the flowers flying.

The court ladies, however, deliberately allow the plum blossom side to be vanquished, acting in accord with the previous commands of the emperor. Then branches and blossoms are broken and strewn, and the ladies fall back in confusion. The cherry blossoms, victory on their faces, cry, "The marriage between the princess and Ri Tōten is now decided!" They raise cries of triumph, and their voices ring through

---

[11] Plum blossoms, because they come out early in the spring, are associated with coldness and chastity. They are also known as the scholar's flower.

the palace like the notes of a thousand song thrushes or a hundred plovers twittering together.

Go Sankei, the president of the council of war, bursts in on their gathering without a word of apology. He is splendidly attired in armor and helmet. Waving his crescent-topped spear, he furiously slashes down plum and cherry blossoms, then bows before the emperor.

GO SANKEI: A moment ago word came that there was fighting by the throne, and war cries echoed through the halls. I came running here, buckling on my armor, alarmed by so extraordinary a disturbance in the palace. But what senselessness do I find! In all the pages of history since the world was created, you will find no such foolish example as this battle of flowers to decide the marriage of your sister and Ri Tōten. Does your majesty not know that if the One Family is loving, the entire state will become loving, but if the One Man is covetous the state will be in disorder? [12] It is customary for the people to follow the preferences of their superiors. When word of this incident spreads, there will be flower tournaments at this place and that, wherever a woodcutter or farmer is planning a marriage for his son or daughter, and these tournaments will develop into quarrels and feuds. It is clear as looking into a mirror that once the blossoms scatter there will be recourse to swords, and real battles will follow the contests of flowers. If now a treacherous subject were to attack the palace, people would suppose, even if his war cries were heard, that it was merely another battle of flowers, and no one would rush to your aid. Then if your august person were cruelly put to the sword by this treacherous subject, the deed would be impious and ignoble, but what would it avail to regret your past folly?

The treacherous subject, the false minister of whom I speak is Ri Tōten. Has your majesty forgotten? When you were young a man named Tei Shiryū [13] incurred your displeasure by urging you to expel the false courtiers. Tei Shiryū was driven into exile as a result. I hear that he now lives at Hirado of Hizen Province in Japan, where he goes by the name of Rōikkan. If Tei Shiryū were to hear of what has happened today, would he not reveal China's shame to the Japanese? A few years ago, when China was suffering from famine, Ri

[12] From the Confucian classic *The Great Learning* (tr. Legge, *Chinese Classics*, I, 376). The One Family is the imperial family, as the One Man is the emperor.

[13] Chêng Chih-lung (1604–61), the father of Coxinga. See Keene, *The Battles of Coxinga*, pp. 45–48.

Tōten used his wiles to steal rice from the granaries of the different provinces. He spread word that he was obliged to accept aid from Tartary because your majesty had no love for your people. He claimed to have saved them himself. He scattered his largesse throughout the country, ingratiating himself with the masses and strengthening the axis of sedition. How foolish of you to be unaware of what has happened!

Ri Tōten gouged out his left eye as a signal to his Tartar confederates. Look at the plaque hanging in this hall of state—*ta ming,* it says, meaning "great" and "bright." The character *ming* is written by placing the symbols for sun and moon side by side.[14] This great Ming is a land of the south and of the yang principle; it is a country of the sun. Tartary is a northern yin country, linked with the moon. Ri Tōten gouged out his left eye, which belongs to yang and corresponds to the sun, as a warrant to his allies that he would deliver this great bright land of the sun into the hands of the Tartars. The envoy understood the meaning at once, and returned joyfully to Tartary. Unless this treacherous subject, guilty of accumulated wickedness and villainy, is at once subjected to the five punishments,[15] this land which has given birth to the sages will soon fall under the yoke of Mongolia,[16] and we shall become their slaves, differing from animals only in that we do not wag tails or have bodies covered with fur. Heaven will be wroth, the gods of our ancestral halls will curse us, and the fault will be attributed to the emperor. Doubt rather that I should miss the earth when striking at it with my fist, than these words of Go Sankei are mistaken. How deplorable your attitude has been!

NARRATOR: The emperor is exceedingly displeased.

EMPEROR: Enough of your lectures on ideographs with that smug look! Such logic could prove that snow was actually black! Everything you say comes from your jealousy of Ri Tōten. You, who for no reason whatsoever have approached my presence in your helmet and armor, are the treacherous subject!

NARRATOR: Rising, he kicks Go Sankei's forehead when, strange to

[14] The character 明 (*ming*) combines 日 (sun) and 月 (moon).

[15] Branding, cutting off of the nose, cutting off of the feet, castration, and death.

[16] The Manchus, the actual conquerors of China, are usually called "Tartars" in this play, but occasionally "Mongols." Their country is called Mongolia here.

relate, there is a repeated rumbling in the palace, and the plaque written in the imperial hand begins to shake. The golden-sword stroke in "great" [17] and the symbol for "sun" in "bright" crumble into powder, a fearsome augury from Heaven. Go Sankei, still unconcerned for his own safety, cries out.

GO SANKEI: Alas! Are your eyes blinded? Have your ears gone deaf? The ideograph for "great" is written by combining "one" and "man". The One Man refers to the Sun of Heaven, the emperor. When a stroke is taken from the One Man, the emperor becomes only half a man. When the symbol for sun is removed from the ideograph for "bright," the country, deprived of the light of the sun, becomes a land of eternal darkness. That plaque was inscribed by the brush of your ancestor, the first emperor of the Ming, as he meditated on the eternal prosperity of his line. Reflect how terrible will be the wrath of the gods of your ancestral temples! Mend your ways, correct your injustices, and preserve your dynasty! Then, though Go Sankei, whose life lies before you, be trampled or kicked to death, he will not complain. I shall not violate the way of a true subject though my body turn to earth, though it turn to ashes!

NARRATOR: He clings to the emperor's robe and cries aloud. Weeping, he remonstrates. Here is a model for all the ages.

At this moment the noise of men and horses echoes from all directions. Horns and gongs are sounded, drums beaten, and war cries shake the earth, loud enough to tilt Heaven itself. Go Sankei, who has expected this disaster, races up to a vantage point and looks out. The mountains and towns swarm with the Tartar hordes. With waving banners and bows and muskets they surround and storm the palace, irresistible as the onrushing tide. Prince Bairoku, commander of the invading host, rides into the palace garden and utters a great shout.

BAIROKU: Hear my words! I lied when I said that the lord of our land, the Great King Junji, had become enamoured of the empress of this country, the Lady Kasei. Our scheme was to cut off the seed of the emperor by capturing his pregnant consort. When Ri Tōten demonstrated his allegiance to our cause by gouging out his eye, we decided to attack without delay. You are no match for us, Go Sankei!

[17] The third stroke ╲ in *ta* 大 . The character is further analyzed by Go Sankei into a combination of — and 人 .

We will seize the emperor and the empress and compel them to bow before us. They will squat in the kitchens of the king of Tartary and prolong their lives by drinking the water we use to wash our rice!

GO SANKEI: What nonsense! For you to attack the Ming court, where not even plants or trees have stirred for 180 years,[18] is as futile as an ant stalking a whale whose bulk bestrides the ocean! Drive them back! Drive them back!

NARRATOR: He races about giving orders to his men, but they amount to no more than a hundred foot soldiers. Not one of the nobles or military lords joins him in his struggle. As he stands in dismay, fists clenched, his wife Ryūkakun leads on the empress with one hand, clutching her baby to her breast with the other.

RYŪKAKUN: Alas! The imperial fortunes are at an end. Everyone, from the highest noble and minister of state down to the lowliest menial sides with Ri Tōten. We are the only friends to the imperial cause. Most mortifying of days!

NARRATOR: She gnashes her teeth in woe.

GO SANKEI: Cease your lamenting. It serves no purpose. The empress is the most precious person, for she lodges in her womb the emperor's seed. I shall cut open an avenue of escape and escort the emperor and the empress to safety. Leave our child with me too. For the present you are to look after the Princess Sendan. Make your way from here to the harbor Kaidō.[19]

RYŪKAKUN: As you command.

NARRATOR: With this brave reply she leads the Princess Sendan by the hand, and together they slip out through the Golden Stream Gate along a narrow path.

GO SANKEI: Now I shall engage the enemy at the main gate and disperse them so that I may lead your majesties to safety. Please do not leave this spot.

NARRATOR: He rushes off with this final injunction. He proclaims himself, "President of the Council of War Go Sankei, first of the subjects of the Ming court," and with his force of less than a hundred men drives into the millions of Mongol troops. As they slash forward reck-

---

[18] The figure 277 years would be more accurate. The phrase about plants and trees means that the dynasty is so stable that nothing in the country is ever disturbed.

[19] Probably an imaginary place name, invented by Chikamatsu.

lessly, the Tartar hordes cry, "Kill them all!" and the fighting rages amidst incessant volleys of bullets and stones from their muskets and catapults.

Ri Tōten and his brother Ri Kaihō profit by the confusion to burst wantonly into the imperial presence. They seize the emperor from both sides. The empress, wondering if this is not some nightmare, clings to them.

EMPRESS: Impious villains! Have you forgotten your obligations to the emperor and the divinity that protects him?

RI TŌTEN: You won't escape either!

NARRATOR: He thrusts her aside and touches his icy blade to the emperor's chest. The emperor's face is wet with tears of wrath.

EMPEROR: It is true, as they say, that the rust on a blade grows from the blade itself. The fire in the cypress forest rises from the cypresses and consumes them. Now I know that the hatred or love a man receives comes from himself. I did not heed the advice of Tei Shiryū or Go Sankei, but was duped by your flattery. I have lost my empire and now I am about to lose my life and leave behind an odious name for all time to come. How foolish I was not to have realized that food sweet to the taste proves harmful in the stomach!

You are no doubt aware that my wife bears in her womb my child, now in its ninth month. Her delivery cannot be long off. I pray you, the one kindness I ask, that you let this child see the light of the sun and moon.

NARRATOR: These are his only words before he is overwhelmed by tears.

RI TŌTEN: No, never! Why did I gouge out my precious eye? Not because of loyalty or duty. It was to throw you off your guard and to demonstrate my allegiance to Tartary. My eye has won me a fief—your head will fetch me a kingdom!

NARRATOR: He pulls the emperor to him and slashes off his head.

RI TŌTEN: Ri Kaihō—I must send this head to the king of Tartary. Bind the empress and bring her with you.

NARRATOR: He rushes off to the invaders' camp. Go Sankei, having slaughtered many of the enemy, has easily opened a path of escape. He returns to the spot where he left the emperor, intending to rescue him, when to his horror he beholds the headless corpse lying on the ground, bathed in crimson, and Ri Kaihō about to lead off the captive empress.

GO SANKEI: I find you in the nick of time! In my battle of vengeance for my sovereign I have arrived too late for the main meal, and will have to content myself with an afternoon snack! [20]

NARRATOR: He flies at Ri Kaihō and splits his skull in two. He cuts the ropes binding the empress and tearfully lifts the emperor's body. Next to the skin he finds the sash and seal, the symbol of enthronement handed down from generation to generation of rulers.

GO SANKEI: Good! As long as the prince about to be born has this, he need not worry about succeeding to the throne.

NARRATOR: He thrusts them into his armor next to the skin.

GO SANKEI: Should I escort the empress to safety first? Or should I first hide the emperor's body?

NARRATOR: His problem is twofold, but he has only one body. As he stands perplexed, the enemy hordes charge at him in wild tumult.

GO SANKEI: I'm ready for you!

NARRATOR: He slashes into their ranks. When they attack he strikes, topples, throws down, and routs the enemy. He runs back to the empress.

GO SANKEI: That will take care of them for the moment. We must hurry. Nothing can be done about the emperor's body. The most important thing is his successor.

NARRATOR: He takes the empress's hand and starts to lead her, when his own child, longing for its mother's breast, begins to howl.

GO SANKEI: Confounded nuisance! But you are my heir.

NARRATOR: He lifts the baby and fastens him to the shaft of his lance.

GO SANKEI: If your father is killed you must grow up and become his successor as a loyal minister to the young prince. You are the last of our line.

NARRATOR: He lifts the infant to his shoulder, then hurries with the empress towards safety. The enemy soldiers press forward to halt the fugitives, but Go Sankei stands his ground and engages them. He slashes and pounds, beating a path of escape. At last they reach the harbor of Kaidō as the tide is receding.

[20] *Toki* (main meal) and *hiji* (afternoon snack) are Buddhist terms. Here Go Sankei means that he has come too late to kill Ri Tōten and must content himself with Ri Kaihō.

Scene Three: The coast at Kaidō.

NARRATOR: Go Sankei has planned to cross to Taisufu [21] from Kaidō, but not a single boat is to be seen by the shore. They start to follow along the coast when suddenly musket fire sweeps down on them like a driving rain from the surrounding woods and mountains. Go Sankei shields the empress, taking bullet after bullet on his stoutly fashioned armor, but—has her destiny run out?—a shot strikes her breast. The jeweled thread of her life is snapped and she breathes her last. Go Sankei stands in dismay, at a loss what to do.

GO SANKEI: Nothing can help the empress mother now, but there is no reason why the imperial seed should perish darkly within her womb.

NARRATOR: He unsheathes his sword and cuts open the empress's robes to the skin. He presses the blade into her abdomen, and makes a cross-shaped incision. A baby's first cry from within the rush of blood comes from a jewellike prince. The occasion is at once joyous and sad. Go Sankei, overcome by helpless tears, rips off the empress's sleeve and uses it to wrap the prince. He lifts the baby in his arms.

GO SANKEI: But wait! If the enemy surrounding us should discover the empress's dead body, they would know that the prince had been spirited away, and they would search till they found him. I would have no chance to rear him to manhood.

NARRATOR: He pauses a moment in earnest thought, then draws his own child to him. He removes the infant's clothes and puts them on the prince. Again he takes up his sword, this time to plunge it through his baby's chest. He pushes the dead child into the empress's abdomen.

GO SANKEI: Noble child! You have been blessed by fortune. You were lucky enough to have been born at a time when you could die in place of a prince destined to be our emperor. You have done well. Do not grieve for the parents you leave behind in this world of delusion. Your parents will not grieve to be parted from you.

NARRATOR: Despite his words, his heart is filled with sorrow. He chokes in tears he conceals with the sleeve of armor in which he cradles the baby prince. How pitiful he seems as he leaves his own son behind!

[21] T'ai-chou-fu, the modern Lin-hai-hsien in Chekiang Province.

Ryūkakun, knowing nothing of this, has guided the Princess Sendan to the harbor mouth. The enemy swarms around them.

RYŪKAKUN: Let us try to go as far as we can.

NARRATOR: They push aside the thickly growing reeds and hide themselves behind them. An Taijin, a captain serving under Ri Tōten, bursts on the scene with a party of soldiers.

AN TAIJIN: I'm sure that our last volley of musket fire struck either the empress or Go Sankei.

NARRATOR: They search the vicinity.

AN TAIJIN: Look! Our shot has killed the empress! Her belly's been ripped open, and we've killed the prince in her womb. Go Sankei, for all his show of loyalty, has deserted his sovereign and destroyed his own reputation. Was he afraid for his life? The villain is dishonored now. Our only task remaining is to search for Go Sankei's wife Ryūkakun and the Princess Sendan. Keep your eyes peeled and win a name for yourselves!

NARRATOR: They spread out in all directions. Among the soldiers is a ruffian called Gōdatsu.

GŌDATSU: I'll capture the Princess Sendan and take all the glory for myself!

NARRATOR: He throws a straw raincoat over his armor and poles a little fishing boat from inlet to inlet.

GŌDATSU: There's something suspicious about these reeds.

NARRATOR: He uses the tip of his oar to spread apart the reeds. Ryūkakun firmly grasps it and pushes back with all her strength. Gōdatsu loses his balance and tumbles head first overboard. He sinks with a splash, and when he struggles to the surface, Ryūkakun strikes him again and again, hard enough to break the oar. When she strikes he sinks, and when he rises she strikes again. She allows him not a moment's breathing space; he is like a snapping turtle swimming in the mud. Finally he dives and makes his escape.

RYŪKAKUN: Your stolen march has done you no good, and it has brought us a boat! This is a case of finding a boat at a crossing! [22]

NARRATOR: She takes up the sword Gōdatsu left lying in the boat, and fastens it by her side. Next she helps the Princess Sendan aboard the boat and is about to climb in herself when Gōdatsu crawls up from somewhere, his armor dripping wet. He leads in pursuit twenty men armed with spears, determined not to let the women escape.

[22] A proverb for finding something when one needs it.

RYŪKAKUN: I certainly have my hands full! Look! Our enemies are coming after us! There's fury in their faces! Please hide in the bottom of the boat while I stave them off.

NARRATOR: She awaits their onslaught brandishing a sword in each hand, the sword she found and the one she had all the time. Gōdatsu soon rushes up.

GŌDATSU: Loathsome woman! I'll pay you back for hitting me with the oar!

NARRATOR: He lunges at her with his long-handled spear.

RYŪKAKUN: And I will pay you back for the sword you left me!

NARRATOR: She slashes right and left, one woman surrounded by over twenty swords. Some men, seagulls of the reeds bewildered on shore, are struck down, no match for her, before they can even flap their wings; others escape with severe wounds. Ryūkakun and Gōdatsu are both badly wounded and covered with blood. They charge back and forth into a clump of reeds, blood streaming into the eyes of both. They strike blindly, uncertain where they aim; their swords strike sparks from the edge of the rocks, sparks as brief as their lives, a frightening spectacle.

Gōdatsu's spear is broken. He hobbles forward and attempts to wrest the sword from Ryūkakun's grasp. In the struggle he loses his footing and falls on his back. At once she pounces on him, driving the blade in, and slices off his head. Ryūkakun smiles, her heart filled with incomparable joy.

RYŪKAKUN: Your highness, are you all right? Is the boat still there?

NARRATOR: She staggers closer.

RYŪKAKUN: I cannot join you in this frightful condition, nor can I withstand the enemy if they attack again. Let the tide take your boat from here wherever it will. I shall stand by on land until you reach the open sea. Tens of thousands of the enemy may attack, but I shall fight on as long as life is left me, as long as my strength stays with me. We shall meet again only if fate wills and we remain alive. May you be safe. I pray to the Buddhas of all the heavens, and especially to the eight great dragon gods,[23] that they will protect the boat of the imperial princess!

NARRATOR: She grasps the crossbar and shoves off the boat. An ebb tide is flowing and carries the boat from shore. Sendan, powerless to control her grief over parting, yields to tears in the salt breeze. Her

---

[23] Gods of the sea who controlled the rain and the waves.

boat, caught by a wind from the offing vouchsafed by the gods, drifts far out to sea.

RYŪKAKUN: What a relief! And what a joy! Now if I prolong my life I shall be alone, and if I die none will journey with me, not even the companion birds.[24] I would escape the sea of life and death, but worry over my husband, my child, my sovereign, remains with me. It is hard to surmount the waves of attachment to this mortal world. But however difficult the sea to cross, the swift boat of my devotion will not break in the breaking waves, though the oars of love and integrity and the rudder of courage be snapped.[25] But do I hear war cries approaching?

NARRATOR: She clutches her swords and staggers about painfully. A storm blowing down from the mountain through the pines on the beach combs her disheveled locks. She stands glaring fiercely about her. Her story has been written down and transmitted as a model for women in Japan and China.

ACT TWO

Scene One: The beach at Hirado, an island off the west coast of Kyushu.
Time: Late autumn of the same year.

NARRATOR: The twittering yellow thrush rests on the corner of the mound. If a man fails to rest in the place meant for him, does it mean that he is inferior to this bird?[26]

There lives in the town of Hirado, in the county of Matsura of Hizen Province in Japan, a young man named Watōnai Sankan[27] who earns his living by casting his line and drawing his nets. His wife follows the same fisher's trade and, like the creature *warekara*[28] that lives

---

[24] Here, as elsewhere in the work, a desire for a play on words leads Chikamatsu into an irrelevant phrase. *Tare wo tomo* (taking whom as a friend) leads into *tomo-chidori* (companion plovers).

[25] This sentence is formed by a series of *engo* (related words) on ships.

[26] From *The Great Learning* (tr. Legge, p. 362). The meaning here would seem to be that Watōnai and Ikkan are admirable in that, like the yellow bird, they know their proper tasks.

[27] This name was invented by Chikamatsu. For more historical information on Coxinga, see Keene, *The Battles of Coxinga*, pp. 44–75.

[28] *Warekara* is at once the name of a sea creature, *Caprella* and a word meaning "of oneself".

in the seaweed, she has of herself, without asking a go-between, joined her pillow to a man's. She is blessed with the name Komutsu—"Little Friend"—and lives on friendly terms with the world. Now the father of this Watōnai was originally not a Japanese. He served as a loyal subject to the great Ming court, where he was known as the Grand Tutor Tei Shiryū. He admonished in vain the foolish emperor and, threatened with banishment, fled instead to the Bay of Tsukushi in the Land of the Rising Sun, where he changed his name to Rōikkan. Marrying a woman who lived by the bay, he begot this son to whom he gave the name of Watōnai, with Wa standing for Japan, his mother's birthplace, and Tō for his father's old home.[29]

Twenty and more springs have elapsed since the boy was born, and autumn is now passing, but November is warm as a second July.[30] Husband and wife go out together in the evening calm, fishing baskets hung from their rakes, to dig clams for their livelihood. They look out over the beach and see the seagulls imprinting their seals in the sand, and the bay plovers clustering on the offshore islets. Watōnai rakes the beach dried by the receding tide, and Komutsu, treading on clams, gathers shells of every kind, indifferent to the water that soaks her skirts. What are the shells that they gather?

Hermit crabs, periwinkles, carpet clams . . . When the bamboo blind-shell is raised by the salt-blowing-shell, I catch a glimpse of a princess-shell and fall in love at first sight. I would like to take my brush and send a letter on a flat-shell. When her red lips-shells part and she smiles-shell, my heart-goes-to-her-shell—ah, what pain-shell! "You draw me to you and I would cling-shell to you, but my love is one-sided as the abalone shell. Oh, cruel one! I could give you a taste of my fist-shell in your monkey-face-shell. Plum blossom-shells, cherry blossom-shells . . ."[31] "Sleeplessly I all alone spend-the-night shell. For whom do I wait-shell? I forget-shell that people-may-see-shell, and only dream of how, when lying together in bed-shell, the joys of marriage will sink-shell into our hearts, and we will celebrate-shell with a triumphant peal-shell the happy beginning of our wedded bliss-shell."

These were the shells that they gather. Among the shells is one, a

---

[29] *Wa* is an ancient name for Japan. *Tō* (T'ang in Chinese), the name of a dynasty, was frequently used for China. *Nai* means "between".

[30] Literally "little sixth moon", meaning Indian summer.

[31] The catalogue of shells is so arranged as to yield a mildly erotic story when the names of the shells are taken into account. The first statement "You draw me . . ." is presumably by the man, and the second "Sleeplessly . . ." by the woman.

huge clam, with its mouth open to the sun. Unaware that someone stands nearby, ready to capture him, the clam is blowing foamy brine. WATŌNAI: Yes, they say that clams sometimes spew out vapor to form castles.[32] This must be an example.

NARRATOR: As he gazes on in fascination, a shrike flying across the seaweed in quest of food swoops down with a curious flapping of the wings. It spots the clam and approaches with angry beak, intent on snapping up the clam with one swift peck. Horrid master shrike! Don't you who chant the sutras realize that you break the command against taking life? And see how the clam immodestly gapes, in flagrant violation of the Buddha's injunction! [33]

The shrike flies at the clam and pecks furiously, but suddenly the shells clamp on the shrike's bill and hold it fast. The pleasure drains all at once from the shrike's face. It tugs frantically with its bill. With a flap of the wings, it shakes its head and edges over to the base of a rock, hoping in its bird wisdom to smash the clam. But the clam digs back into the sand, struggling to drag down into a puddle of sea water its prize. The shrike, straining its feathers, flies up a dozen feet, only to fall with the clam's weight. It rises quickly again, to fall just as abruptly. The shrike struggles desperately, beating its wings a hundred times, standing its feathers on end.

Watōnai, absorbed, throws down his rake.

WATŌNAI: Extraordinary! I understand now why the priest discovered his true nature in the snow that broke the bamboos—and how, by cutting off his arm he learned the meaning of the teachings brought by the Master from the West.[34] I have studied at my father's command the Chinese texts of military strategy, and examined the principles underlying the success or failure in battle of the great Japanese generals

[32] One variety of *hamaguri* (clam) was said to be a kind of dragon which could emit a vaporous castle. See Hozumi Ikan *Naniwa Miyage* (in *Jōruri Kenkyū Bunken Shūsei*), p. 182.

[33] The chirps of the shrike were said to resemble the chanting of Buddhist sutras. The clam was violating the command against keeping one's mouth open—i.e., looseness of speech.

[34] A reference to the story of Hui-k'o (d. 593). When Hui-k'o went to see the great Zen teacher Bodhidharma to ask for instruction, the teacher would not see him. Hui-k'o continued to wait in his garden even though it snowed so heavily that the bamboos broke under the weight of the snow. Bodhidharma, moved to pity, asked what he wanted. Hui-k'o asked for instruction, but was refused. He thereupon cut off his arm and placed it before the master to prove his sincerity. Chikamatsu has misused this story as an example of sudden enlightenment.

of ancient and modern times. I have devoted my attention to problems in tactics. But only now have I gained sudden enlightenment into the profoundest secret of the science, thanks to this battle between a shrike and a clam.

The clam, secure in the hardness of its shells, did not realize that a shrike would attack. The shrike, proud of its sharp beak, did not foresee that the clam would snap shut its mouth. The shells will not let go, and the shrike, straining all its energies to free itself, has no time to look behind. Nothing could be simpler than for me to seize both of them in one swoop. The hardness of the clam's shells will be of no avail, and the shrike's sharp beak will not frighten me. This is the secret of military tactics: to provoke a quarrel between two adversaries, and then catch both when they least expect it. This was in China the strategy behind the vertical and horizontal alliances the first emperor of the Ch'in used to swallow up the Six Kingdoms.[35] When we read the *Taiheiki*[36] of Japan, it tells how the Emperor Godaigo ruled the country laxly, like the clam with its shells open. A shrike named the Lay Priest of Sagami beat his wings in Kamakura; his arrogant beak was sharp. He attacked at Yoshino and Chihaya and forced the clam to blow salt water, only for his beak to be caught in an attack by the two shells called Kusunoki Masashige and Nitta Yoshisada.[37] Takauji, a master of martial strategy, struck at shrike and clam, profiting by their preoccupation, and seized empty shells and clam together.[38]

I have heard that in the land of my father Ikkan's birth a battle is now raging between China and Tartary, exactly like that between shrike and clam. If I were to go to China and attack, applying what I have now learned to the present struggle, I am sure that I could swallow up China and Tartary both in one gulp!

NARRATOR: He racks his brains with schemes of conquest, not taking his eyes from the shrike and the clam. The determination which stirs in this warrior promises splendid deeds. What could be more natural than that this man should cross to China, conquer China and Tartary,

[35] The stratagem was advocated by Chang I, a counselor of the state of Ch'in, and succeeded in winning all China for the ruler of Ch'in.

[36] A chronicle written about 1360; translated by H. C. McCullough.

[37] Kusunoki Masashige (1294–1336) and Nitta Yoshisada (1301–38) were loyal generals of the Emperor Godaigo. They defeated Hōjō Takatoki ("the Lay Priest of Sagami"), but were ultimately vanquished by Ashikaga Takauji (1305–58).

[38] Not an exact parallel—if the shells are Kusunoki and Nitta, the shrike (Takatoki) is no longer around to be captured by Takauji.

and gain glory abroad and at home? This young man is no other than the future Coxinga, prince of Empei.[39]

KOMUTSU: Look! The tide is already coming in. What are you staring at?

NARRATOR: She runs up.

KOMUTSU: Well! The shrike and the clam are kissing! This is the first I knew they were married. Shame on them—in broad daylight, like dogs! I'll separate them somehow.

NARRATOR: She pulls out a hairpin and prizes the shell apart. The shrike, delighted, heads for the reeds, while the clam buries itself in the sand as the tide flows in.

WATŌNAI: It looks like rain. Let's go back.

NARRATOR: He happens to glance out at the end of the sand bar, and sees a rudderless boat of curious construction drifting towards them.

WATŌNAI: That's not a whaling boat. I wonder if it's a Chinese tea boat? [40]

KOMUTSU: I have no idea.

NARRATOR: They examine the boat and discover inside a high-born lady of sixteen or more years, who looks like a Chinese. Her face is a lotus blossom, her eyebrows willow leaves. Her sleeves are wet with a tide of tears, and the sea winds have washed the rouge and powder from her face that is pale and drawn. She is touchingly lovely, like the first flowers of spring wilted by the rain.[41] Komutsu speaks in a whisper.

KOMUTSU: She must be a Chinese empress, the kind they draw in pictures, who's had a love affair and been exiled.

WATŌNAI: Yes, that's a good guess. I made the mistake of thinking that she might be the ghost of Yang Kuei-fei,[42] and it frightened me. Anyway, she's certainly a lovely girl, isn't she?

KOMUTSU: You horrid man! Do Chinese women attract you? If your father'd stayed all along in China, you'd have been born there too, and you'd be sleeping with a woman like that in your arms. But unluckily for you, you were born in Japan, and you're saddled with a wife like me. I feel sorry for you!

[39] Empei is Yen-p'ing in Chinese. I have used Japanese pronunciations of the Chinese names which figure in the play, but retained Chinese pronunciations for historical names.
[40] A "tea boat" was a kind of sampan.
[41] I have omitted the phrase, not intended by Chikamatsu to be comic, "with a nose and mouth attached."
[42] A celebrated Chinese beauty (718-756). See below, p. 117.

WATŌNAI: Don't be silly! No matter how pretty a Chinese woman may be, her clothes and the way she does her hair make me think I'm looking at Benzaiten! [43] I could never get to sleep with one—I'd feel much too on edge!

NARRATOR: He laughs. As they talk the lady steps on shore and beckons them.

SENDAN: Japanese! Japanese! *Na mu kya ra chon nō to ra ya a ya!* [44]

NARRATOR: Komutsu bursts out laughing.

KOMUTSU: What sutra is *that?*

NARRATOR: She holds her sides with amusement.

WATŌNAI: You mustn't laugh! She said, "Japanese, come here. I have something to request of you."

NARRATOR: He brushes Komutsu aside and goes to the lady, who is blinded with tears.

SENDAN: Great Ming *chin shin nyō ro.* Sir, *ken ku ru mei ta ka rin kan kyū, sai mō su ga sun hei su ru,* on the other hand, *kon ta ka rin ton na, a ri shi te ken san hai ro. To ra ya a ya, to ra ya a ya.*

NARRATOR: These are her only words before she melts in tears again. Komutsu plops down on the beach, convulsed with laughter, unable to endure more. Watōnai, who learned his father's tongue, touches his hands to the ground and bows his head.

WATŌNAI: *U su u su u sa su ha mō, sa ki ga chin bu ri ka ku san kin nai ro. Kin nyō, kin nyō.*

NARRATOR: He claps his hands, then takes the lady's hands in his, most intimately. His tears of sympathy suggest that they are old friends. Komutsu, enraged, catches the breast of his kimono.

KOMUTSU: See here, you! I don't want to hear any more of your Chinese talk. For all your flirtations, when did you manage to get in touch with her in China? You've extended your operations too far afield! And as for you, with your *to ra ya a ya,* how dare you go *kinnyō-kinnyō*-ing to my precious husband? I won't give you the chance to taste what a Japanese man is like. Try a taste of this instead!

NARRATOR: She brandishes her rake, but Watōnai snatches it away.

WATŌNAI: Open your eyes before you start being jealous! This is the Princess Sendan, the younger sister of the emperor of China, my fa-

---

[43] A Buddhist goddess of beauty, known in Sanskrit as Sarasvatī.

[44] The words, as used here, have no meaning, and merely represent what Chinese sounds like to a Japanese. For the derivation see Keene, *The Battles of Coxinga,* p. 184.

ther's former master he has so often told us about. The storms of a revolution have blown her here. We cannot abandon her in this pitiful condition. But if we take her directly home, we'll have to bother with the village headman's permission, and the governor's office is sure to investigate. The best plan is to ask my father's advice. Go home and bring Father here at once. Quickly, before people see!

NARRATOR: Komutsu claps her hands.

KOMUTSU: The poor dear! I've heard how ladies of noble birth have met with stormy winds even in Japan. How much worse it must be for a princess from China to be brought to such a sorry state! Some deep connection between master and retainer must have guided her boat ashore here, out of all the many harbors. I'll call Father at once. You poor thing, *to ra ya a ya, kin nyō, kin nyō.*

NARRATOR: Her eyes fill with tears as she leaves on the road home.

Ikkan and his wife, unaware of what has happened, are walking along the beach on their return from the Sumiyoshi shrine of Matsura where they have worshiped following a strange and wonderful dream. Watōnai calls them to him.

WATŌNAI: The Princess Sendan has fled the disorders in China, and her boat has been stranded here. See what a piteous state she is in!

NARRATOR: Before he has finished speaking, Ikkan and his wife bow their heads to the ground.

IKKAN: I believe that your highness may have heard of me. I was formerly known as Tei Shiryū. My present wife and my son are Japanese, but I should not be acting as a loyal subject if I failed to repay old obligations. I am bent with years, but my son is well versed in martial matters and, as you can see, he is of a naturally powerful build. He is bold and invincible, a hero who will restore the dynasty of the great Ming and bring peace to the late emperor in the other world. Please be of good cheer.

NARRATOR: He speaks reassuringly. The princess is moved to tears.

SENDAN: Are you indeed the Tei Shiryū of whom I have heard so much? Ri Tōten treacherously allied himself with Tartary. He killed my brother, the emperor, and usurped the country. I too would have been killed had it not been for the loyal protection of Go Sankei and his wife. Their efforts have preserved to this day a life which I would not begrudge. I put myself in your hands, helpless and uncertain as the dew.

NARRATOR: These are her only words before she melts again in tears. Only because of some lasting connection are these reiterated words of regret over the past exchanged between strangers. Watōnai's mother can hardly wring out her sleeve for the tears.

MOTHER: I see now it must have been as a sign that we would hear such tidings that my husband and I had the same revelation in dreams this morning. It plainly foretold that a battle would be waged two thousand leagues from here,[45] followed by a victory in the west. Watōnai, you must interpret this dream and bear it in mind as you strive in loyal service for the success of the imperial cause. What do you say?

NARRATOR: Watōnai answers respectfully.

WATŌNAI: A few moments ago on this beach I witnessed an extraordinary encounter between a shrike and a clam. It has enlightened me about the profoundest secret of military strategy. The prophecy that victory would come in the west a thousand leagues from here must refer to China, a country situated a thousand leagues over the rough waves to the west of Japan. The ideograph for strategy is written with the symbol for "water" and the symbol for "to leave".[46] This was clearly a divine message enjoining me to entrust myself to the waters of the rising tide and leave Japanese soil at once. My fortune is the "hexagram of the general." "The general" stands for an army. The hexagram is arranged with the trigram for earth above and that for water below. One yang controls many yin,[47] it says, meaning that I alone shall be general commanding tens of thousands of troops. I shall leave Japan immediately, on the rising tide indicated by the symbol for water, and push on to Nanking and Peking. I shall join counsel with Go Sankei, if he still survives in this mortal world, and crush the traitorous followers of Ri Tōten. Gathering an army round me, I shall counterattack Tartary and twist the Tartars by the pigtails on their

[45] The distance between Japan and China is variously estimated at one, two, and three thousand *ri*. To keep the meaning vague, I have translated *ri* as "league".

[46] The symbols are 氵 (water) and 去 (to leave). Combined they form 法 (strategy).

[47] The seventh hexagram in *I-ching* (Book of changes). Legge says of it (*Yi King*, p. 72), "The conduct of military expeditions in a feudal kingdom, and we may say, generally, is denoted by the hexagram Sze." The hexagram has one yang (unbroken) line and five yin (divided) lines.

shaven pates.[48] I'll behead them all! I'll drive them back, cut them down, and then raise a hymn of victory for the long prosperity of the Ming! These are the plans that fill my soul. They say that "opportunities of time vouchsafed by Heaven are not equal to advantages of situation afforded by the Earth, and advantages of situation afforded by the Earth are not equal to the union arising from the accord of Men." [49] And again, "Good or bad fortune depends on man and not on the stars." I shall set sail without further delay, and persuade the barbarians of islands along the way to join my forces. Then I shall do battle in the manner I have planned. To the front!

NARRATOR: In his bold figure they seem to behold the Empress Jingū standing fiercely at the helm as she set off to conquer Korea.[50]

His father is greatly impressed.

IKKAN: What noble and promising sentiments! Indeed, the text is true which says that a single flower seed does not rot in the ground, but grows at last into a thousand blossoms.[51] You are truly a son of Ikkan! Your mother and I should offer to accompany the princess in the same boat, but if we are too many we shall attract attention, and there is the danger that we may be arrested at one of the points of shipping control. We shall therefore sail secretly instead from the Bay of Fujitsu.[52] You depart from here and leave the princess at some convenient island on the way. Then change course and catch up with us. They say that the gods dwell in honest heads; a divine wind will surely guide over the sea so loyal a father and son. Let us meet at the Bamboo Forest of a Thousand Leagues, famous throughout China. Wait for us there. Now hasten on your way!

NARRATOR: Husband and wife take leave of the princess and set off on their distant journey. Watōnai takes the princess by the hand and leads her aboard the Chinese boat. He is about to push off when his wife runs up, all out of breath. She seizes the hawser.

KOMUTSU: Your father and mother weren't home. I thought something funny was up, and I see I was right. You and your father planned

---

[48] The Tartars shaved their heads except for a tuft at the top which hung behind as a pigtail.

[49] From *The Book of Mencius,* translated by Legge (*Chinese Classics,* I, 208).

[50] The conquest of Korea by Jingū (also called Jingō) apparently occurred in the fourth century A.D.

[51] From the Nō play *Semimaru.* See Sanari, *Yōkyoku Taikan,* iii, 1680.

[52] The coast of Fujitsu-gun in the present Saga Prefecture.

this long ago. You sent for a wife from his country, and now the four of you are going off to China with all our property, leaving me behind! This is too brutal of you, too heartless! What did I do to displease you? We promised each other we'd go together not merely to China or Korea, but to India or to the ends of the clouds. We were joined by pledges and oaths locked in our hearts, and not by go-betweens or formalities. For the love you once bore me, however weary of me you may have become, take me aboard the boat with you. I won't complain though you throw me into the waves five or ten leagues from shore and I become food for sharks. Please let me die at my husband's hands, Tōnai.

NARRATOR: She beats on the prow, she weeps, she pleads with him, and gives no sign of releasing the hawser.

WATŌNAI: Your bawling face will bring me bad luck, just when we're starting on an important mission. Be off—or I'll teach you a lesson!

NARRATOR: He menaces her with an oar. The princess, alarmed, clings to him, but he brushes aside her restraining hand and beats the side of the boat hard enough to break the oar. Komutsu thrusts herself under the blows intended only as a threat.

KOMUTSU: Beat me to death—that's all I ask!

NARRATOR: She falls on the beach and rolls over in anguish, wailing at the top of her lungs.

KOMUTSU: And I still can't die! Very well! My trouble all along has been that I'm too good-natured. I'll throw myself to the bottom of the sea, and my fury will turn into a serpent of jealousy. The love I once bore you will today become hatred. I'll have my revenge!

NARRATOR: She picks up some stones and drops them into her hanging sleeves. She starts to climb a cliff over the sea, when Watōnai rushes up after her and takes her in his arms.

WATŌNAI: Don't act so rashly! I'm sure now that I can depend on you. I shall leave the princess in your care until the warfare in China ends and peace is restored. It was my intention to leave her here in Japan, but I had to test you, a woman of low birth, to see if you were worthy. That is why I deliberately acted so cruelly. Now I entrust you with the princess, the equal in importance of all 400 districts of China— that should prove that your husband's heart has not changed. It will be a hundred times more exacting to serve the princess than to serve your father-in-law or your husband. I ask this most seriously—it is a matter of life and death. When peace is restored in China I will send a ship for the princess, and I want you to escort her.

NARRATOR: Komutsu listens obediently to his soothing words.

KOMUTSU: Don't worry about anything here. May all go well with you!

NARRATOR: She speaks bravely, but her woman's heart weakens.

KOMUTSU: Not even one night together before you leave? What a nightmare separation this is!

NARRATOR: She clings to her husband's sleeve and weeps aloud, inconsolable. Watōnai too is choked with emotion, and his eyes cloud over in sympathy. For a moment both are torn by conflicting emotions.

WATŌNAI: We can't keep saying good-by indefinitely. I must leave you. Farewell!

NARRATOR: He takes his leave. Sendan is also in tears.

SENDAN: I will await your boat.[53] Then I shall return to my country with your wife. I hope it will come soon.

NARRATOR: Watōnai bows in assent; then, still weeping, he pushes off the boat. Komutsu again catches the hawser.

KOMUTSU: I have something else to tell you. Wait just a moment.

NARRATOR: She stops him.

WATŌNAI: Unreasonable woman!

NARRATOR: He cuts the rope and rows the boat out to the deep. She follows him helplessly, till her body is soaked in the waves. She can only raise her hand and call to the boat, though by now it is too distant for her cries to be heard. She runs back on shore and climbs a stony crag. She watches on tiptoes as the boat moves ever farther out to sea.

KOMUTSU: I feel now like the women for whom they named the Watching Wife Mountain of China and the Scarf-waving Mountain of Japan.[54] I shall not move. I shall not leave this spot, though I turn to stone, though I become a part of the mountain.

NARRATOR: She assures him of her love, weeping with unstinted tears. They call to each other, but the salt spray hides their figures, and the waves of the open sea interrupt their voices. The sea gulls and beach plovers hovering offshore join their cries of sorrow over parting.

[53] Literally, "I shall await the welcoming palanquin."
[54] A legend tells of a woman who climbed a mountain in Anhwei Province in China to watch for her husband's return. She remained there so long that she eventually turned to stone. The "Scarf-waving Mountain" relates to the wife of Ōtomo no Sadehiko, a fifth-century courtier, who waved to her husband's ship when it left for Korea.

Scene Two: The Bamboo Forest of a Thousand Leagues.

NARRATOR: Father and son part, bound for their uncertain destination. Their boats, leaving behind Tsukushi of burning sea fire [55] hidden in clouds, meet with a divine wind that carries them through the myriad waves to arrive on the shores of Cathay at one and the same hour. Tei Shiryū Ikkan, in honor of his homecoming, changes to a costume of Chinese brocades. He turns to his wife and son.

IKKAN: This is my native land, but the times have changed, and the dynasty is no longer the same. The entire country, thanks to Ri Tōten's machinations, has been enslaved by the Tartar barbarians. Who of all the friends and family I once knew is left? There is no way to tell. How can I raise a standard for loyal troops to follow when I am not sure where Go Sankei may be, or even if he is still alive? Where shall I find a castle in which to entrench our forces? I know of none.

Yet, when I departed this country in the fifth year of Tenkei [56] and crossed the seas to Japan, I left behind in her nurse's sleeve a daughter barely two years old. Her mother died in childbirth, and I, her father, have been separated from her by the broad barrier of the sea. The girl has never known father or mother, and she has grown as plants and trees grow, by the grace of the rain and dew. Heaven and Earth have been her parents and her succor. Traveling merchants have told me that she has reached womanhood and become the wife of the lord of a castle, a prince named Gojōgun Kanki. I have no one else to turn to. If only my daughter is willing to help us, out of love for her father, I'm sure that it will be simple to ask Kanki's cooperation. His castle is 180 leagues from here. People will suspect us if we travel together, so I shall journey alone, by a different road. Watōnai, take your mother. Use your intelligence: if you tell people that you've been shipwrecked from a Japanese fishing vessel, they'll let you stay in their houses. You can catch up later if you fall behind. Ahead of us lies the famous Bamboo Forest of a Thousand Leagues, the haunt of tigers. Beyond this huge forest is the Jinyō River where monkeys live. Next you'll see

[55] *Shiranuhi* (sea fire) is used both as an epithet for Tsukushi (Kyushu) and as a pivot-word, where it means "unknown" (destination).
[56] 1625.

a tall mountain of majestic aspect called the Red Cliff. That was where
Su Tung-p'o was exiled in days of old.[57] Wait for me at the Red Cliff,
where we will make our future plans.

NARRATOR: Not knowing which direction to follow, they take the
sun shining through the white clouds for their guide and part to
east and west. Watōnai, in obedience to his father's instructions,
keeps an eye open for houses where he may hide. He steadfastly trudges
forward, his mother on his back. He jumps and leaps over unscalable
rocks and boulders, the roots of massy trees, and swift currents but,
though he speeds ahead swift as a bird in flight, China is a land of
immense distances, and he wanders into the vast bamboo forest, far
from the habitations of men. Watōnai is baffled and bewildered.

WATŌNAI: Mother, I can tell by the strain in my legs that we must
have come forty or fifty leagues, but we have met neither man nor
monkey. The farther we go, the deeper we get in the forest. Ah, I
have it! This must be the work of Chinese foxes. They see that we
Japanese don't know the way, and they're playing tricks on us. If
they want to bewitch us, let them! We have no other inn on our
journey—we'll stay wherever they take us, and we'll be glad to share
in a dish of rice and red beans![58]

NARRATOR: He pushes and tramples through the underbrush and
tall bamboos, penetrating ever deeper into the forest when—strange
to tell—thousands of voices suddenly echo, together with a noise of
hand drums and bass drums, bugles and trumpets, coming closer as
if in attack.

WATŌNAI: Good heavens! Have they discovered us? Are those the
advancing drums of an enemy surrounding us? Or is it the work of
foxes?

NARRATOR: He stands perplexed when a gale all at once arises, blowing fiercely enough to scoop holes in the ground and curl back the
bamboo leaves. The bamboo stalks broken by the wind are like swords,
and the scene horrifying beyond description. Watōnai is not in the least
perturbed.

WATŌNAI: I know what this is—a Chinese tiger hunt. Those gongs
and drums were the beaters. These are the hunting grounds of the

[57] *The Red Cliff* is a prose poem in two parts by Su Tung-p'o (1036-1101). He was
exiled to various places, but the Red Cliff (in modern Hupei Province) was not one of
them.
[58] Rice boiled with red beans was believed to be a favorite dish of foxes. In children's
stories one finds accounts of people bewitched by foxes who are treated to this dish.

Thousand Leagues. They say that when a tiger roars a wind rises. I'm sure that this storm must be the work of some wild beast. Yang Hsiang, one of the twenty-four examples of filial piety, escaped danger from a ferocious tiger because of his devotion to his parents. I am not his equal in piety, but my courage is braced by my loyalty. This will be the first test of my strength since my coming to China. But it would be unmanly to face a tiger with my sword, knowing that the blade is imbued with the strength of the Japanese gods. I can crush with one blow of my fist an elephant or a demon, let alone a tiger!

NARRATOR: He tucks up his skirts from behind and readies himself. As he stands guard over his mother, he is a sight to inspire terror even in the Indian lion, the king of beasts.

Exactly as he predicted, a raging tiger appears on the heels of the storm. It rubs its muzzle against the base of a ringed bamboo, and sharpens its claws on a jutting rock, glaring at the strangers all the while. The tiger snaps its jaws angrily, but Watōnai remains unimpressed. He strikes the tiger with his left hand, and fends it off with his right. Watōnai dodges as the tiger attacks with a twisting motion. The tiger falters and Watōnai nimbly leaps on its back. Now up, now down, they engage in a life-and-death struggle, a test of endurance. Watōnai shouts under the effort, and the tiger, his fur bristling, roars in fury, a noise as of mountains crumbling.

Watōnai's hair is disheveled, and half the tiger's fur has been pulled out. Both are out of breath. When Watōnai clambers on a boulder to catch his breath, the tiger, exhausted, hangs its head among the rocks. Its heavy panting echoes like some powerful bellows. Watōnai's mother rushes up from her shelter in the bamboo grove.

MOTHER: Watōnai! You were born in the Land of the Gods and you mustn't harm the body, hair, and skin you received from them in a contest with a brute beast. Japan is far away, but the gods dwell in your body. Why shouldn't this sacred charm from the Great Shrine by the Isuzu River [59] be effective now?

NARRATOR: She offers him the charm she wears next to her skin.

WATŌNAI: Indeed, it is as you say.

NARRATOR: He accepts the charm reverently and points it at the tiger. He lifts the charm, when—what is the mysterious power of the Land of the Gods!—the tiger, the very embodiment of ferocity, suddenly droops its tail, hangs its ears, and draws in its legs timidly. It

---

[59] The Great Shrine at Ise stands by this river.

creeps into a cave in the rocks, trembling with fear. Watōnai, seizing the tiger by the base of its tail, flings it backwards, forces it down. When it recoils, he leaps on it and presses it beneath his feet, showing the divine strength of the god Susanoo when he flayed the piebald colt of Heaven.[60] How awe-inspiring is the majestic power of the goddess Amaterasu!

At this moment a swarm of beaters rushes up. One of them, obviously the chief, shouts.

AN TAIJIN: Where have *you* come from? Vagabond! How dare you deny me my glory? This tiger is one we've been hunting so that we might offer it to the king of Tartary as a present from our exalted master, the general of the right Ri Tōten. Surrender it at once! If you refuse, you're a dead man! Ho, officers!

NARRATOR: Watōnai smiles with pleasure at mention of Ri Tōten.

WATŌNAI: They say that even a devil counts as a human being! You certainly talk the part of a bold man! I was born in great Japan, and you've said one word too many in calling me a vagabond. If you want the tiger so badly, ask your master Ri Tōten or Tokoroten,[61] or whatever his name is, to come and beg for it! I've business with him and must see him personally. Otherwise you'll never get your tiger.

NARRATOR: He glares at the man.

AN TAIJIN: Don't let him say another word! Kill him!

NARRATOR: The men all draw their swords.

WATŌNAI: I'm ready for you!

NARRATOR: He places the charm on the tiger's head and stations the beast beside his mother. The tiger lies motionless, as though rooted to the spot.

WATŌNAI: Now I have nothing to worry about!

NARRATOR: He lifts his broadsword and, charging into the throng, slashes his way irresistibly in every direction, rolling the men back. An Taijin, the chief of the beaters, counterattacks, leading his officers.

AN TAIJIN: Kill the old hag too!

NARRATOR: They make a beeline for her with flailing swords, but—a further sign of divine protection—the gods lend their strength to the tiger. It springs up and, quivering, bares its teeth. It leaps with a

---

[60] A reference to the story in the first book of the *Kojiki* telling of how the god Susanoo, to spite his sister Amaterasu, flayed a piebald colt backwards and threw it into her halls.
[61] Watōnai is making fun of Ri Tōten's name. *Tokoroten* is a kind of jellied noodle served cold in summertime.

fierce roar at the enemy. An Taijin and the beaters cry, "We're no match for him!" They fling at the tiger their hunting spears, rough lances, and whatever else comes to hand, and slash with their swords. The tiger, possessed of divine strength, leaps about at will, snatching their swords in mid-air with his jaws and dashing them to splinters against the rocks. The glint of the blades scatters like a hail of jewels or slivers of ice. The officers, with no more weapons to wield, are clearly beaten, and they flee in confusion. Watōnai appears behind them. With a shout of "I won't let you go!" he grips An Taijin's neck and lifts him high in the air. He whirls him round and round, then flings him like a ripe persimmon against a rock. An Taijin's body is shattered and he perishes. Now if the officers attempt to retreat they are confronted by the jaws of the ferocious tiger, and if they go forward Watōnai, bold as a guardian king, menaces them.

OFFICERS: Forgive us, please. We crave your pardon.

NARRATOR: They join their hands in supplication and weep bitterly, their faces pressed to the ground. Watōnai strokes the tiger's head.

WATŌNAI: Vile creatures! You who despise the Japanese for coming from a small country—have you learned now the meaning of Japanese prowess, before which even tigers tremble? I am the son of Tei Shiryū, of whom you have no doubt heard. I am the Watōnai who grew up at Hirado in Kyushu. I met there by chance the Princess Sendan, the sister of the late emperor, and I returned to my father's country hoping to restore order and thereby repay the debt of three lifetimes.[62] Join me, if you value your lives. Refuse, and you become food for the tiger! Will it be yes or no?

NARRATOR: He presses them for an answer.

OFFICERS: Why should we say no? We served the king of Tartary and Ri Tōten only because we feared for our lives. From now on we shall be your followers. We beg your indulgence.

NARRATOR: They bow till their noses scrape the ground.

WATŌNAI: Hurrah! But if you're to be my men, you'll have to shave your foreheads in the Japanese manner. Once you've had your coming of age ceremony, change your names. Then you can serve me.

NARRATOR: He orders them to remove their short swords—even these

---

[62] A familiar saying had it that the relations between parent and child lasted one lifetime, those between husband and wife two lifetimes, and those between ruler and subject three lifetimes.

can be used in an emergency for razors. His mother helps collect
the blades. Together they shave at a breakneck pace the heads lined
up before them, not troubling to sprinkle or massage the scalps. The
razors slash away with abandon, sometimes going so far they leave
only a fringe of hair on the sides or the crown. The shaving is completed in the flash of an eye, and the victims, despite a couple of
desperate strokes of the comb, are left with only an unkempt tangle
of hair. Their heads are Japanese, their beards Tartar, and their bodies
Chinese. They exchange looks of consternation. Then the shaven heads
feel the wind, and soon they have caught cold. They sneeze again
and again, with running noses and tears like driving rain. Mother
and son burst out laughing.

WATŌNAI: My followers are all matched now! Take new names in
the Japanese style, on the order of something-*zaemon* or something-
bei, or using numbers, from *tarō* and *jirō* all the way to *jūrō.*[63] Put
the place you come from at the head of your name. Then form two
ranks and start moving.

NARRATOR: "Yes, sir" is the reply. The first to set out are Chang-
chowzaemon, Cambodiaemon, Luzonbei, Tonkinbei, Siamtarō,
Champajirō, Chaulshirō, Borneogorō, Unsunrokurō, Sunkichikurō,
Moghulzaemon, Jakartabei, Santomehachirō, and Englandbei.[64] His
new followers to the fore, the rear of Watōnai's train is brought up by
draft horses and his mother's striped steed. He helps his mother onto
the tiger's back and wins a name for filial piety, as soon he will win
the country. His fame spreads to both China and Japan, as his legs in
the saddle and stirrups when he jumps on the tiger's back; he displays his might to the world for a thousand leagues round.

ACT THREE

*Scene One: The Castle of Lions. Outside the Great Gate.
Time: Early spring, 1645.*

NARRATOR:

Even the benevolent ruler cannot support a worthless minister;

---

[63] Familiar suffixes to Japanese personal names. The eldest son often had a name ending
in *tarō* (first son), and subsequent sons might be given names ending in *jirō, saburō,
shirō,* etc., standing for second, third, or fourth sons. *Jūrō* would be the tenth son.
[64] There is disagreement about some of the place names here given. Unsun was a game
of cards introduced by the Dutch. Sunkichi is unknown.

Even the kindest father cannot love a good-for-nothing child.[65] Though the ways of Japan and China differ in many respects, in essence they are one: father and son, hastening on divergent roads, do not wander astray, for they follow the true path.[66] The parents and son, after meeting as planned at the foot of the Red Cliff, travel together to the Castle of Lions, the seat of Gojōgun Kanki, about whom all they know is that he is Ikkan's son-in-law. The castle exceeds their expectations: the stone walls towering on high are crowned by roof tiles, sparkling with the frost of the still-cold spring night, and at the crest dolphins wave their fins in the sky. The indigo water of the moat coils into the distant Yellow River like an enormous rope. The castle gate is tightly bolted, and from within the walls a night watchman's gong noisily rings out. Every loophole in the wall is provided with a crossbow, and catapults installed here and there are ready to be fired in time of danger. This is a fortress unmatched for strength by any in Japan. Ikkan is dismayed.

IKKAN: In these troubled times, when the castle is so strictly defended, I doubt that anyone will believe my words even if I knock boldly at the gate in the middle of the night and announce that Kanki's father-in-law, a man unknown to anyone, has arrived from Japan. Even if my daughter should hear me, it will be no easy matter to gain admittance to the castle, no matter how many proofs I may offer that I am her father, separated from her when she was two years old, her father who went to Japan. What shall I do?

NARRATOR: He murmurs unhappily. Watōnai cries out at once.

WATŌNAI: It's too late now to be surprised! Ever since leaving Japan I have been resigned to having no allies except myself. Rather than make friendly overtures—"I am your long-lost father-in-law!" "My dear son-in-law" and the like—only to suffer some humiliation, we ought to make a direct proposal: "Can we rely on you or can't we?" If he says "No," he becomes our enemy on the spot. His wife—the daughter you left when she was two—is my half sister, it's true, but if she had any affection for her father you'd think that she'd have wanted to know what was happening to him in Japan and would

---

[65] From a poem by Ts'ao Chih (192–232). Here, as in the poem that opens the second act, the case of Watōnai and Ikkan is the opposite to that given: Watōnai is a dutiful son and Ikkan is a valuable minister.

[66] Two meanings are compressed here: the ways of Japan and China are different, but in essence their teaching are the same; and the roads that father and son follow are different, but they reach the same destination.

have sent letters. But there weren't any. We can't depend on her. I'll stage a series of attacks with the barbarians I conquered in the bamboo forest as the nucleus of my force. In no time at all I'll pick up another fifty or a hundred thousand men. There's no use in asking favors. I'll kick down the castle gate and twist off the head of my unfilial sister. Then I'll have a fight to the finish with your son-in-law Kanki!

NARRATOR: He jumps up, ready for action, but his mother restrains him by clinging to him.

MOTHER: I don't know what's in the girl's heart, but it is customary for women to obey their husbands and not to do as they please. She is your father's daughter and of the same seed as yourself. I am the only stranger. Though we have always been separated by thousands of leagues of ocean and mountains, I cannot escape being called her stepmother.[67] It's inconceivable that the girl should not long in her heart for her father and her brother. But if you force your way into the castle, people will say that it was because the girl's Japanese stepmother envied her. It will be a disgrace not only to me but to Japan.

You have conceived the noble plan of destroying the powerful Tartar enemy and restoring the Ming dynasty, though only a commoner yourself. You should forget about personal disgrace and endure the resentment you feel. Try to win others to your side. I have heard that the essence of military strategy is to gain as your ally even a single private from the enemy camp. How much truer is this of Kanki, the lord of a castle and commanding general of a whole region! Do you think it will be easy to persuade him to join us? Control your emotions and ask him to admit you to the castle!

NARRATOR: She cautions him. Watōnai stands outside the gate and shouts.

WATŌNAI: I have something to discuss privately with General Kanki. Open the gate!

NARRATOR: He beats on the gate and the sound echoes within the castle walls.

The soldiers on guard shout variously.

SOLDIERS: Our master, General Kanki, left yesterday by command of the great king. We have no information when he'll return. You'd like

---

[67] In Japan (as elsewhere) the stepmother is generally depicted as an envious, disagreeable woman.

to meet him personally? What impudence, whoever you are, to make such a request in the middle of the night, when he's away! Speak up, if you've something to say. We'll tell him when he gets back.

NARRATOR: Ikkan answers in a low voice.

IKKAN: My message may not be relayed. If Lord Kanki is absent, I should like to meet his wife and address myself to her. She will surely understand if you inform her that I have come from Japan.

NARRATOR: Hardly has he spoken than the castle resounds with angry cries.

SOLDIERS: What effrontery! The rogue wants to see our general's lady! We've never even seen her ourselves—and he's a Japanese! Beware!

NARRATOR: They wave their long-handled lanterns, and beat gongs and cymbals. The crowd of soldiers on the wall all train their muskets on the visitors.

SOLDIERS: Release the catapults! Crush the intruders! Fuses! Bullets!

NARRATOR: They mill around in tumult. Kanki's wife in her apartments must have heard their disturbance. She rushes to the gate.

KINSHŌJO: Stop this commotion! I shall listen to what they have to say, and until I give the command to fire, you are not to shoot. Do nothing rash!

You outside the gates! I am Kinshōjo, the wife of General Kanki. The entire country bows before the great king of Tartary. My husband, in keeping with the times, has joined the staff of the great king, and has been entrusted with this castle. I do not understand why you wish to see me when my husband is away and the strictest precautions are observed. But anyone from Japan is dear to me. Tell me who you are. I long to hear.

NARRATOR: Even as she speaks she wonders, "Can it be my father? Why should he have come?" She feels anxious and frightened, but nostalgic memories are uppermost in her mind.

KINSHŌJO: Soldiers! Do nothing rash! Don't fire your muskets accidentally!

NARRATOR: Her fears are understandable. Ikkan's first glimpse of his daughter's face under the misty spring moon is clouded by tears. He raises his thickened voice.

IKKAN: Forgive me for speaking so abruptly, but was not your father Tei Shiryū of the Ming? Your mother died in childbirth, and your father, incurring the emperor's wrath, fled to Japan. At the time you were but two years old, and could not understand the sorrow of parting from your father, but you must have heard what happened from your nurse's gossip. I am your father, Tei Shiryū. I have spent long years at the Bay of Hirado in Hizen, a province of Japan, and my name is now Rōikkan. This man is your younger brother, born in Japan, and this is your new mother. I have something to tell and to ask of you in private. That is why I have come, not concealing the shame of my reduced circumstances. Would you please have the gate opened?

NARRATOR: His words of earnest persuasion strike home. Kinshōjo wonders, "Is it indeed my father?" She would like to run down to him, cling to him, gaze into his face. Her heart is torn a thousand ways, but she remains every inch the wife of Kanki, the lord of a castle. She holds back her tears lest the soldiers see.

KINSHŌJO: I remember everything as you describe it, but your arguments are unconvincing without some proofs. I should like to learn what proofs you may have that you are my father.

NARRATOR: The soldiers at once cry out.

SOLDIER A: Proof! Furnish proof!

SOLDIER B: His only proof is to say that he's her father!

SOLDIER C: He's a villain!

NARRATOR: They all point the barrels of their matchlocks at Tei Shiryū. Watōnai runs between his father and the soldiers.

WATŌNAI: If you even pretend to shoot your damned guns, I'll slaughter you!

SOLDIERS: Don't let him escape either!

NARRATOR: They lift the caps of their matchlocks and cover the party from all sides. With rising intensity they press Ikkan for proofs, and the situation seems perilous, when Ikkan raises his hands.

IKKAN: I have it! The proof must be in your possession! When I was about to leave China I had my portrait painted, thinking that it would serve as a memento of me when you were grown. I left this picture with your nurse. Old age has changed me, but some vestiges of my former appearance must remain. Compare the picture and my face, and remove your doubts!

KINSHŌJO: Those words are already proof!

NARRATOR: Standing by the high railing, she unfolds the portrait which has never left her person, and takes out her mirror. She reflects in the mirror her father's face illuminated by the moonlight, and closely compares and matches it with the portrait. In the picture the face has its former luster and glossy sidelocks; in the mirror is the present gaunt old age. The head is now covered with snow, but left unchanged, just as once they were, are the eyes and mouth, which closely resemble her own features. The mole on her forehead inherited from her father is indisputable proof that they are father and daughter.

KINSHŌJO: Are you truly my father? How I have longed for you! How dear you are! I was told only that my mother lay under the sod in the other world, and that my father was in Japan. I sought word, but I had no one to help me. I knew that Japan was at the eastern end of the world, and so I worshiped the rising sun at dawn as my father. At dusk I would spread out a map of the world, and say to myself, "This is China, and here is Japan. My father is here!" On a map Japan seems so close, but it is more than three thousand leagues from here, they say. I had given up all thought of seeing you in this world and, hoping we might meet in the world of the dead, I awaited the future life even before I died. I passed my days in sighs and my nights in tears. The days and nights of twenty years have been hard to bear. How grateful I am that you have kindly stayed alive, and that I can behold my father!

NARRATOR: She weeps for joy, not caring who might hear. Ikkan, choking with tears, clings to the gate tower. He looks up and she looks down, their hearts too full for speech. Only their tears have no end. Watōnai, for all his impetuous martial spirit, is overcome like his mother by emotion, and even the unfeeling Tartar soldiers dampen the rope matches of their guns with overflowing tears. After a while Ikkan speaks.

IKKAN: We have come to make an important and secret request of Kanki. First I should like to discuss it with you. Please have the gate opened and admit us to the castle.

KINSHŌJO: Normally I should of course invite you in, without a word from you, but the country is still in the midst of a war, and by order of the king of Tartary it is strictly forbidden to allow foreigners—even close relatives—within the castles. But this is surely a special case. Soldiers! What do you say?

NARRATOR: The obdurate Chinese cry out.

SOLDIERS: No! Impossible! Never! Leave at once! *Bin ḳan ta satsu bu on bu on!* [68]

NARRATOR: They aim their muskets again. The visitors, not expecting such treatment, are in despair, but Watōnai's mother comes forward.

MOTHER: You are right—an order from the great king may not be disobeyed. But you need not worry about an old woman like myself. All I ask is a word with the lady. Please admit me alone. This will truly be the kindness of a lifetime.

NARRATOR: She joins her hands in supplication, but the soldiers will not listen.

SOLDIERS: No! Nothing exempted women from the order. . . . But we will be reasonable. You must be bound like a criminal all the while you are within the castle walls. If we admit you under this condition, our general will have an excuse to offer and we ourselves will be absolved if the king of Tartary should hear of it. Hurry—tie on the ropes! If you refuse, leave at once! *Bin ḳan ta satsu bu on bu on!*

NARRATOR: Watōnai's eyes flash fire.

WATŌNAI: Dirty Chinese! Where are your ears? Are you all deaf? This is the wife of Tei Shiryū Ikkan—my mother, and the same as a mother to your lady too. How dare you suggest binding her with ropes like a dog or cat on a leash? No Japanese will tolerate such nonsense. It makes no great difference even if you won't let us inside this bothersome place. Let's go!

NARRATOR: He starts to lead his mother away, but she shakes off his hand.

MOTHER: Have you forgotten what I told you a few moments ago? A person who has an important service to ask of others must expect to be subjected to unpleasant experiences of every kind and even to humiliation. As long as our request is granted, I shall not mind being fettered hand and foot, much less bound with ropes—it will be like getting gold in return for broken tiles.[69] Japan is a small country, but her men and women do not abandon a just cause. Please put the ropes on me, Ikkan.

---

[68] Nonsense language, intended to sound like menacing Chinese.

[69] A proverb. The ends of Japanese tiles were round and had markings on them like those on a coin; this may have been the origin of the expression.

NARRATOR: Watōnai, shamed, has no choice but to take out the rope he keeps by his waist for an emergency. He binds his mother at elbows and wrists. Mother and son exchange glances and force a smile—a sign of the gallant training of a Japanese. It is hard for Kinshōjo to bear the sight, but she hides her grief.

KINSHŌJO: Everything is governed by the times, and the laws of a country may not be disobeyed. Have no fear about your mother while she is in my care. I do not know what her request may be, but I shall hear it through, and I shall transmit her words to my husband Kanki with the prayer that he grant your wishes.

The water in the moat around this castle has its source in a conduit in the garden by my dressing chamber, and flows eventually into the Yellow River. If my husband Kanki hears me and grants your request, I shall dissolve some powder in the conduit. The river water flowing white will tell you that all has gone well. In that case, enter the castle in good cheer. But if he does not grant your request, I shall dissolve some rouge in the water. The river water flowing red will tell you of failure. Go then to the gate and escort your mother from here. Watch the river water and you will see by the white damask or Chinese crimson whether good or ill fortune is your lot. Farewell!

NARRATOR: The moonlit gate is opened and the mother is led inside. She stands at the threshold of life and death, but instead of the Gate of Enlightenment, she is at the Gate of Delusion of this world.[70] The bolt drops with an ominous thud.

Kinshōjo's eyes grow dim: weakness is the way of the Chinese woman. Neither Watōnai nor Ikkan weeps: this is the way of the Japanese warrior. The opening and closing of the great gate resound like the firing of a catapult, the way of Tartary. The single echo makes them feel a huge distance separates them.

Scene Two: Inside Kanki's Residence.

NARRATOR: Only on journeying to distant China, a country she had never visited even in dreams, does the mother first learn what it means to have a daughter. They are joined by bonds of affection so strong

[70] Buddhist terms; instead of passing into the realm of enlightenment the mother is about to go to a place where she will suffer.

that the mother submits to criminal fetters, a rare instance even in foreign countries. Rare too, as the plum blossoms first opening in the snow, is their meeting; no interpreter is needed for the voices of the song thrushes, alike in note whether in China or Japan. Kinshōjo, deeply attentive to her mother, leads her to a room in her apartments. She arranges double layers of cushions and triple layers of quilts, politely offers delicacies from the mountains and sea and famous wines; her courtesy would do honor to heaven itself. But the bonds at elbows and wrists make the mother look like a criminal guilty of the Ten Villainies and the Five Inhuman Acts,[71] a sight too pitiful to behold. Kinshōjo waits on her devotedly, gentle as to her own mother, admirable in her solicitude.

Her maidservants gather round.

FIRST MAID: Have you ever seen a Japanese woman before? Her eyes and nose are like ours, but what a funny way she does her hair! See how peculiarly her clothes are sewn! I suppose the young women must dress the same. Her skirts and hem billow all the way out. Why, at the first gust of wind you could see all the way up to her thighs! Isn't it shameful?

SECOND MAID: I don't agree. If I have to be born as a woman again, I want to be a Japanese. I'll tell you why. Japan is called the Land of Great Gentleness.[72] Wouldn't a country where everyone is gentle be wonderful for a woman?

THIRD MAID: Yes, it certainly sounds so.

NARRATOR: They narrow their eyes enviously and nod. Kinshōjo approaches.

KINSHŌJO: Now what are you gossiping about with such pleasure?— Filial affection and duty both make me feel greater obligation to this mother who did not bear me than to my real mother. But, alas, I am forced by the laws of the country to bind her like a criminal. And I am worried lest my husband be blamed if the king of Tartary hears that we admitted her. Torn between fears for both, my role is the hardest to play. I ask you all to assist me.

[71] The Ten Villainies were the killing of living beings, theft, adultery, lying, the use of obscene language, cursing, being double-tongued, covetousness, anger, and foolishness. The Five Inhuman Acts were patricide, matricide, wounding Buddha's person, killing his immediate disciple, and murdering a Buddhist priest.

[72] The name Yamato is written with characters which mean literally "great gentleness".

I'm told that Japanese food is quite unlike our own. Ask my mother what she would like, and prepare it for her.

MAID: If it please you, my lady, we prepared a meal most carefully —rice cooked with longans, soup made with duck and fried beancurd, pork in sweet sauce, steamed lamb, and beef-paste cakes. We offered these dishes to her ladyship, but she only said, "How disagreeable! I don't like such food at all. I can't manage it with my hands tied. Please make something simple—*musubi* will do." I had no idea what kind of food *musubi* might be. I gathered everyone and asked their opinion. Somebody said that in Japan they call a *sumō* wrestler a *musubi*.[73] I searched everywhere for one, but it's a poor season for wrestlers, and I couldn't find a one to suit her taste.

NARRATOR: A carriage rumbles outside and the shout goes up, "His excellency has returned!" Chests of clothes are borne ahead of the carriage, and a splendid silken parasol shades Kanki—a dignified procession worthy of his high name. Kinshōjo goes out to meet him.

KINSHŌJO: You've returned earlier than I expected. What happened at court?

KANKI: The great king of Tartary was highly pleased with my achievements, and he granted a promotion in excess of my deserts. I have been appointed banner leader of one hundred thousand horsemen, with the rank of general of cavalry. He bestowed on me the headgear and court costume of a prince, and commanded me to perform important services. No higher honor could come to our house.

KINSHŌJO: I congratulate you. Good fortune has come twice to our house today. I have often told you how much I miss my father and long for him. Today he came to our gate with my Japanese mother and brother. He said that he had a request to make of you, but I told him that you were away. My father and brother, in deference to the strict laws of the country, have departed, but I have kept my mother with me. I feared, however, that the government might hear of this, and she was therefore bound with ropes before she entered the castle. I have offered her entertainment in the women's pavilion, but you can imagine how sad it makes me to see in criminal bonds my mother —though I am not of her flesh and blood.

KANKI: You were wise to have her bound. Now I have an excuse

---

[73] *Musubi* are cold rice balls; one class of wrestler is today called *ko-musubi*.

to offer if the government should learn of this. Treat her with the utmost kindness. But I should like to meet her myself. Please lead me to her.

NARRATOR: His voice must have carried: the mother cries out from the double doors.

MOTHER: Kinshōjo, has Lord Kanki returned? He does me too great an honor. It is for me to go to him.

NARRATOR: Her figure as she comes forward suggests an ancient pine twisted and bound with wisteria vine. Kanki's eyes are filled with pity as he watches her struggle painfully towards him.

KANKI: It is true—a mother will journey ten thousand leagues over mountains and rivers because she has a child somewhere in the world. But, alas, we are compelled by the laws of our times to bind you in this fashion. Wife, make sure that the ropes do not hurt your mother. I mean not the least disrespect towards so rare a guest. I promise that I shall grant whatever you may request, providing that it is within my competence. Tell me—there is no need to hesitate.

NARRATOR: His manner is extremely gentle. The old mother's expression relaxes.

MOTHER: Thank you. I feel I can trust you. Why should I hesitate, now that I have your assurance? I should like to tell you privately our important request. Please come closer.

NARRATOR: Her voice drops to a whisper.

MOTHER: Longing for our daughter has not been our only reason for coming to China. Early last winter the Princess Sendan, the younger sister of the Ming emperor, was blown ashore in a small boat at a place called the Beach of Matsura in Hizen Province. She told us that China had been seized by the Tartars. Your father was formerly a minister at the Ming court, and my son Watōnai, though he follows a humble fisherman's calling, has studied the texts of military science of both China and Japan. As soon as they heard the princess's story, they decided to overthrow the great king of Tartary and restore the former dynasty with the princess on the throne. We left the princess for the time being in Japan, and came ourselves to China. But, alas, how distressing it is to find that everything, even the plants and trees, sways before the Tartars. No one wishes to join the adherents of the Ming. Only one man can we trust to be Watōnai's right arm—you, Kanki. I implore you, sir—lend us your strength. I bow before you.

NARRATOR: She forces her forehead down to her knees; she seems possessed of but a single determination. Kanki is greatly surprised.

KANKI: So this Watōnai of Japan I've been hearing about is Kinshōjo's brother and the son of Tei Shiryū Ikkan! Even in China we're impressed by his bravery. His plan is promising and the obvious course. My forefathers were all vassals of the Ming, but after the death of the emperor there was no sovereign I could serve. I had no choice but to accept the rewards of Tartary. I was resigned to spending my days in this fashion, but your request now exactly fulfills my hopes. I should like to declare myself your ally on the spot, but the matter requires some further consideration, and I am not at liberty to assent immediately. I shall seriously consider your proposal and then make my reply.

NARRATOR: The mother interrupts.

MOTHER: How cowardly of you! You contradict yourself! Once so important a matter is mentioned, it becomes common knowledge. Supposing word leaks out while you are deliberating our proposal —no amount of regret will restore our cause if such a slip leads to defeat. We will bear you no grievance if you refuse, but whether your answer is yes or no, make it at once!

NARRATOR: She presses him for a reply.

KANKI: If you insist on an immediate answer, it is quite simple. Kanki most assuredly will be Watōnai's ally.

NARRATOR: Hardly has he finished these words than he catches Kinshōjo by the front of her kimono and pulls her to him. He draws his sword and presses it to her throat. The old mother rushes over in alarm and forces herself between them. She kicks away Kanki's hand that holds her daughter, then with her back pushes Kinshōjo down and lies over her in protection. She cries out in a loud voice.

MOTHER: Monster! What does this mean? Does Chinese custom compel you to stab your wife when you are asked a favor? Or is this rage directed at your wife because you were obliged by her relative to hear an offensive request? Or is it madness? Wicked man—you would kill your wife before her mother's eyes, the very first time I come to see her! I can imagine how you must behave on ordinary days! If you don't wish to join us, don't! My precious daughter, you have a mother now. You have nothing to fear any more. Hold tight to your mother!

NARRATOR: She sacrifices herself to become an intervening wall protecting her daughter. Kinshōjo cannot understand her husband's motives, but she is grateful for her mother's love.

KINSHŌJO: Don't hurt yourself!

NARRATOR: These are her only words; the two choke with tears. Kanki jumps back.

KANKI: Your doubts are natural, but I assure you that I am neither a villain nor mad. Yesterday the king of Tartary summoned me. He said, "An insignificant wretch named Watōnai has recently come here from Japan intending to overthrow the king of Tartary and restore the dynasty of the Ming. He is resourceful and well versed in military strategy, though a man of low birth and base demeanor. Who will punish this villain?"

Finally he chose me from among all the nobles present, and appointed me general of cavalry with a command of one hundred thousand men. I of course never dreamt that Watōnai was my wife's brother. I answered boldly, "Watōnai may know as much about military strategy as Kusunoki, or whatever that Japanese general's name was, and he may be bold as Asahina or Benkei, but I have mastered the essence of Chu-ko Liang's strategy.[74] I shall borrow the secrets of Fan K'uai and Hsiang Yü to pursue and rout him in a single engagement. I shall return with Watōnai's shaven head borne aloft on a pike."

If, after boasting in this manner, I should calmly become your son's ally without having crossed swords or shot a single arrow, I am sure that the Tartars would say—knowing Kanki is not a man to be frightened by tales of Japanese martial prowess—that I lost my courage and forgot my duties as a soldier because I was tied to my wife's apron strings and influenced by her relatives. If such is their gossip, my sons, grandsons, and even my remote descendants will be unable to escape disgrace. I would kill my dearly beloved wife in order to be able to join Watōnai cleanly—not influenced by his relation to my wife, and revering still the principles of justice and fidelity.

Kinshōjo—your mother's words when she stopped me were filled with compassion. The point of your husband's sword was tempered by a sense of loyalty. Give up your life, for your mother's love and for loyalty!

[74] Kusunoki Masashige, Asahina Yoshihide, and Musashibō Benkei were all Japanese military heroes. Chu-ko Liang and the two men mentioned in the next sentence were famous Chinese strategists.

NARRATOR: These are the unadorned words of a soldier.

KINSHŌJO: I understand. I am capable of such loyalty. I do not regret sacrificing for the sake of filial piety this body I have received from my parents.

NARRATOR: She pushes her mother aside and steps forward. She opens the front of her kimono, and draws to her the icy blade so terrible to behold.

MOTHER: Alas!

NARRATOR: She rushes up and tries to separate husband and wife, but in vain; she cannot use her hands to intervene. She catches her daughter's sleeve with her teeth and pulls her back, only for Kanki to come closer. She takes the husband's sleeve in her mouth, but the daughter approaches again, determined to die. Frantic as a mother cat carrying her kittens to a new nest, her eyes dim with the strain, and she falls with a cry. The mother seems oblivious to what happens around her. Kinshōjo clings to her.

KINSHŌJO: I never knew my mother before, and when I met her at last, I failed to perform a single act of daughterly affection. How shall I repay her for all her kindness? Please let me die instead, Mother.

NARRATOR: She pleads, laments, and bursts into tears.

MOTHER: What a sad thing to say! You have three parents, two in this world and one in the world of the dead. To your other two parents you owe the great debt of having been brought into this world. I am the only one who has failed to show you kindness or generosity. I shall not be able to rid myself of the name of a stepmother, however I try. If I allow you to die now, people will say that your Japanese stepmother hated her Chinese stepdaughter so much—though they were separated by three thousand leagues—that she had her put to death before her eyes. Such a report would disgrace not only me but Japan, for people would say, judging the country by my acts, that the Japanese were cruel-hearted. The sun that shines on China and the sun that shines on Japan are not two different lights, but the Land of the Rising Sun is its origin, and there you will find humanity, justice, and the other constant virtues. Could I, having been born in the Land of the Gods, where mercy is honored above all virtues, look on as my daughter is killed and then still go on living? I pray that these ropes that bind me will reveal themselves as the sacred ropes of the Japanese gods and strangle me on the spot. Then, though my corpse be exposed in a foreign country, may the ropes lead my soul to Japan!

NARRATOR: She raises her voice in tearful pleading, a voice filled with understanding, love, and pathos. Kinshōjo clings to her, and the mother's sleeve is wetted by the tears that both shed. Kanki too is persuaded by the mother's reasoning, and yields to helpless tears. After a while he strikes his chair impatiently.

KANKI: It can't be helped, then. I can do nothing to change matters. Your mother has refused to accept my plan. From this day forth Watōnai and I are enemies. But I do not wish it to be supposed that I detain our mother here as a hostage. Prepare a palanquin for her, and send her wherever she wishes to go.

KINSHŌJO: No, it won't be necessary to send her anywhere. I promised my brother that if I had good news I would drop white powder in this conduit flowing to the Yellow River, or, if his wish was not granted, that I would color the water with rouge. I shall dissolve some rouge in the water, and her companions will come to fetch her when they see the water flowing red.

NARRATOR: She goes into her chamber. Watōnai's mother is lost in thought, as she wonders what to tell her husband and son when she returns, now that everything has gone contrary to their hopes; her helpless tears of blood make a scarlet brocade, even before the rouge is set flowing. Kinshōjo in the meanwhile is dissolving rouge in an agate bowl.

KINSHŌJO: Thus the brocade bridge is cut before the father and daughter could cross.[75] Now is the moment of farewells.

NARRATOR: The rouge slips into the moonlit waters of the spring and rushes like the crimson leaves of autumn through the turbulent waters, telling the sad news. The bubbles in the garden stream, dyed the same hue, flow crimson through the conduit to the waters of the Yellow River. Watōnai sits on the bank, his straw raincoat thrown over him, watching the surface of the river to see if the water flows red or white.

WATŌNAI: Great heavens! The rouge is flowing! He's refused my request! I can't trust my mother to that villain Kanki who won't join me!

[75] Reference to poem 283 in the Kokinshū: "In Tatsuta River the red leaves seem to flow by in confused patterns. If I should cross, the brocade would be cut through the center."

NARRATOR: His feet rush forward furiously up the rapids of the river. When he reaches the moat at his destination, he leaps across, climbs the inner wall, tramples down wattled fences and lattice railings, and finally arrives at the spring within the garden of the women's apartments of Kanki's castle.

WATŌNAI: What a relief—Mother's safe!

NARRATOR: He flies to her and cuts the ropes that bind her. He plants himself squarely before Kanki.

WATŌNAI: So you're that bearded Chinese of a Kanki! I tied up my mother, the only one I'll ever have in heaven or on earth, because I honored you for what I thought you were, and because I wanted you for my ally. But the respect I paid you seems to have gone to your head. Is it because of my inadequacy as a general that you refuse to be my ally? I expected you to follow me, if only because your wife is my sister. I, Watōnai, peerless in all Japan, now make my request directly—answer me!

NARRATOR: He lays his hand on his sword hilt and draws himself up.

KANKI: You are all the less likely to succeed if you mention your relationship to my wife. You may be without peer in Japan, but I am the unique Kanki of China. I am not the kind of general who makes alliances because of his wife's influence, but I have no ground for divorcing her. Nor am I disposed to wait patiently for her to die. Take advantage of the favorable breeze and leave at once. Or would you prefer to give me your head as a memento?

WATŌNAI: No! I'll take yours back to Japan as a souvenir of my visit!

NARRATOR: Both are about to draw their swords when Kinshōjo cries out.

KINSHŌJO: See! You won't have to wait for me to die! Here is the source of the crimson water!

NARRATOR: She opens the front of her robe to reveal that she has stabbed herself, slashing diagonally with her dagger from under her breast to her liver. The mother cries out and swoons at the sight of the wound bathed in crimson. Watōnai is also dumbfounded, and even Kinshōjo's husband, who had been ready to kill her, is stunned. Kinshōjo speaks painfully.

KINSHŌJO: Mother would not let me be killed for fear of the disgrace it might bring to Japan. But if I begrudge my life and fail to help my parents and my brother, it will be a disgrace to China. (*To Kanki.*) Now that I have stabbed myself, no one will slander you by saying that you were under your wife's influence. Kanki, please join my father and brother and become a source of strength to them. Tell my father of this too.—Please say no more. Oh, I am in pain!

NARRATOR: These are her only words before she loses consciousness. Kanki hides his tears.

KANKI: Nobly done! I promise that your suicide will not have been in vain.

NARRATOR: He bows his head before Watōnai.

KANKI: My ancestors were vassals of the Ming, and I should gladly have joined you, but I feared that people might say I had been led astray by a relative of my wife. She has killed herself in order to encourage me on the path of justice. I can now become your ally honorably. I look up to you as my commanding general, and I shall offer you a new name, one fit for a supreme prince. I give you the name Coxinga, lord of the imperial surname, Tei Seikō, prince of Empei.[76] Pray wear the robes of your office.

NARRATOR: Kanki draws forth from a Chinese chest, that opens as Coxinga's fortunes have opened, a scarlet court robe of double-thickness brocade, the sleeves of gauzy and figured silks, a ceremonial hat, shoes with floral patterns, a belt set with coral and amber, and a sword of polished gold. A silken parasol is lifted above Coxinga's head, and a hundred thousand or more troops line up before him, armored sleeve against sleeve, bearing imperial flags with pendant streamers, conical ensigns, shields, spears, bows, and muskets: it seems as though the king of Yüeh had come a second time to Kuai-chi Mountain.[77]

Coxinga's mother cries out joyfully.

MOTHER: What a glorious day! My hopes have been realized! See, Kinshōjo—because of your sacrifice the prayers of my husband and son have been granted. But these prayers are not ours alone—they are shared by the whole world. This dagger is a mere nine and a half inches long, but your suicide has determined the destiny of all China. For me to prolong my life now would render false my first words, and bring further shame on Japan.

[76] For the historical circumstances behind Coxinga's names, see Keene, *The Battles of Coxinga*, p. 46.

[77] See n. 9, above.

NARRATOR: She seizes her daughter's dagger and plunges it into her own throat. Everyone exclaims in horror, but she calls out.

MOTHER: Don't come any closer!

NARRATOR: She glares fiercely about her.

MOTHER: Kanki, Coxinga. Under no circumstances must you lament or grieve over the death of your mother and her daughter. Consider the king of Tartary as the enemy of us both, and you will be strengthened in your vengeance. Do not forget these last words of a mother whose kindness consisted in not allowing your determination to relent. (To Watōnai.) Your father Ikkan is still alive, and you will not want for a parent. Your mother exhorts you by dying; your father, living on, will continue to instruct you. With such guidance you should become a great general with perfect accomplishments.—My thoughts of this fleeting world go no farther.

NARRATOR: She thrusts the dagger in again and twists it, severing the bundle of her liver.[78]

MOTHER: Kinshōjo, do you feel no regret at leaving this world?

KINSHŌJO: What regret should I feel?

NARRATOR: Her words are brave, but regret lingers for the husband she leaves behind. Mother and daughter take each other's hands and nestle together. They look up and down Coxinga's robes of office, then expire at the same moment, the happy smiles on their faces a memento for this world.

Coxinga, so bold that he might be mistaken for a devil, and Kanki, courageous as a dragon or tiger, are overwhelmed by tears. But Coxinga is determined not to disobey his mother's injunctions, and Kanki not to violate his wife's noble purpose. Coxinga is ashamed to weep before Kanki, and Kanki before Coxinga; they hide their downcast faces.

Along the road over which the sad remains are borne to the grave, the army sets out for battle. The quick and the dead take the same road. For Coxinga his mother's last words were like a sermon to Buddha;[79] his father's instructions will be an iron bar in a devil's hands. When he fights he will triumph; when he attacks he will conquer all before him. Here is a warrior endowed with wisdom and love, a marvel of the ages.

[78] It was believed in Japan that the liver had seven lobes joined together at the top.

[79] A proverbial expression of unnecessary instruction: Coxinga is determined to restore the Ming even without his mother's admonition. The iron bar in the devil's hands is another proverbial phrase, meaning to make stronger what is already strong.

The banks of a pool which holds a jewel cannot be broken;
The pond where a dragon lives will never run dry.[80]
The country which has produced such a hero is a well-ordered
country, and its prince is a true prince. Here is the prodigy of Japan,
a man who illuminates a foreign land with the brilliance of his martial
talents.

ACT FOUR

Scene One: Before the Shrine of Sumiyoshi in Matsura.
Time: Autumn of the same year.

NARRATOR: The days and nights at Komutsu's house by the Beach of
Matsura have been spent in anxious waiting for news from China.
The Chinese princess living with Komutsu has become the subject
of the neighbors' gossip; they suspect that she may be a countryless
wanderer from the isles where the waves of China and Japan come
together.[81]

When Komutsu learned that her husband had changed his name
to Coxinga, lord of the imperial surname, and become the commanding general of many tens of thousands of troops, her heart leapt with
excitement, and she at once assumed male attire. Her sidelocks are
now combed back to form a thick queue, and her glossy backlocks
hang loosely behind: she might be the son of a Shinto priest or an
ointment seller,[82] but hardly a woman. She wears light blue breeches
and a cloak, and carries a wooden sword in a vermilion scabbard with
a scarlet sword knot. Her rouged lips are like a flower, her face white
with snowy powder. Her wicker hat is pulled deep over her face,
but her skirts are lifted high as she steps lightly as a plover along the
beach on her daily visit of prayers to the Sumiyoshi shrine of Matsura.

She arrives before the shrine and joins her hands in fervent prayer:

[80] This passage, quoted from the Chinese classic *Hsün-tzu*, means here that a country
which has produced a hero like Coxinga is invincible, just as a pond which holds a
dragon can never run dry.

[81] *Chikura* designated the region between Japan and China, and is sometimes identified
with the island of Tsushima.

[82] The reference is not clear, but it has been suggested that a Shinto priest would be
especially well groomed. Ointment sellers (particularly those of Seikenji) were young
men whose full head of hair and dandified appearance attracted customers. See Statler,
Japanese Inn, pp. 158–59.

"May my vows be fulfilled!" The next instant, still kneeling, she has whipped out her sword, a feat of dexterity. She jumps up and, wooden sword held high, assaults with bold shouts her opponent, a sacred pine. Swift as summer lightning or the lion in his leap, her hands and feet move nimbly as she wields her broadsword, now high, now low, skillfully feinting and dodging. She charges in and fells with a stroke of her wooden blade a branch from the ancient tree. Here indeed is a latter-day Ushiwaka.[83]

The Princess Sendan—how long has she been watching Komutsu here?—runs up from the forest shadows.

SENDAN: Komutsu—every day at the same hour you leave the house in that strange costume. Today at last I have followed you and discovered where you went. Who taught you to use a sword? I marvel at your skill.

KOMUTSU: I've never had a teacher. I merely imitate what I've observed of my husband's sword practice.

We don't know when word may be coming from China, but I intend, even if no ship is sent for us, to accompany you over the seas. I have been praying to the god here for a sign whether we would be successful or fail, and look! I cut a branch from the pine with a wooden sword, exactly as if I had used a steel blade! It must be a sign that the god has granted my prayers! A merchant ship happens to be sailing today for China—let's take passage aboard her!

SENDAN: With great pleasure. I am sure that all will go well. Please take me back to China as soon as possible.

NARRATOR: She is overjoyed.

KOMUTSU: Have no fears. Sumiyoshi, the god of this shrine, is the protecting divinity of the sea lanes. When the Empress Jingū embarked on her conquest of Korea, he used his ebb-tide pearl and flood-tide pearl [84] to guard her ship. That is why they call him also the god of ships. Many years ago a man from China named Haku Rakuten [85] crossed to the Islands of the Dragonfly,[86] thinking to test the wisdom of Japan. As soon as he saw the scenery before his eyes he wrote a poem:

---

[83] The youthful name of Minamoto Yoshitsune (1159–89).

[84] These treasures are enshrined at the Matsura shrine of Sumiyoshi today.

[85] The Japanese pronunciation of Po Lo-t'ien (or Po Chü-i). For this legend, see Waley, *The Nō Plays of Japan,* pp. 205–13. The two poems in fact have nothing to do with Po Chü-i.

[86] A poetic name for Japan.

Green moss donned like a cloak
Lies on the shoulders of the rocks.
White clouds like a sash
Girdle the mountain's waist.

The great god Sumiyoshi, appearing in the guise of a humble old fisherman, recited a poem in reply:

Strange, that the rocks have no sash,
Though they wear a cloak of moss,
And that the cloakless mountain
Should have to wear a girdle! [87]

Rakuten, at a loss to match this poem, returned at once to his country, they say. My traveling robe will be the moss cloak the god sang of in his poem, the god who protects our country. Let us be on our way!

NARRATOR: They set off together. Their path across the water stretches distantly before them.

Scene Two: The journey of the Princess Sendan from Hirado to China.

NARRATOR:

In a Chinese hairdo, a Satsuma comb,
In a Shimada hairdo, a Chinese comb:
Yamato and Cathay are blended here.[88]
How uncertainly they face the journey ahead!
On their way by boat and by land
They must keep with them their bamboo hats
And pillows folded inside their kimonos
On which the dreams of many nights will unfold,
Resolved to voyage a thousand leagues:
A woman's courage is roused by love for a man.

KOMUTSU:

I leave on a journey that takes me from home,
Yours is a journey back to your land.
How different our lots, but yours is the brighter!

[87] The poem is a satirical rejoiner based on the conceit that "cloaks" and "sashes" should go together.
[88] Sendan wears a Japanese comb in her hair and Komutsu wears a Chinese comb in hers; in this way the two countries are united.

NARRATOR:

> Sendan is strengthened by Komutsu's reproach,
> And plucks up courage for the voyage to China.
> How distant her thoughts now range!

SENDAN:

> Why should she, with a husband and parents, grieve?
> The daybreak moon itself will be the same,
> But she will remember with many regrets
> The moon they shared in their marriage chamber.

NARRATOR:

> At Ōmura Bay the beach wind brings a shower
> That splashes but to clear, as tears do not,
> Tears they conceal and with trailing sleeves wipe
> At Mirror Shrine, where they leave their reflections.
> Will people see at Seaweed Bay that they weep not?
> They stare westward at the course of the moon,
> The distant sky of their destination.

KOMUTSU:

> When shall we return? Heaven-flying geese,
> Tempt him, tempt my husband back to me.
> Twenty-five the years that we've been pledged,[89]
> Twenty-five, like the strings of my lute.
> I'll play, and when in Hakozaki's pines
> I hear he pines for me, I'll hurry forward.

NARRATOR:

> Along the beach the children of fisherfolk
> Who gather drifting seaweed are clustered,
> Playing jacks and marbles, odd or even,
> Counting three, four, five—happy, childish games.
> Even the water plays at hide-and-seek
> On its way to the Pool of Seven Rapids,[90]
> Hiding the reflections of old-time lovers.
> The children sing, "Before the devil comes!" [91]
> —The women's sleeves are wet with tears that do not dry.
> They wait at Matsura River for the China boat;

[89] Perhaps meaning that Watōnai and Komutsu were destined from birth to be married.
[90] A series of numbers runs through the lines, from three to seven. The pool adjoins the Matsura River.
[91] "The devil" is the "it" in a game of hide-and-seek.

The harbor is swept by winds from Nearby Bay.
The princess glances at the harbor shore:
In Kuriya River, where nets are hauled from the bank,
Aboard a fishing boat rocked by the waves,
A boy with parted hair [92] is fast asleep,
His net not lowered, a string dangling from his pole.

SENDAN: Say there, my lad! We are travelers bound for China. Please take us part of the way aboard your boat.

BOY: That's simple enough! One of you, I see, is Chinese, and the other from Tsukushi. There must be someone you love in China for you ladies to be traveling there! I'm sure you're yearning for lovers two thousand leagues away.[93] This is not the night of the full moon, but now, while no one can see, come quickly aboard my boat. It will sail like the moon through the sky.

NARRATOR: He punts his boat closer with his water-wise pole.

BOTH WOMEN: What strange chance is this?

NARRATOR: They board his boat, and at once he rows out towards their unknown destination. The white waves calm, and their boat glides over the smooth surface of the sea.

SENDAN: What are all those islands we can see? Would you please tell a stranger as a memento of this journey?

NARRATOR: The boy steps up to the prow and points in the distance over the broad expanse of sea.

BOY: Listen well, travelers! First, stretching off out there, are the twelve islands of Kikai, one group of five and the other of seven. That one, where flocks of white birds are poised, is Whitestone Island, and there, where the smoke rises, is Sulphur Island. The tall island to the south hung with mist is Chido. And that island is called Two Gods because in ancient times two gods sported there, the goddess Amaterasu dancing to Sumiyoshi's flute. What say you to that, my Chinese lady?

NARRATOR: Even as he speaks they have left Japan behind, and the islands ahead, or what seem to be islands, are peaks of clouds; what seem to be mountains rise in the sky and not in the sea. No wind stirs, but the little skiff races ahead as once the bird boat and rock

[92] In ancient times, as we may gather from works of art, boys wore their hair parted in the middle and tied at the ears. This style, completely out of fashion in Chikamatsu's day, suggests that the boy in the boat has something supernatural about him.

[93] Allusion to lines by Po Chü-i: "When on the night of the fifteenth moonlight bathes anew the sky, I think of old friends two thousand leagues away."

boat of Heaven [94] flew through the sky. Mountains appear to the west, where no mountains had been. Faster than the moon, apace with the sun, they reach the habor of Sung-chiang [95] where men are still fishing for sea bass in an autumn wind exactly like the wind that blew when they left the Land of the Rising Sun. They step ashore from the boat.

SENDAN: Our passage has been smooth as if we sat in our parlor, truly thanks to you, my lad. Who might you be who have carried us in an instant across the high seas?

BOY: You talk as if I were a mortal man! I am without a name, but people call me the Boy of the Sea from Sumiyoshi because I have dwelled from ancient times in the Land of the Rising Sun.[96] I say good-by to you now and go back to Sumiyoshi, where I shall await your return to Japan.

NARRATOR: He rows his skiff back from the shore with the evening waves, and favored by the breeze he moves out to the open sea, far out to the open sea.

Scene Three: The Mountain of the Nine Immortals.

NARRATOR: It is related how T'ao-chu Kung served Kou Chien. He shut himself up at Kuai-chi Mountain where he plotted various stratagems, finally crushing the king of Wu and satisfying Kou Chien's dreams of revenge.[97]

In ancient days, in times far removed from the present, there was such an example; today this is Go Sankei's fate. He wanders from mountain to cloud-covered mountain, hiding his identity and rearing the prince. With the reversal of his fortunes, he has learned to sleep on moss for his mattress; the willows in front of the palace and the blossoms before the royal halls have given way to withered trees on mountain peaks. When the evening mists settle, Go Sankei makes a blanket of his body to warm the infant prince; and for the prince to ride in, he fashions a handcart of ivy vines in place of a brocaded

---

[94] Boats used by the Japanese gods in the old legends.

[95] Sung-chiang was famous for its sea bass. Chikamatsu undoubtedly learned this fact from Su Tung-p'o's poem *The Red Cliff*.

[96] The name Sumiyoshi contains the word *sumi* (dwelled).

[97] T'ao-chu Kung was another name for Fan Li. His loyal service to the king of Yüeh. Kou Chien, is described in n. 9, above.

palanquin. When the morning dews lie thick, the prince rides on the shoulders of the valley monkeys. Two years have passed, quickly as yesterday turning to today. Their nights are spent in mountains, their days are passed in mountains. Go Sankei in his journeys hides his own name and the prince's face from the eyes of men. The rainbow bridge to the world has been broken by clouds; the cries of the crows and night birds deep in the mountains, and even the voices of the parrots [98] screeching at the tops of the trees suggest nothing of the past.

Go Sankei has been pushing his way through bamboo underbrush, and through thickets of black pine and cypress, far from any water, deep in the mountains. He wearily struggles up a steep mountain road towards the towering summit of the Mountain of Nine Immortals in Hsing-hua-fu, known to him only by name. As he pauses a while he notices two old men with shaggy eyebrows and white hair, seemingly in perfect harmony with the pine breeze, as friends who have lived together long years. They have put a *go* [99] board on a rock before them, and are utterly absorbed in their game, watching the black and white stones form scattered pockets or diagonal lines like flights of geese over the 361 intersections. Their thoughts move freely, like a spider's thread in the air, and their bodies have become empty cocoons on a withered branch. This is the art of conversing by hand, far removed from the usages of the world.

GO SANKEI: Can this be the pure world of Brahma? [100]

NARRATOR: He transfers the prince to a ledge in the rocks and, leaning his chin on a withered stump, gazes in fascination on the game, purified of the dust of worldly concern. Carried away, he cries out.

GO SANKEI: Old gentlemen, I should like a word with you. I am interested to see you play the game of *go*. Is there some special pleasure to be found in this contest played without the help of the Three Friends—music, poetry, and wine?

NARRATOR: One old man, not seeming to answer, speaks.

OLD MAN: If it looks like a *go* board to you, it is a *go* board, and for

---

[98] The parrot was an exotic bird, and Chikamatsu therefore places it for local color in the Chinese mountains.

[99] A game played with black and white stones on a board. Proficiency in the game is believed to be akin to a mastery of military tactics.

[100] A stage of enlightenment at which one transcends all earthly desires, reached in this case by absorption in the game of *go*.

the eye that sees *go* stones, they are merely *go* stones. But there is a text which likens the world to a *go* board. For those who see with their minds, the center of the universe is here. From this vantage point, what will cloud our view of the mountains, rivers, grasses, or trees of all China? The ninety intersections in each quarter of the board represent the ninety days of each of the four seasons. Together they come to 360.[101] How foolish of you not to realize that we spend one day on each intersection!

GO SANKEI: Extraordinary! But why should you two oppose each other as your sole pleasure in heaven and earth?

OLD MAN: If there were not both yin and yang there would be no order in creation.

GO SANKEI: And the result of your contest?

OLD MAN: Does not the good or bad fortune of mankind depend on the chance of the moment?

GO SANKEI: And the black and the white?

OLD MAN: The night and the day.

GO SANKEI: What are the rules of the game?

OLD MAN: The stratagems of war.

GO SANKEI: Breaking up formations, checking, opening offensives . . .

NARRATOR: In *go* as in war the sparks are set flying. The black and the white may be likened to crows in restless flight or to clusters of snowy herons. How natural that before this spectacle a king of old lost track of the days and the nights, and his axe handle rotted before he knew it!

The old man speaks again.

OLD MAN: A heroic general named Coxinga has crossed here from Japan and taken up the Ming cause. He is now in the midst of a battle. The scene of the fighting is far from here, but the power of vision that comes from concentration on *go* will permit you to see how the battle progresses, plainly before your eyes.

NARRATOR: His voice and the mountain wind echo in the sound of the *go* stones. Go Sankei suddenly realizes where he is.

GO SANKEI: This must be the Mountain of the Nine Immortals that commands a view of all China!

[101] There are actually 361 intersections, ninety in each quarter plus one in the middle, but Chikamatsu says 360 here because he wishes to make a parallel with the 360 days in a year of the lunar calendar.

NARRATOR: He gazes at a distant peak, faintly visible—or is it a cloud? The veil of mist descends to the foot of the mountain, where it is blown away by a spring breeze, to reveal a mid-April sky.[102] He can clearly see a castle swathed in the brocade of mingled willow shoots and cherry blossoms. What man of what country has fortified himself here? The gates are high and the moat is deep. Shielding walls have been erected around the encampment, and an imposing tower rises boldly at the heart of the fortress. The soaring larks and the wild geese returning, mistaking the many-colored pennants for flowers, might approach to rest their wings. In the gentle sunlight of a spring morning, flags marked with the sun and the moon display the fair name of Japan to the world. It hardly need be said that this is Shih-t'ou Castle, captured by Coxinga, prince of Empei.

Here are white sandalwood bows, muskets, Korean spears, lances, and halberds; flags large and small incline to one another; conical ensigns, shrine banners, and the general's standard flap in the wind. They tint the heavens in every hue, as if the wisteria, azaleas and primroses of the season are reflected skywards. But even as Go Sankei watches the flowers blossom and fall, the days of spring are piling up like stones on a *go* board.

The young leaves have grown out and turned a deep green, and through a rift in the clearing clouds appears the Cloud Gate Pass to Nanking. Cuckoos fly singing from the gate and verbena hedges grow tall as tents. It is mid-summer of the year.

GO SANKEI: For thirty leagues around felled trees have been laid, points towards the enemy. The generals of the pass Saryōko and Uryōko guard it with three thousand troops.

OLD MAN: The stars on their helmets shine.

GO SANKEI: They beat their drums wildly.

OLD MAN: Even if one could i-

GO SANKEI: -mi-

BOTH OLD MEN: -tate the crowing of the cocks, one could never get through such a stronghold.[103] Swords are thick as pampas grass in a summer meadow, and rope matches glow like fire-

---

[102] The battles to be narrated occur in the four seasons, beginning with spring, with appropriate descriptions for each.

[103] From a poem (*Goshūishū*, no. 940) by Sei Shōnagon: "The dawn has not come; even though you imitate the crowing of the cock, you won't be able to get through Ōsaka Pass where we might meet." The allusion is to the story of a nobleman who

flies in a marsh. Not even a bird could slip through the gate of this imposing barrier.

NARRATOR: Coxinga was reared in Japan, and it would be easier for him to smash through this barrier, even if it were fortified with iron and stone, than for a child to break a single thickness of paper window. But drawing to mind the catalpa bow of Musashibō Benkei who, long ago in the Bunji era [104] of his country, tricked the barrier keeper at Ataka, a glorious martial exploit, he winks a signal to his men and cries.

COXINGA: Hear ye! Hear ye! This is the foot of Mount Li, the site of the grave of Yang Kuei-fei.[105] We are itinerant priests gathering funds wherewith to build again the T'ai-chen Palace. Listen to our Book of Gifts and pray subscribe, O gatekeeper.

NARRATOR: He produces an attendance roll of his troops and, praying in his heart for the success of his forces and the downfall of the enemy, he reads aloud.

COXINGA: The autumn moon of enlightment lies hidden by pitiless clouds from the Tartars and rebels, but none can yet raise them from their long uncertain dream of life and death. Here in days gone by lived an emperor whose name was Hsüan Tsung. When he lost the beautiful princess he dearly loved, he could not master his longing, and tears, like strings of pearls, flowed from his eyes. Then, turning his thoughts to her repose in the world of the dead, he built in her memory the T'ai-chen Palace. I, a descendant of the magician from Lin-ch'iung, grieving that so holy a place should come to ruin, am soliciting funds throughout the land. Those who fight on the enemy's side even in a single battle will have their heads transfixed by our spears; those who fight for us will raise shouts of triumph after the victory. I bow my head in devotion and respect.

NARRATOR: He reads, loud enough to make the heavens resound. Saryōko and Uryōko, the guardians of the barrier, cry out.

---

actually succeeded in getting through the barrier at night by imitating a cock's crows so skillfully that the barrier keeper opened the gate, thinking it was dawn. The effect of divided speech here was achieved by several chanters performing the different parts.
[104] The Bunji era was 1185–89. The following passage is based on a scene in the Nō play *Ataka*. The Kabuki version in *Kanjinchō* is well known.
[105] Coxinga changes the names in the passage from *Ataka* to suitable Chinese ones, substituting Yang Kuei-fei for the consort of the Emperor Shōmu and the T'ai-chen Palace for the Tōdaiji.

SARYŌKO AND URYŌKO: Look! Coxinga has flown like a summer moth into the flames!

NARRATOR: They attack, humming like cicadas in a treetop. Coxinga smiles at their folly.

COXINGA: Fan K'uai's style was not so remarkable—see how Asahina of Japan used to break down gates!

NARRATOR: He rips through the gate bar and the tangle of felled trees. He knocks down those who oppose him and, catching those who flee, tosses them like pebbles. He slays Saryōko and Uryōko and easily passes the barrier. The months and days too are passing on the *go* board, and an autumn wind can be heard blowing from the barrier. The mists clear over the mountain castle where the Tartar general Prince Kairi is entrenched. Before the castle is a precipice, and behind it is the sea. Coxinga, noting the carelessness that reliance on the fortress breeds, stages an attack this autumn night. As he rides his horse the bit tinkles clearly, like the cry of an insect awaiting the moon. His troops stealthily advance to the castle moat. Suddenly, as one man, they raise thousands of paper lanterns on poles. It is like seeing the thousand suns and moons of a thousand worlds in one instant, and the soldiers of the castle, dumfounded, scurry about in wild consternation. They buckle their helmets around their knees, don their armor upside down, carry their horses on their backs. Shouting hysterically, they throw open the front gate of the castle, and pour out, waving their swords. The attackers raise war cries to the accompaniment of horns and gongs. Coxinga signals his men with his commander's fan.

The Japanese style of battle command includes Yoshitsune's method of attacking and crushing the enemy, and Kusunoki's of catching the enemy off guard and then striking.

Here, as at the rout of Kurikara, the downhill charge at Ichinotani, or the battle on the beach at Yashima, the attackers are irresistible, and the enemy, cut to pieces, withdraws towards the castle. "Now is our chance!" cries Coxinga, and in the evening darkness his men light hand grenades, the secret Japanese weapon, which they hurl at the enemy. The roar of the explosion is loud enough to make one think Mount Shumi [106] is crumbling. From the battlements and tower pour smoke thick as from the shore where fishermen burn salt or from a charcoal kiln. The flames suggest masses of crimson leaves in autumn,

[106] Sumeru, the central mountain of the Buddhist universe.

or the Hsien-yang Palace reduced to ashes by the torch of the man from Ch'u.[107]

Coxinga, raising a shout of victory, pulls back his horse's reins, and rides round and round in triumph; and, as the months and days roll around, faithful in their course, the early winter rains have begun to fall. The rains lift to reveal a high-gated citadel by a hill. This is Ch'ang-lo Castle in Foochow, captured by Coxinga. The glittering tiles at the eaves give the color of jewels to the first hail, falling and piling. A night storm mingled with sleet blows. How wonderful to see the walls and towers buried in the snow!

Coxinga has captured thirty-eight other strongholds in Min, Ken, and other provinces.[108] In anticipation of the future visit of the crown prince, he has erected outworks at different places, and provided them with military stores and garrisons. His might may be sensed in the air itself.

These sights are so clearly visible to Go Sankei that he feels he can almost touch them. In his excess of joy he forgets himself and the others with him, and clasping the crown prince in his arms, rushes off towards the castled mountain. The two old men stay him.

FIRST OLD MAN: How foolish of you! All you have witnessed, though it seemed to take place directly before your eyes, has in fact occurred hundreds of leagues away. You may think that but a moment has passed since you came to this mountain, but you have spent here the springs and autumns of five whole years. You do not suspect, do you, that these battles you have watched were fought during the four seasons of four different years. Even as I speak, the months and the days are passing. See how the prince has grown, and look well at your own face reflected in the water. The water is pure, and the reflection will be true. I, who stand reflected in the mirror of your loyal and faithful heart, am the first sovereign of the Ming.

SECOND OLD MAN: And I am Liu Po-wen of Ch'ing-t'ien.[109]

BOTH OLD MEN: Our home is the moon, where the leaves of the laurel, blown over,

---

[107] The Hsien-yang Palace was the residence of Ch'in Shih-huang, the first emperor of China. It was burnt by Hsiang Yü, "the man from Ch'u" (233–202 B.C.).

[108] Either Min or Ken might refer to Fukien Province; probably Chikamatsu was none too sure of his Chinese geography.

[109] Usually known as Liu Chi (1311–75), one of the most celebrated among the counselors of the founder of the Ming dynasty.

SECOND OLD MAN: Appear to the eyes that see true the waxing

FIRST OLD MAN: And the waning, but

SECOND OLD MAN: The ordinary man, confused of mind, takes it for a mere contest between *go* stones.[110]

FIRST OLD MAN: The fish swimming in the water

SECOND OLD MAN: Mistakes it for a fishhook.

FIRST OLD MAN: The bird soaring above the clouds

SECOND OLD MAN: Is frightened, thinking it a bow.

FIRST OLD MAN: The moon does not descend,

SECOND OLD MAN: Nor do the waters rise.

BOTH OLD MEN: Behold the abiding moon whose light waxes but to wane, and wanes but to wax again. Though hidden a while in clouds, in the end it will be free and illumine the world.[111] The day will soon dawn when the crown prince assumes his office, with the help of the divine strength of Japan, the Land of the Rising Sun.

NARRATOR: Their voices blend with the wind through the pines. For a moment their images linger on, but they too presently vanish in the wind from the peak of the pine-clad mountain.

Go Sankei, dazed, wonders if he has dreamed, but he has not been sleeping. And, a sign that five years have indeed elapsed, a long beard has grown on his face. The prince's appearance has changed in the wink of an eye: he has the height and bearing of a seven-year-old. His voice calling, "Go Sankei, Go Sankei!" is grave beyond his years, and recalls to Go Sankei the first cries of the song thrush heard deep in snow-covered mountains. He bows his head in response, then worships Heaven and Earth, so overjoyed that his legs are unsteady, and he feels again that he may be dreaming.

He brings his hands together reverently before the prince.

GO SANKEI: I have heard reports that Coxinga, the only son of the former minister Tei Shiryū, has come from Japan and raised a loyal army in our cause. His military exploits during the past five years have been brilliant, and he has already retaken half the empire of the great Ming. I should like to communicate with Coxinga, and inform him that your highness is here.

[110] The dark side of the leaves of the laurel creates the impression of the waning moon; the ignorant man, not realizing this, imagines that he sees black *go* stones triumphing over white *go* stones when the moon wanes.

[111] The moon here stands for the Ming power.

NARRATOR: Scarcely has he spoken than from the other side of the valley a voice calls.

IKKAN: Is that not Go Sankei, president of the council of war, across the valley? Go Sankei! Go Sankei!

NARRATOR: Go Sankei gazes in the direction of the voice.

GO SANKEI: Are you Tei Shiryū, the former minister?

IKKAN: Go Sankei! What a miracle that we should both be alive and able to meet here! My son Coxinga's wife has escorted the Princess Sendan to China from Japan.

NARRATOR: He beckons, and the princess comes forward.

SENDAN: Dear Go Sankei! I escaped in a drifting boat thanks to your wife Ryūkakun's self-sacrificing devotion, and I was carried by the wind over a sea of griefs to Japan. Now, the kindness of Ikkan and his family has brought us the blessing of this extraordinary reunion! Where is Ryūkakun? What has become of your baby? I should like to see them as soon as possible. Please take me to them.

NARRATOR: Her longing is natural.

GO SANKEI: Alas, my wife perished from the severe wounds she received at the time. The empress also lost her life to the enemy guns, and I cut open her womb to deliver her child. Later I killed my own son to throw the enemy off the track. Since then I have been rearing the prince safely in these mountains. He is already seven years old. He is with me now.

NARRATOR: The princess utters a cry of dismay at the news, and falls to the ground where she weeps, heedless of the others' eyes; her grief stirs them to pity.

Ikkan turns back to the foot of the mountain.

IKKAN: Look! That villain Prince Bairoku has discovered the princess, and he has come now in pursuit with thousands of men. I shall summon up the strength left in these old bones, stand my ground, and defend her to the death!

NARRATOR: His words are brave, but the princess's life is in danger.

IKKAN: If only I could escape with her to the other side of the valley! But I don't know my way in these mountains. Is there no way across?

GO SANKEI: No, it is sixty leagues around the mountains, and the gorge is bottomless. I cannot lead you here, nor can I cross the valley to you. What shall we do? What is there to do?

NARRATOR: He bows to the empty air.

GO SANKAI: First Emperor of the Ming and Liu Po-wen of Ch'ing-t'ien who showed yourselves but a moment ago in a miraculous revelation! Vouchsafe your wondrous, immortal strength and rescue us from this grave peril!

NARRATOR: The crown prince prays by his side in single-hearted devotion. The princess and Komutsu also join their hands in prayer.

SENDAN *and* KOMUTSU: Hail to the great god Sumiyoshi of Japan, gatherer of happiness boundless as the sea!

NARRATOR: They earnestly pray with undivided hearts. Heaven is moved and Earth hears their prayers: from a crevice in the mountains a stream of cloud issues forth and trails idly across the gorge to form a bridge in the sky. Is this the bridge the magpies built with their wings for the lovers to cross? [112] It spans the abyss like the stone bridge of Kume, built by the god of Katsuragi, though night has not fallen.[113] They climb to the peak on the other side of the valley as in a dream, with no sensation of crossing the bridge or even of moving. Their legs tremble under them.

Soon afterwards the rebel soldiers surge up in swarms.

SOLDIERS: Look—the crown prince and Go Sankei too! What an unexpected haul! We've cast our nets for sardines and come up with a whale! They're fair targets for us! Get your bows and muskets ready! Shoot them down! Kill them!

NARRATOR: They jostle together in wild excitement. Prince Bairoku shouts his commands.

BAIROKU: Wait! They have plenty of room behind them to escape. Bows and muskets can't take care of them. Look—a cloud bridge! That's something I've never seen before. No doubt Coxinga's brought it from Japan, this abacus bridge or folding bridge or whatever it is. What a clumsy piece of strategy—providing his enemy with a weapon! Follow me, men! Over the bridge!

NARRATOR: More than five hundred soldiers storm eagerly onto the bridge, shouting and pushing to be first across. When they are about at the mid-point, a mountain wind and a valley wind spring up and

---

[112] A famous Chinese legend tells how on one night of the year the magpies build a bridge with their wings over which the Herd Boy and the Weaving Girl (two stars) cross to meet.

[113] Because the god of Katsuragi was so ugly that he was ashamed to be seen by day, he built his bridge at night.

blow to shreds the bridge of clouds. The general and his men plummet one after the other to the bottom of the gorge, where heads are split and skulls are crushed. Groaning and shrieking, they pile ever higher. Go Sankei and Tei Shiryū cry, "Victory! Hurrah! Wonderful!" They seize rocks, logs, whatever comes to hand, and fling them at the Tartars until not a man is left alive. In a moment's time the enemy horde is converted to mincemeat. Only the general, Prince Bairoku, has managed to escape, climbing up a vine that grows along the base of the cliff. Go Sankei lifts the *go* board of the immortals and shouts.

GO SANKEI: This *go* board has been kneaded of taro root, and is harder than stone. It's bitter, and I daresay it won't suit your taste, but how about a bite? You've only one *go* stone left to play, and you're not much of an opponent now! See what a strong game is like!

NARRATOR: When Bairoku shows his head, Go Sankei smacks it squarely; when he shows his face, Go Sankei strikes it smartly. He belabors Bairoku with repeated blows, till brains and skull are smashed to bits, and he perishes.

IKKAN: You've fulfilled my hopes! There's a similar example in Japanese history too, Tadanobu and his *go* board at Yoshino.[114] Tadanobu's board was of *kaya* wood,[115] this of taro root from the Mountain of Nine Immortals.

The time has come for our side to take the offensive. Let us surround, infiltrate, cut off, and corner them, arrest and pursue.[116] When sure that victory is ours in our struggle, we will pick up the enemy pieces. We will restore the country and the dynasty, the reward for our labors. The path of loyalty lies this way, the way is before us.

NARRATOR: Together they enter the Castle of Foochow.

[114] Tadanobu figures in various old *jōruri* plays. In one, he is caught by his enemies at the house of a Kyoto lady and defends himself with a *go* board.
[115] *Torreya* wood.
[116] "Surround", "infiltrate", and the rest are technical terms of *go*.

ACT FIVE

Scene One: Coxinga's camp in Dragon-horse Fields, Kiangsi Province.

NARRATOR: No man can take Mount T'ai under his arm and leap over the north sea, but it is not impossible for a king to act like a king.[117]

Coxinga, the prince of Empei, uses his troops masterfully, as though he turned them in the palm of his hand. He has reduced over fifty cities, and his military strength grows day by day. His wife has brought the Princess Sendan from Japan, and Go Sankei has accompanied the crown prince in his progress from the Mountain of the Nine Immortals. Coxinga has offered the prince the imperial sash and seal, and proclaimed him the Emperor Eiryaku.[118] He has raised a wooden encampment half a mile square in the Dragon-horse Fields, and encircled it with camp curtains, outer tents, and brocade hangings. Sacred wands with paper streamers from the two shrines of Ise in Japan fly over the camp, inviting the divine presence. Coxinga has installed the crown prince in a palace of his own.

Now Coxinga sits on a camp stool in the center of the fort. To his left and right sit President of the Council of War Go Sankei and the General of Cavalry Kanki. They have been exchanging views on the decisive struggle between Tartary and the Ming. Go Sankei takes up his military fan.

GO SANKEI: The best plans are those which arrive at great results from insignificant beginnings.

NARRATOR: He holds up a bamboo tube.

GO SANKEI: I have stuffed this tube with honey and a great number of hornets. We should prepare thousands of tubes like this, and give them to our front-line troops to carry. They will advance, pretending to do battle, only to retreat and abandon the tubes on contact with the enemy. The Tartar hordes, with their usual gluttony, will suppose that the tubes contain food, and will undoubtedly retrieve them. As soon as they remove the stoppers, tens of thousands of hornets will swarm out

[117] An allusion to *The Book of Mencius* (tr. Legge, *Chinese Classics*, I, 142): "In such a thing as taking the T'ai mountain under your arm and leaping over the north sea with it, if you say to people, 'I am not able to do it,' that is a real case of not being able."
[118] Chinese pronunciation: Yung Li. For an account of this pretender, see Keene, *The Battles of Coxinga*, p. 53.

and sting the rebels viciously. While they are staggering about in confusion, our troops should return and attack from all directions. Look!

NARRATOR: He removes the stopper and a great many hornets fly out, buzzing their wings.

GO SANKEI: The rebel soldiers, once they realize what has happened, will make fun of the tubes. They will say, "What a childish trick to deceive us! Let's burn the lot and make them ashamed of themselves!" They will pile up the tubes and set them on fire. In an instant the gunpowder prepared at the bottom of the tubes will explode with a roar. There won't be a soldier left for half a league around.

NARRATOR: He touches a rope match to the tube. At once it sputters forth flames that suggest his device will indeed work.

Kanki brings forward a basket filled with fruit.

KANKI: I am impressed by Go Sankei's unusual plan, but I also have a suggestion. We should make two or three thousand baskets of this kind, and fill them with poisoned sweetmeats, rice balls, and appetizers. We should dispose these baskets at various places inside the camp, and lure the enemy close to our lines. Then we should retreat about ten leagues, pretending to have been defeated in battle. The Tartars, flushed with victory, will enter the camp after one of their usual long marches. When their eyes light on the food, the officers and men will imagine that they have come to a mountain of treasures, and they will surely struggle to see who will be first to grab the food and swallow it. As soon as it touches their lips, one after another they will vomit up poisoned blood. We will slaughter them without staining our swords.

NARRATOR: Both have taxed their ingenuity in military stratagems. The plans they offer differ considerably. Coxinga nods.

COXINGA: Your suggestions both have merit. Indeed, they are beyond criticism. However, my mother's last words have penetrated my soul, and I cannot forget them. "Consider the king of Tartary as your mother's enemy, Coxinga, and your wife's enemy, Kanki, and carry out your great plan! We have died so that you would not relent in your determination." Her words have soaked into my bones and permeate my entire being. I have never forgotten them for an instant. What need have we of elaborate stratagems? I shall attack boldly, challenge both the king of Tartary and Ri Tōten at close quarters, then cut them to shreds. If I fail to kill them in this fashion, I shall be guilty of unfilial conduct towards my mother, though I perform a million other martial feats, though I prove myself loyal to my sovereign and just to my fellow men.

NARRATOR: Tears pour from his mirror-clear eyes. All present, from Go Sankei and Kanki downwards, wet their sleeves with tears.

COXINGA: My mother, though a woman, did not forget her native land. She thought to her last breath of the honor of Japan, revering the country of her birth. I too was born in Japan, and I shall not abandon my country. Behold! I humbly beg the great goddess Amaterasu to vouchsafe her protection. The divine strength of Japan has enabled me to rise from the common people, capture many cities, and to become now a prince of the Chinese empire, honored by all. That is why I insisted that the barbarians I subdued in the bamboo forest must have their heads shaved in the Japanese style. I shall put them in the van of my forces and give out that they are reinforcements from Japan. The Tartar barbarians will be frightened at the news, for they know that the Japanese excel in the use of bow and arrow, and are peerlessly trained in all the martial arts. While the Tartars hesitate, intimidated, we shall launch a massive attack and seize the city. This is the plan my wife and I have devised together. (*To Komutsu.*) Minamoto no Ushiwaka! [119] Lead your soldiers here!

NARRATOR: He lifts his commander's fan, and Komutsu shouts a word of assent. She comes forward, her hair tied with a paper cord. Her troops, their heads blue from a close shaving in the Japanese manner, present a colorful sight in their Chinese brocades.

The princess rushes forth from the curtains of the temporary palace.

SENDAN: Coxinga, this is your father's ensign, and here is a note in his writing—a most upsetting message.

NARRATOR: Coxinga kneels to receive the letter, and reads aloud.

COXINGA (*reads*): "I returned to China, foolishly imagining that I might repay my debt to the emperor of the Ming, but I have achieved nothing, have won no glory. What pleasure may I expect from the years of old age left me? Tonight I shall go to the walls of Nanking and, dying in battle, shall leave a fair name in Japan and China. I shall die in my seventy-third year. Tei Shiryū Ikkan."

NARRATOR: Even before he has finished reading, Coxinga springs to his feet.

[119] Komutsu is called Ushiwaka because of her masculine garb. See n. 83, above.

COXINGA: My hatred for the enemy is complete. My mother's enemy is now my father's enemy too. I need no stratagems. What will military tactics avail me? Whatever you may choose to do, I, Coxinga, can wait no longer. Alone I shall ride into the city of Nanking and twist off the heads of the king of Tartary and Ri Tōten. I shall die fighting where my father falls, and journey with my parents to the world of the dead. Farewell for this life!

NARRATOR: He starts off precipitously, but the two generals catch him by the sleeves.

KANKI: How inconsiderate of you! The Tartars are the enemies of my wife and my father-in-law.

GO SANKEI: And the enemies of my wife and baby.

COXINGA: You're right. They are enemies to all of us equally. We three will take on the enemies of the whole world! Come on!

NARRATOR: They rush off together. The most powerful demon or god of ill fortune would not have dared face the points of their swords.

Scene Two: The Tartar camp.

NARRATOR: Tei Shiryū Rōikkan bravely sets out, attired for the dark mists of evening in armor braided of black leather. He creeps up to the outer walls of Nanking and raps on the great wooden gate.

IKKAN: I am Coxinga's father, Ikkan. I am old and my knees buckle under me. I cannot fight like a man in his prime, yet when the young men talk of battle I cannot listen idly. I have ventured here in the hope I might find a quick death and end my life as I had always planned. Grant me the favor, Ri Tōten, of showing yourself, and taking this white-haired head! This is all I ask before I die.

NARRATOR: In answer to his shout, a strapping fellow six feet tall calls from the castle.

MAN: Nobly said, Ikkan. I'll take you on!

NARRATOR: He pushes open the gate and emerges swinging his sword.

IKKAN: I'm ready!

NARRATOR: They exchange two or three blows of the sword, when Ikkan suddenly closes and lops off his opponent's head. Much displeased, he shouts loudly.

IKKAN: I am old, but I will not yield my head to a common soldier of his kind! Ri Tōten, come out and fight! I'll deal with anyone else as I did with this man.

NARRATOR: He stands glaring at the wall. The great king of Tartary shows himself on the tower of the Shou-yang Gate.

KING: That villain is Rōikkan, Coxinga's father. I have many things to ask him. Don't kill him, but capture him and bring him to me.

NARRATOR: Forty or fifty men shout assent. They surround Ikkan with their clubs and beat him mercilessly, without allowing him the chance to defend himself. They twist him to the ground, tie him, and drag him off into the castle. Ikkan is chagrined beyond words.

Soon afterwards Kanki and Go Sankei with Coxinga at the fore race up to the front gate of the city. Behind them sixty thousand and more troops led by Komutsu, the general of the rear guard, press eagerly forward, resolved that today they will fight to the finish. Coxinga issues his commands.

COXINGA: We still do not know whether my father is dead or alive. We must be extremely careful. There are twelve major gates and thirty-six smaller ones around the walls of Nanking, and if we leave even one unguarded, the enemy is sure to escape through it. Keep a sharp lookout on all sides, then let's attack!

NARRATOR: At a signal they fall into position, strike their quivers, and raise war cries loud enough to overturn Heaven itself.

Komutsu advances to the fore, wielding a short sword in the Ushiwaka style with the skill born of constant practice.

KOMUTSU: I will take on any opponent, whoever he may be, when or where he may choose, providing he is willing to die!

NARRATOR: Proclaiming herself boldly, she charges into the enemy ranks and furiously does battle.

Many of the rebel soldiers are slain, but the city of Nanking, in which seven hundred thousand troops are entrenched, shows no sign of capitulating. Coxinga, hoping to discover somehow whether his father is dead or alive, races around the walls, but without success. He advances to the front ranks and shouts.

COXINGA: Never in the five years since coming to China, in all my numerous battles, have I fought without swords. Today, for a change, I shall not lay my hand on my sword hilt. You Tartars who are such masters of horsemanship and pride yourselves on your skill with your swords, come out and fight!

NARRATOR: Such is his challenge.

TARTARS: Kill the loathsome braggart!

NARRATOR: They rush out at him, howling as they attack. Coxinga pulls his assailants to him. He wrenches away their swords, beats and crushes them. He wrests away lances, spears, and halberds, twisting, bending, and snapping the blades. If the onrushing villains touch his legs, he tramples them to death; if they touch his hands, he twists and strangles them, spurning their bodies like pebbles before him. Mounted warriors he catches horse and all, and toys with them a moment before tossing the horses like jackstones. He mixes human jackstones, horse jackstones, and stone jackstones in a display of strength that does not seem human. The Tartars, for all their vaunted prowess, are forced to retreat, and the fall of the city seems imminent when Ri Tōten shows himself, the king of Tartary before him, and with them Ikkan, bound to the face of a shield.

RI TŌTEN: Coxinga, you crawled forth from your insignificant country of Japan and ravaged all China. Not content with capturing cities at various places, you've dared approach the seat of the great king. Your outrageous insolence has compelled us to bind your father in this fashion. Shall we cut his belly in the Japanese manner? Or will you and your father agree to return to Japan immediately? If you agree, we'll spare Ikkan's life. Otherwise, we'll slit him open now before your eyes. Make your answer, one way or the other!

NARRATOR: He shouts the demand. Coxinga until this moment has been in high spirits, but suddenly his head spins, his strength ebbs, and he seems utterly dejected. His troops are disheartened, and the camp becomes utterly still. Ikkan gnashes his teeth.

IKKAN: Coxinga! Do you hesitate? Have you lost your courage? What use would it be for me, a man over seventy, to prolong his life? Have you forgotten how you praised your mother's dying words? You will be disgraced for all ages to come if it is said that, having virtually achieved your great goal, you allowed worry over the life of a wrinkled old man to bring you to failure. And think of the name you will give your country! Will it not be a disgrace to Japan if Japanese acquire abroad the unfortunate reputation of being so weak emotionally that they abide by no principles? Your mother, though she was a woman, respected her country, and gave up her life sooner than bring disgrace to Japan. Have you forgotten? Now that you have reached this critical moment, you must not flicker an eye, not even if your father is hacked to bits before you. You must charge the enemy, carry out your plan, and restore the dynasty of the Ming! Where have you lost your resolution? Ahhh—you are a weakling, you are contemptible!

NARRATOR: He stamps in fury, rebuking his son. Coxinga, stung by his father's words, plucks up his courage and makes a rush at the great king. Ri Tōten at once presses his sword against Ikkan. Coxinga's senses fail him. He stands stockstill, unable to move, his legs trembling under him. Even had Mount Shumi crumbled over his head, at this moment he would not have noticed. Coxinga seems utterly beside himself. Kanki and Go Sankei, exchanging glances, rush up and prostrate themselves before the king of Tartary.

KANKI *and* GO SANKEI: Great king, we have been successful until this moment, but your fortunes are the stronger. Coxinga's luck ran out when his father was captured, and we can hope for nothing more from such a general. If you will but spare our lives, we will take Coxinga's head and offer it to you. Grant us your answer, backed with your oath.

NARRATOR: The king of Tartary at once replies.

KING: Splendid! Splendid!

NARRATOR: They spring on him even as he speaks and, kicking him to the ground, grasp him by the throat. Coxinga the next instant leaps forward and twists off his father's bonds. He seizes Ri Tōten and, pushing him onto the shield where his father had been tied, he binds Ri Tōten in the same manner, at elbows and wrists. The three heroes look at one another and raise a shout of joy that echoes through the entire country. The soldiers, once more in high spirits, escort the crown prince and the Princess Sendan to the spot.

COXINGA: I shall punish these rogues in your presence. This one is the king of Tartary. Though his is a land of barbarians, I shall send him back to his country alive, after first tying him to a stake and whipping him.

NARRATOR: His men divide to left and right, with 500 whips for each side. When they have thrashed the king until he is half dead, they let him escape.

COXINGA: And now we come to Ri Tōten, the cause of all our griefs, a monster guilty of the Eight Grave Crimes,[120] the Five Inhuman Acts,

---

[120] The Eight Great Crimes were crimes of treason and great atrocity as defined by the Taihō penal code of A.D. 701. For the Ten Villainies and the Five Inhuman Acts, see n. 71, above.

the Ten Villainies. I myself shall cut off his head, so that there will be no resentment among us. Kanki, Go Sankei—cut off his arms!

NARRATOR: Standing on three sides of Ri Tōten, they raise their swords with a great shout, and in one motion slice off his head and arms.

They wish the Emperor Eiryaku a reign of ten thousand years, and offer prayers for the peace and safety of the country. This joy they owe to the divine, the martial, and the saintly virtues of the emperor of Great Japan, a land endowed with these perpetual blessings, which will prosper forever as her people prosper. All pray that by this benefaction the five grains will continue to ripen in abundance, and that the emperor's reign will endure a hundred million years.

THE UPROOTED PINE

First performed on the day after New Year of the third year of Kyōhō (February 1, 1718). The title of the play in Japanese, *Nebiki no kadomatsu*, contains an elaborate play on words. It may mean a pine tree, uprooted entirely to symbolize longevity and hung at gates at New Year; it may also refer to a "Pine," the highest rank of courtesan, who is "uprooted" or ransomed from service in a brothel. The title and probably also the ending may be explained in terms of the New Year festivities which accompanied the first performance of the play.

Cast of Characters

YOJIBEI of Yamazaki
JŌKAN, his father, a rich merchant
JIBUEMON, his father-in-law, a samurai
YOHEI, a poor young man
HIKOSUKE, a tobacco merchant
KUROZAEMON, host at the Izutsu House, a teahouse
KAN'EMON, owner of Azuma's contract
SHINSUKE, a boy
AZUMA, a courtesan of the highest rank
OKIKU, Yojibei's wife
OKAYA, a "Chaser"
OLD WOMAN, Yohei's mother
COURTESANS' MAIDS, "LAUNCHES," "TOWBOATS," "DEBUTANTES," and other prostitutes of different ranks

ACT ONE

Scene One: A street in the Shimmachi Licensed Quarter of Osaka.

Time: New Year, 1718.

NARRATOR:

Like the white jewels of the waterfall
Tumbling from the peak of Mount Tsukuba,[1]
The shuttlecock goes bounding back and forth,
One, two, three, four, five, six, seven, eight,
Nine-house Street [2] is where the mated battledores [3]
Polish the shuttlecock to its full luster
As the courtesans' maids, now sprouting first leaves,
Will be polished by love.

They send the shuttlecock back and forth lazily three, four, five times, young pines with enlacing branches, and their drawling tones [4] are familiar to the New Year pines, to those kept Pines who pine for their customers; in Shimmachi on the first Day of the Rat [5] of this year the green deepens in the Pines so numerous that the uprooting of Pines on this day will never cease, though a thousand generations pass.[6]

MAID: Shinsuke! You insist on batting the shuttlecock even when I tell you I don't want you to. Now look what you've done! You've knocked it into the pine tree. Bring it down again!

NARRATOR: She clings to his sleeve.

SHINSUKE: Let go of my sleeve! You should've known in the first place that it'd get knocked up if you let a man at it. What's so strange?

NARRATOR: He shakes his sleeve free and claps his hands.

---

[1] The name Tsukuba suggests the words *tsuku* (to strike) and *ha* (feather), words related to "shuttlecock" which follows.

[2] Name of a section of the Shimmachi Licensed Quarter.

[3] At New Year people played at battledore and shuttlecock. The battledores were paired, one decorated with the picture of a prince, and the other with that of a princess.

[4] Courtesans' maids (*kamuro*) prolonged the last syllable of their words; the text has *mi-i* and *yo-o* for *mi* (three) and *yo* (four).

[5] On the first Day of the Rat (*hatsune*) people formerly went out into the fields to uproot young pines as part of the New Year festivities. *Hatsune*, written with different characters, also means "first sleep [day]," when courtesans met their customers for the first time in the year.

[6] When uprooting pines it was customary to pray for a thousand generations of happiness. The sentence otherwise contains puns on the pine tree, the Pine (the highest rank of courtesan) and the verb "to pine for".

SHINSUKE: Ha-ha! That's none of my concern! The red of my eye to you!

NARRATOR: He runs inside the house.

MAIDS: Don't let him escape! Catch him!

NARRATOR: They fly after him in a manner befitting a quarrel that started over a shuttlecock.

Beautiful enough to entice the first sprouts of love through the valley snows white as their feet, wearing sleeves of mist fragrant with rare incense and sashes bright as rainbows, cloaks of clouds draped on their shoulders, the Launches and Debutantes sally forth in full glory.

> Indigo and saffron, pale hues, light blues,
> Woven silks, embroidered silks,
> Every kind of dyeing in figured patterns,
> Triple-dyed and double-dyed,
> Dappled silk of azure and dappled silk of green,
> Purple silks dappled with snows of passing years
> And griefs that crimson silks, like poppies, make us forget.[7]

A procession in dazzling colors moves along Echigo Street. The three thoroughfares are bright with a triple flush of spring, the season when the Pines put forth Young Shoots and the Plum begins to flower.[8] The Chasers' new aprons glow sunrise scarlet under an intoxicated sky, and men get drunk on this year's first cups of saké. The courtesans toast the New Year at their houses, then set out together on calls of thanks: the clatter of their sandals strikes up a tune of spring. Among them no flower is the peer of Azuma, the famous Pine of the Wisteria House, who rules the Quarter as purple rules the colors.[9] Her eyes flash love and wisdom, her whole appearance as she promenades so brims with tenderness that passers in the street must stop to gaze, and even the wild geese, deserting the spring blossoms for the north, turn back to the Quarter for one last glimpse.

An old woman of seventy, unashamed of either her station or her age, an old cotton bonnet pulled around her face, and wrapped, in

---

[7] A pun on *keshi* (the poppy) and *keshi* (to obliterate [the griefs of past years]). Purple was the color worn by senior courtesans (here, Azuma). The passage contains numerous other plays on words and allusions.

[8] "Young shoots" were *kamuro* expected to become future "Pines"; the second rank of courtesans were known as "Plum trees".

[9] Purple from ancient times was considered the most noble color. It is associated here with the name "Wisteria House".

honor of the spring no doubt, in a wadded cloak of greenish-brown,[10] redeemed from the depths of a pawnshop, rubs her sleeve against Azuma and trails on her heels. Okaya, the Chaser, calls in a loud voice.

OKAYA: Look here, old woman! Why, when you have a great, broad street to walk on must you go creeping after the lady, as if you were the old dame in *Takasago* [11] and you'd been separated from your husband? You're an eyesore and a nuisance. And who is that young man sneaking behind you? I don't suppose he carries your palanquin. Is he your accomplice? Out of the way, both of you, at once!

NARRATOR: She pushes her aside, but the old woman is not provoked.

OLD WOMAN: Ah, you may well say that. Please pardon me. I know it's presumptuous of me, but I have something to discuss privately with the great Azuma. I've been wandering all over the Quarter looking for her. Please grant me this kindness. It will help me even in the world to come. Oh, I feel so ashamed! I'm sure that the exalted lady must think a wrinkled old crone like myself is nothing but a curiosity-seeker.

OKAYA: You're quite a clever talker, but it's an old, old trick to watch for a courtesan going by in her full finery and then to announce that you're her aunt or her grandmother. But that's what a Chaser is for. My eyes are quite sharp—watch out!

OLD WOMAN: Please don't say such dreadful things. Do I look as if I'm trying to trick her?—Ah, it's a curse to be poor. My husband was Yozaemon of the Naniwa-ya, a man well known in Semba, with a thousand *kamme* at his beck and call. But he fell behind in payments on the exchange and he was forced to shut up his shop in Osaka and move to Yawata, where he died. The old woman before you was his wife, and this young man with his face covered is his only son. The boy was brought up in a household where he was warmed by the steam from a cauldron of a thousand *kamme*, but now he hasn't as much as a string of copper coins to his name. Yohei, Hard-luck Yohei,[12] they call him, and he's a day laborer earning just enough to see him through each day.—Yes, I can see why you might think I was up to some trickery.

[10] Literally, "*uguisu*-brown". The *uguisu* is a bird of greenish-brown hue which sings in the springtime.

[11] A Nō play about a faithful old couple, translated in *Japanese Noh Drama*, published by Nippon Gakujutsu Shinkōkai.

[12] He should be called Naniwaya Yohei, after the name of his father's shop, but the name Naniwa is shortened to *nan*, meaning "hard luck".

NARRATOR: Tears shine in her eyes as she rambles on, an old woman's wont. Even as she tells this story no one has asked to hear, she seems lost in old memories. The "Towboats" and courtesans' maids answer boldly.

MAIDS: Oh, is it about you, granny, that they sing in the dance tunes— "Yah, yah, Yamazaki, Yamazaki, Yohei's ma from Yamazaki. Some money, please, she says, I truly need the money."—Come again the day before yesterday!

NARRATOR: They laugh, but Azuma meanwhile has been weeping in sympathy.

AZUMA: What are you all laughing about? When someone's down on his luck, it doesn't matter whether or not it's because of love, we in the profession never turn our backs. Dear, sweet old lady! I'm touched that you should have put your trust in me. I swear by the providence of courtesans that I will hear you. But it's so crowded here. (*To Towboat.*) Shigeyama, please hire a place in one of those little shops on the side street off Ageya Lane. We can talk there. Come with me.

NARRATOR: She takes her hand; the old woman weeps.

OLD WOMAN: Thank you, thank you very much. I'm sure you must be wondering what request an old woman of my years could make of you. Yohei—he's a rascal, but he's the moon and stars of my life—was sent here to Shimmachi by his employer to deliver a letter. He saw you then, Azuma, and he fell in love at first sight. (*She laughs uneasily.*) It's embarrassing for a mother to talk about such a thing, but the boy is sick from love. I've scolded him time and again, I've told him that the landlord and the neighbors would hear of it and that it was a sure sign that he'd be holding out a beggar's bowl before long. I thought of chasing him from the house for once and for all. But then I recalled that if we had our former fortunes the young man would be in the midst of affairs with all kinds of kept women and mistresses. Forgive me for saying so, but we could have bought him the exclusive favors of even the highest rank of courtesan for a year or two at a time without feeling any financial strain. That's the style of living he was brought up in. I love him and I wish I could do something to help, but my own feeble struggles and my son's hopes have been overpowered by the enemy called Money. I seemed to have no choice but to look on helplessly as my son's life wasted away. Finally I told him, "Don't worry, love is Azuma's business. I'll beg her to drink a cup of saké with you. And with that you must break off your attachment." I've brought him with me, and I've trailed after you, all out of love for my son. If a mother's life were worth the price of a courtesan for a single night, I would cheerfully kill myself here and now. I don't mean to force you, but won't you please drink a little saké from this cup?

NARRATOR: She produces from her sleeve a small saké bottle filled to overflowing with maternal love, and a chipped saké cup painted in lacquer with a design of monkeys. The others smile, but their laughter soon turns to tears; even the Chaser, who does not know what weeping means, is so moved she looks the other way.

The more she hears, the more Azuma droops her head.

AZUMA: You're a very knowing old lady. Words quite fail me. Where has Yohei gone? I'd like to see his face. Ask him to come here.

NARRATOR: The old woman feels as though in one instant her life has been prolonged a thousand years, like the New Year pine in whose shadow Hard-luck Yohei has been hiding. Called to, he creeps out embarrassedly, his finger in his mouth. Azuma takes his sleeve and pulls him towards her.

AZUMA: It's an honor for a woman of my profession when even some casual customer says, "I've fallen for you," though it's only an empty phrase. I am happy to have stirred pangs of love in a man built like Kimpira himself.[13] Thank you. I should like to have you as my lover always, and to offer you my body and soul, but I am so deeply pledged to another man that I am not free to exchange even so much as a few words of love with anyone else. His name is Yojibei of Yamazaki. From my first night in this profession we have exhausted love's pleasures and sorrows together. I am a courtesan in name only. You might more properly call us husband and wife, for we are so close that no one can come between us. But now that I've heard your mother's earnest request and know your feelings, I wouldn't be content merely to exchange a cup of saké with you here, standing up, and have done with it. Shigeyama—bring me the packet I left with you.

NARRATOR: The Towboat with a word of assent takes from her sleeve an object wrapped in silk. Even without her saying so they know it contains ten or more pieces of gold.

AZUMA: This money has a special meaning for my dear Yojibei and

[13] Kimpira was the name of the hero of a kind of roughhouse Kabuki and puppet play, very popular in the seventeenth century in Edo.

myself, but I offer it to you, madam. Please use it to buy whatever clothes Yohei needs to cut a splendid figure in this Quarter. (*To Yohei*.) Selling her body to even the most casual customers means nothing to a prostitute. We two have never shared pillows, it is true, but let us drink one cup of saké together and with it wash away your months and years of unhappy memories.

NARRATOR: Yohei takes the money Azuma offers and throws it at her feet.

YOHEI: How heartless of you! How utterly devoid of understanding! I'm not in love with your money. Do you despise me because I'm poor and think you can shut my mouth with your gold? We live in a house so small—seven and a half mats, including the kitchen—that you might take it for the temporary quarters of the God of Poverty, and I wear the same thin clothes even in the dead of winter. But could I dare show my face anywhere if people said that I took money from a prostitute to visit the brothels? You've misjudged me badly, Azuma, if you think I was pretending to be in love so that I could take your money. I'm ashamed to have exposed my mother, a woman over seventy, to the contemptuous stares of all these people. Please forgive me, Mother.

NARRATOR: He stifles his sobs.

YOHEI: But come to think of it, how foolish I am to be so bitter! You'll soon be ransomed by Yojibei and become his wife. Supposing some day I go to your house as a day laborer—it will be very awkward for you if I gossip with the servants. You were wise to consider carefully such possibilities. But don't worry. I'm quite resigned. And here's proof that when I say I love you, they're not just shallow words.

NARRATOR: He unsheathes the dirk at his waist and is about to cut off his little finger when Azuma clutches his arm.

AZUMA: Stop, please! It was my mistake.

NARRATOR: She at last restrains him.

AZUMA: I was wrong to offer you money, but it was not because I am so ignoble as to think of my future convenience or reputation. Yojibei has a proper wife, his childhood sweetheart, and his father is a notoriously uncompromising old gentleman. I can't describe the domestic troubles that I have occasioned. Between his wife's jealousy and his father's complaints, ever since the twentieth of last month when I met Yojibei for a minute I've had nothing but the letters saying he couldn't meet me which he sent through the palanquin bearers and teahouse people. I've been obliged to take care of their gifts and to offer Yojibei's New Year presents to me! My contract still has some time to run, but I've extended it in order to raise some money. The more I try to hide his failings, the more acutely I feel the torments of never being able to extricate myself from this place. Pity Azuma, who is fated to become an old woman in the Quarter.

NARRATOR: She discloses her shame and her grief. The tears she inadvertently sheds ill accord with the New Year, but on her face they do not seem ugly. She removes her thin outer kimono, the sleeves so soaked with tears she must wring them out, and unties her sash, revealing a jet-black crested robe thick enough to keep the warmth of her lover's bed the night they met from cooling till they meet again.

AZUMA: This underrobe belongs to Yojibei. I have never taken it from my person for even a moment. My whole heart goes with it— wear the robe and consider yourself my acknowledged customer.

NARRATOR: She removes the underrobe and gives it to Yohei.

YOHEI: This is true kindness. My love has been fulfilled.

NARRATOR: He presses the robe to his forehead and can only weep. His mother has been listening in bewilderment.

OLD WOMAN: What a complicated business it is coming to terms with a courtesan!

NARRATOR: How lovable she seems as she strains to catch their words! Yohei wipes away his tears.

YOHEI: Only since we met have I have learned what real tears are. Yojibei is a lucky man to have your love. He won't find another woman like you, not if he wears out a pair of iron sandals in the search. I'll return the kimono and accept instead the money you kindly offered.

NARRATOR: But his mother sharply slaps his hand as he reached for the coins.

OLD WOMAN: How unmanly of you! That's not what you were saying before! Are you trying to blemish the reputation of the house of Naniwa? You mean villain!

NARRATOR: Yohei shakes his head at her words of reproach.

YOHEI: No, I'm not acting out of greed. It would dishonor me if I abandoned Azuma and Yojibei, now that I know how much they mean to each other. This money, unless I accept it, will end up as presents for the teahouse and become worthless as dust. These may look like gold coins, but actually they are the oil wrung from Azuma's body.[14] I accept responsibility for the money, and with the oil of my body I'll start an oil business. I'll leave at once for Edo, a place where you can make or lose a fortune in no time. I'll turn these ten gold coins into a hundred, a hundred into two hundred, two hundred into five hundred—once the profits start rolling in, I'll turn my fortune into a thousand pieces of gold quick as shooting an arrow. The Kantō trade and its tricks have always been a specialty of our family. I'll never live down the disgrace unless I can repay the affection shown me today by ransoming Azuma and seeing her joyfully united to Yojibei. I have so often thought, "If only I had the money I would buy here and sell there"—my head is full of ideas. Half a gold piece will more than cover my expenses to Edo. Mother, if I can leave you with your brother-in-law in Yokobori, it'll ease my mind. I'll send money from Edo before long. My success will mean Azuma's deliverance and Yojibei's dreams come true.

NARRATOR: Here is a man of uncommon ability: in one leap he covers a thousand miles.

AZUMA: The more I hear, the more confidence you inspire. To think —you love me yourself, but you're going to leave now for Edo so that you may join me forever to Yojibei! You are the god who will bring us together! Let me drink a parting cup with you and tell you my thanks most warmly. We'll go to the Izutsu House. Would your mother like to join us?

OLD WOMAN: No, if Yohei has what he wants, I ask nothing more. I feel as if I've attained Buddhahood while still alive. Lady Courtesan, good-by. I hope that you'll always be kind to Yohei.

NARRATOR: She taps Yohei's back.

OLD WOMAN: You're a lucky boy. Are you happy? Are you happy, son?

NARRATOR: With lighthearted words she eases his tension; the mother plays jester to her son's great patron. Here is a guest who enjoys more affection from Azuma than the most lavish spender. As the mother hurries back home through the bustling, lively street, long chests filled with courtesans' belongings jostle by on their way to the tea-houses.

CHASER: Look, Azuma, that bothersome man is coming this way.

[14] The images are drawn from the pressing of oil from rapeseed.

TOWBOAT: You're right. It's that loud Hikosuke, and he's walking so unsteadily he must be dead drunk. If he sees us we'll be in for his usual abuse.

Scene Two: The Izutsu House, a teahouse in Shimmachi.

NARRATOR: They pull Azuma into the Izutsu House, drawn by its protection, and whisper to the proprietress what has happened. The latter answers merely, "I understand," and Yohei, in Yojibei's borrowed robe, becomes a patron for the nonce. He plunges into the unfamiliar hurly-burly of the teahouse; trembling with love, he cuts a pitiful figure.

Hikosuke's gait is unsteady with drink, but his eyes are still sharp. He takes up the whole street as he reels along, *hakama* and jacket askew, and stumbles unceremoniously into the Izutsu House. Azuma clenches her teeth on her pipe, and silently stares in the opposite direction. Yohei, hoping to escape notice, buries his head in the quilts of the foot warmer. He is engulfed in layer upon layer of damask, but even more numerous are the thoughts that beset him. Hikosuke pulls the hostess aside.

HIKOSUKE: Most esteemed procuress, kindly listen carefully to what I say. I beg to inform you of my best wishes for the New Year season.[15] That's what they all say—but me, I'm so drunk on New Year's saké that I'm going to beg to inform you instead of all of my grievances. You don't want to hear? They're very interesting, I promise. You— that Chaser over there—you listen too, attentively. Yes, you can call her my lady Azuma, the great courtesan, all you please, but when you come down to it, she's just a high-priced whore—right? No, you can't deny it. Well, on top of that, she sells herself to Yojibei of Yamazaki. Why doesn't she sell herself to me, Hikosuke the tobacco merchant? I've never asked her to come down on her price, no, not a penny, not a fraction of a penny. Who does she think I am? I proudly claim the honor to be an unrelated descendant of the Emperor Kammu,[16] Hikosuke the tobacco merchant, a native of Hattori in the province of Settsu, and I've got a shop with a thirty-foot frontage in

---

[15] Hikosuke gives the stereotyped New Year's greeting, then twists it.

[16] *Mutai* (unrelated descendant) is a play on *kutai* (ninth-generation descendant), found in the Nō play *Funa-Benkei* in the line, "I am the ghost of Tomomori, a ninth-generation descendant of the Emperor Kammu." Hikosuke is being humorous.

Osaka. Doesn't she realize what a rich man I am? No, it's impossible for her not to know, if I must say so myself. I spent a fortune on Takahashi from Shimabara in Kyoto, and got her to send me a lock of her hair. And I gave a pile of money to Takao from Fushimi,[17] who cut her nails to the quick to prove how much she loved me. Why, girls have been glad to slice pieces from their ears and noses for me—that's how big a patron I am. But to have Yojibei get the better of me and be refused three, no, four times by Azuma of the Wisteria House—that doesn't leave my pride a leg to stand on. Not half a leg. Well, I've grabbed her now, and I'm going to keep her for three days, starting this minute. This'll be my first purchase of that high-priced whore, but I'm willing to bet that if I scatter around enough pieces of gold and silver, Azuma will come round to my tune. Anyway, I'm buying her.

NARRATOR: He leans suggestively against Azuma. She slaps his cheeks smartly to disabuse him of the notion.

AZUMA: I don't want to hear any more of your empty boasting. I suppose that your Takahashi and Takao, or whatever their names are, really do cut their hair and pull out their fingernails even for a fool like you, providing you give them the money. I don't know about Kyoto or Fushimi, but a Shimmachi courtesan is of a different breed. I'm sure that no matter what happens—even if I have to spend the rest of my life paying house fees for the privilege of not answering your call—I'm not the kind of prostitute to be manipulated by a rotten scoundrel like you with the lever of your money. If you're as bold as you talk, see how far you get at winning over Azuma.

NARRATOR: She stands abruptly.

HIKOSUKE: Your pride makes me fall for you all the more. I'll show you how Hikosuke wins you over. You'll turn to my tune, yes, you will. That Chaser's face is turning round and round, the room is turning round, round and round like the old woman of the mountains who went round and round from mountain to mountain. This is fun. Yes, by hook or by crook, I'll take you to a back room, Azuma.

NARRATOR: He drags her with the violence that drunkenness and his native brute strength supply. The Towboat cries out in dismay and tugs him back, but Hikosuke blows a frontal gale at her, pushes the

---

[17] Takahashi was the name of a courtesan from the Shimabara Licensed Quarter in Kyoto. Takao is from the Fushimi Licensed Quarter.

hostess off to one side, and tosses the Chaser before him, sending all scattering in confusion like falling plum blossoms.

Hard-luck Yohei has always been quick-tempered, and though he grits his teeth, he can now endure no more. He thrusts his arms out of the quilts and firmly gripping Hikosuke's ankle, twists it powerfully.

HIKOSUKE: Ow, wow! My ankle is coming off!

NARRATOR: His brows contract in pain, but still he babbles on.

HIKOSUKE: There must be a wolf in the foot warmer.

NARRATOR: He tries to kick his foot free, but Yohei knocks him over. Sweeping aside the quilting, he leaps out and stands there, legs astride, his lemon-sour face thrust before the nose of Hikosuke, who stinks like an overripe persimmon.

HIKOSUKE: Who's this blackguard?

YOHEI: Open your eyes, if you can, and you'll see. I'm a human being, a man. Take a good look at what a real man looks like. And who are you, swine?

HIKOSUKE: A man called Hikosuke the tobacco merchant. Take a good look.

YOHEI: How dare you call yourself a man? Stop pretending! What kind of man plucks his brows [18] and then torments these poor prostitutes? If you're so sure you're a man, have it out with me! Are you afraid? I'll teach you what a fight among real men is like.

NARRATOR: He throws himself on Hikosuke, jerks him up by the wrists and, lifting him over his shoulder, sends him spinning head over heels, to land with a thud on his belly. Yohei follows this with seven or eight kicks in the small of Hikosuke's back, after which he stands humming to himself, his arms folded in satisfaction. Azuma and the others suppress smiles of amusement which come to their lips, then look dismayed, thinking of possible consequences. Hikosuke finally struggles to his feet.

HIKOSUKE: I understand. You're one of Yojibei's spies. That's why you've trampled on me. Yojibei of Yamazaki, remember this! I've been trampled on, but seven tenths of the victory belongs to me—my person and fortune have been stamped out, so early in the New Year. Besides, this is the Year of the Dog, and dogs lie on the ground—

[18] A man who plucked his brows daily was considered to be unusually well-groomed and dashing.

I've been doing exactly what the divination signs decree.[19] South-southeast be my lucky direction!

NARRATOR: Squaring his elbows, he boldly strides off.

CHASER: If he talks that big even after he's been licked, what must he be like when he's trampled on somebody else?

NARRATOR: The sound of laughter grows boisterous, and the tea-house begins to bustle with the excitement of the first buying of prostitutes of the New Year. Samisens sound in the kitchen under the decorations, and behind the stairs is a grab bag. The man of the year[20] scatters beans for good luck and cries, "A woman who sleeps with Daikoku of the hammer head[21] for her lover will have luck through the year. Paste Ebisu charms in the kitchen,[22] hang dried bream, kumquats, citrons, and oranges, and all will be well. Here are lucky products from everywhere—zebra grass from Yoshino, dried chestnuts, sea lentils (the genuine article), lacquered trays of sweetmeats." He offers saké in unglazed cups, but the others say, "Just a moment. First let us pray that this year will be more prosperous than last, and that the hostess will be younger than ever!" The first water of the New Year bubbles forth with joyous abandon at the Izutsu House.[23]

Yojibei of Yamazaki, who has crossed the mountain of love[24] and attained the ultimate refinement in courtship, enters the Quarter from the West Gate, hurrying his palanquin. The bearers lustily shout, "The great patron has come!" At once the people of the house, barefoot as they are, rush out with cries of welcome, all the way to the gate, to give him the reception due a god of good fortune. They lead Yojibei

[19] In order to "avoid calamities" it was necessary to observe the astrological information in the old calendars; this included lucky and unlucky directions and appropriate conduct for the year.

[20] A man designated to perform the rites at *setsubun* (the beginning of spring) on behalf of the entire family. He scatters beans and cries, "Out with devils and in with good luck!"

[21] Daikoku, a god of good luck, carries a mallet and stands on a sack of rice. There is a pun on *ine* (rice) and *ne* (sleep).

[22] Ebisu is another god of good luck, and the items enumerated all have felicitous associations.

[23] The name Izutsu-ya means literally "Well Curb House". Here the association is made between "first water" and "well".

[24] The place name Yamazaki contains the word *yama* (mountain). "Mountain of love" refers to someone with a great deal of experience in love.

in with joyous shouts, and take him to a back room where a heater is ready. The master brings the lacquered tray, the mistress a jug of saké, and the daughter of the house an unglazed cup.

KUROZAEMON: Look—even an old creature like myself is celebrating today, and Azuma is in full glory. We've managed to pay our year-end bills very comfortably, thank you. How about some of this spiced tea to start things off? Azuma has an unusual story to tell you.

NARRATOR: Azuma introduces Yohei to Yojibei and relates all that has happened.

YOJIBEI: I've had my troubles with Hikosuke in the past, and I was wondering what I ought to do about him. Thank you, Yohei, for helping me out. I hope that we'll always be good friends. But please don't bow to me that way—relax!

NARRATOR: Such is his greeting. Yohei is embarrassed by the unfamiliar surroundings and by a way of speech which he is unaccustomed to use or to hear. But most of all he is afflicted by numbness in his legs from sitting too long in one posture, and all he can utter is moans.

YOJIBEI: Your strength is a great asset, and your plan of going to Edo a fine one. Don't worry about Azuma. Concentrate instead on making a respectable fortune for yourself. Come back to Osaka when you're successful. In honor of your departure we'll spend tonight (*sings*) "in drinking and in song—who knows what the morrow will bring?"

YOHEI: It'll be pitch dark before we know it, and I know my mother worries when it gets so late. I'm much obliged for your kindness. Yojibei, Azuma, and all you other people, I'm sorry to have caused so much trouble. I'll be leaving now.

NARRATOR: He stands.

YOJIBEI: Why are you in such a big hurry? Surely there's no harm in relaxing this one night.

YOHEI: No, if I give myself an inch I'll take a mile. Carelessness is the enemy of success.

NARRATOR: He unfastens his sash and prepares to return Yojibei's kimono, but Azuma stops him.

AZUMA: You mustn't stand on ceremony in this cold weather. Keep the kimono, just as it is.—On your way to Edo there's the River Ōikawa. They say it's a dangerous place. Do be careful. We'll be waiting for the good news that you've arrived safely. And we'll see you again very soon.

NARRATOR: These are her parting words. Yojibei also sees him off.

YOJIBEI: Yohei, please consider that you have a brother in Yamazaki, and that you can depend on me.

YOHEI: Excuse my presumption, but I wish you'd also consider you have a brother in Edo. Let us write each other so we'll know that we're both all right.

NARRATOR: After they have parted, the doors and *shōji* are shut. The moon lies fast asleep in a pool of clouds, and storm winds snore in the pines. The closing drum has sounded by the time that Yohei takes two or three slow steps along Nine House Street; the Quarter is still. Hikosuke, the tobacco merchant, is lying in wait. He imagines that he recognizes Yojibei from the crest on the kimono, and darting up from behind stabs at Yohei, who nimbly leaps aside.

YOHEI: Here's the clown of the evening! Were you hoping for a return match?

NARRATOR: He charges and, knocking Hikosuke to the ground, slashes at him, the point of his dagger held downwards. Hikosuke, struck between the eyes, writhes in anguish on the ground and screams, "Murder!"

YOHEI: If they find me I'll never make my fortune.

NARRATOR: Yohei, who normally would never turn his back on an enemy, makes his escape, swift as the wind. The Quarter suddenly erupts in a tumult, with frantic shouts of "Get a stick!" "A rake!" "Lanterns, somebody!" "Shut the gates!" Hikosuke shrieks confusedly.

HIKOSUKE: Yojibei of Yamazaki stabbed me! He's at the Izutsu House.

NARRATOR: Yojibei, hearing the cry, realizes at once what has happened. He steps forward.

YOJIBEI: Here I am, if anybody wants Yojibei.

NARRATOR: Hikosuke, guided by the voice, grabs Yojibei from behind and holds him tightly.

HIKOSUKE: I've caught my assailant. I've got him pinned. (*To Yojibei.*) Don't try to start anything now.

NARRATOR: Azuma, the Towboat, and the Chaser rush out frantically, and try to calm Hikosuke, but he only grips Yojibei more firmly. The women burst into tears, but to no avail; Yojibei's fate stands in doubt.

ACT TWO

Scene: Jōkan's house in Yamazaki.
Time: Some weeks later.

NARRATOR: What strange curiosity stirred in that man of old the desire to behold "the moon of exile" though guilty of no crime?[25] So wonders Yojibei, confined by order of the magistrate to quarters unvisited even by the sun, for the quarrel in Nine House Street in which Hikosuke was wounded. Once the assailant was identified as Yojibei of Yamazaki, his sense of honor kept him from revealing Yohei's guilt, and he took the punishment on himself. Yojibei has been left in the custody of his father Jōkan, and life or death depends on whether his accuser's wounds heal or he dies. Uncertain as the pools and shoals of Asuka River, Yojibei helplessly awaits what the morrow will bring. Of all the household his wife Okiku is the most distraught.

OKIKU: He's never known a single day of hardship. I'm afraid this confinement will bring on some sickness. If only I could comfort him in some way!

NARRATOR: She toasts rice cakes for him, and they burn like the flames of longing in her breast. She follows along the garden path to Yojibei's quarters and opens the *shōji*. Yojibei, his face pale, stares blankly at the floor in utter dejection.

OKIKU: You haven't eaten for two or three days. If anything hurts you, you should take some medicine.—You see what a constant source of worry your short temper has been. If by some chance I had been unfaithful, it would have been normal for you to strike down the other man or even kill him. But after all, a prostitute is an article for sale, and Azuma has to sell herself to any number of men. This trouble has all started from your foolish jealousy. Or is it because you consider Azuma no less precious than myself? If I had suspected that was the case, I'd never have let you set foot out of the house. I'm only sorry now that I wasn't more jealous.

NARRATOR: Bitterness is mixed in her tears of indignation.

---

[25] Refers to an anecdote about Minamoto no Akimoto (1000–47) related in *Tsuredzuregusa* by Yoshida Kenkō (Sansom translation, p. 12). Akimoto, having read many poems written by men in exile bewailing their fates, thought he too would like to know what it felt like to be exiled.

YOJIBEI: Please don't say such things. I feel more ashamed before you than before all the rest of the world. But, as the Hachiman Temple at Iwashimizu is my witness, it wasn't I who stabbed Hikosuke. He deliberately started the fight, determined that I wouldn't escape—the result is the same as if I actually stabbed him. Besides, the real assailant is a man I'm under obligation to, and I intend to go on saying, even if I drop into hell, that I stabbed Hikosuke. If he dies, I'll be killed—I'm resigned to that. And yet, you know, his wounds are not so serious. It's clear as a mirror that this is a trick to extort money from me. My life obviously can be bought, but it seems that no money will be forthcoming from the coffers here. The day I was confined was the anniversary of my mother's death, a sure sign that this has all been a punishment for my having been such a bad son.

NARRATOR: He bows his head, a piteous sight.

OKIKU: Yes, my father has said the same thing. "I don't understand Jōkan. A man can't be miserly all the time. It may cost him a thousand or even two thousand pieces of gold, but is that too much to pay for the life of his only son? If he'd put aside his greed, the matter could be settled quickly. It's a great shame. If only I weren't a former samurai myself—" He's so upset that he keeps rambling on in that strain. He'll probably be coming again today. I'll speak to him privately and urge him to make your father feel ashamed of himself. I'm sure he'll yield then, no matter how stingy he is. Oh, I hear my father's voice now. I'll have good news soon.

YOJIBEI: Are you going already? Come back to see me later. My poor dear! I know how lonely you must be.

NARRATOR: Their faces are downcast, but he shuts the *shōji* to stop the tears. The light from the opened *shōji* made his heart all the darker.

Kajita Jibuemon comes on the ferry over the River Yodo to visit Yojibei every day. Because of his daughter he thinks about his son-in-law, worries his old heart for him, but Yojibei's own father Jōkan seems unconcerned.

JŌKAN: I'm glad to see you, Jibu. Let's get back to our game of chess, the one we began yesterday. Please come in.

JIBUEMON: Really, Jōkan, this is too much. I drag my aged limbs here every day because I'm worried about Yojibei, not to play chess. What does it matter who wins the game? Put it away, please.

JŌKAN: No, that fool must be left to his own fate.—The pieces are all just where they were yesterday. Come, play the game.

JIBUEMON: Well, this will be the last one, whoever wins. I'm under a handicap playing against an opponent who's had all last night to stare at the board. Is it your move? Go ahead.

JŌKAN: First I'll move this pawn in front of my rook.

JIBUEMON: Are you after my queen? I'll move it over here.

NARRATOR: Jōkan raps his head.

JŌKAN: Blast it! My knight's trapped.

"When I galloped my horse
Down into the deep paddy-fields,
Though I drew the reins
He wouldn't get up,
Though I whipped him,
He wouldn't go on;
Even his head disappeared." [26]

What a predicament!

NARRATOR: He ponders the situation. Okiku comes up beside the board.

OKIKU: Father, don't you see that if the other side gets beaten, your side is beaten too? You'll never settle the contest as long as you remain at odds. Only one piece is in trouble, and Jōkan has plenty of gold and silver in reserve.[27] If he would forget his greed and merely disburse a little of his treasure, his knight would be saved. Please, I beg you, try to think of some way of dislodging his gold and silver. Do you understand me?

NARRATOR: She tugs at his sleeve. Jibuemon nods.

JIBUEMON: Ah-ha! Thank you for the advice. I'll do as you say.

NARRATOR: But Jōkan ignores this exchange.

JŌKAN: You mustn't help him just because he's your father. I'll put this pawn here for protection.

JIBUEMON: What have you in reserve?

JŌKAN: Three gold, three silver, and some pawns. If I make good

---

[26] A quotation from the Nō play *Kanehira*. The general Kiso no Yoshinaka, attempting to escape his enemies, rides into a quagmire and is trapped. Here suggested by the predicament of Jōkan's knight, literally a "horse". See Sanari, *Yōkyoku Taikan*, I, 728.

[27] In *shōgi*, a game rather similar to chess, one unusual feature is that captured enemy pieces may be held in reserve and then used as the occasion arises to help one's own side. "Gold" and "silver" are the names of two pieces in *shōgi*.

use of the pawns, I'm sure my gold and silver will multiply. Aren't you jealous of such a rich man?

JIBUEMON: Before you start bragging of your riches—my bishop is threatening you. If I move it here, you'll have to lay down some gold and silver.

JŌKAN: No, I won't part with any. I'd rather lose my knight.

NARRATOR: Jibuemon is at the end of his patience.

JIBUEMON: What a miser you are! What will you do with all the gold and silver you're clutching there? Do you plan to take it to the next world? Look here. If I pull back this rook so, your king, the one and only you have, will be cornered, confined to his quarters, you might say, and in no time he'll be lost. Don't you want to protect him by laying down some gold and silver?

JŌKAN: I'm perfectly well aware that I'm stingy. But I don't care whether the king is driven into a corner or trapped in the middle of the board—I'm not letting any gold or silver out of my hands. I'll show you how much trouble I can create with my pawns!

JIBUEMON: Wouldn't you be sorry if, while you're busy with your pawns, your king in turn were beheaded by a pawn? [28]

JŌKAN: It wouldn't matter. But first I'd try to escape.

JIBUEMON: In the meanwhile your king may be transfixed by a spear.[29] Would you still refuse to part with your treasure?

JŌKAN: It wouldn't be worth it. Even if my king is run through, even if his head is exposed on a prison gate, I won't give up my gold and silver.

NARRATOR: His greed is drawn taut like pieces marshaled in strongest array. Okiku watches in distress. She covers her tears with her hand, like a player unwilling to divulge his reserves: it seems as though Yojibei's life has been checkmated.

Jibuemon, wrath written on his face, snatches up the pieces on the board and throws them squarely at Jōkan's forehead. Okiku is astonished, but Jōkan does not move a muscle. Jibuemon edges up to him.

JIBUEMON: For shame, Jōkan! Fathers-in-law are essentially strangers, and it's a waste of breath, I know, to talk with a man so indifferent

---

[28] Refers to an old expression describing the humiliation of a warrior who is killed in battle by a common soldier—here meaning Hikosuke.

[29] A "spear" is a *shōgi* piece which advances in straight lines forward—here the word probably refers to some official judgment against Yojibei.

to shame that he doesn't object even when chess pieces are thrown in his face. But I have been trying to tell you indirectly, under pretext of talking about the chess game, that you should use your money to reach a settlement with Hikosuke and save Yojibei's life. I can't believe that you failed to understand me. How can you refuse to part with your money, even if it means that his head will be taken by a menial or he'll be stabbed! Do you find it so interesting or amusing to infuriate me? You have an only son and I an only daughter. No one can take the place of either. I love my son-in-law as my own child. Don't you think of his wife as your daughter too? You don't care at all, do you, that if Yojibei is beheaded my poor Okiku will be broken-hearted? Ah, you make me seethe with rage!

My wife tried to stop the marriage when they were first engaged. She insisted that Okiku would do better to marry a samurai, even a poor one, and that if she married a businessman, no matter how rich he might be, they would never get along together. I argued with her. I told her that Jōkan of Yamazaki was a well-known man, accepted even in samurai circles. I had my way, but of late my wife has been reproaching me. Thanks to your stinginess and your cruelty, I have quarreled with my wife after we have spent fifty years together. But I don't suppose that a man who refuses to part with his money to save his own son's life would care even if his relatives were dying of starvation. I'm no longer a samurai myself, but members of my family are still full-fledged samurai. What an unspeakable thing to have besmirched our family name by joining it in marriage to that of such an obstinate fool!

NARRATOR: He sobs and weeps. Jōkan blinks his eyes for the tears.

JŌKAN: A samurai's child is reared by samurai parents and becomes a samurai himself because they teach him the warrior's code. A merchant's child is reared by merchant parents and becomes a merchant because they teach him the ways of commerce. A samurai seeks a fair name in disregard of profit, but a merchant, with no thought to his reputation, gathers profits and amasses a fortune. This is the way of life proper for each. With sicknesses too, each one, no matter how grave or difficult to cure, has an appropriate treatment. If a man's life is in danger because he has broken the law, it won't help to douse him in ginseng infusions, but he can be saved by money. This trouble would never have arisen if only Yojibei had realized that money is so precious a treasure that it can even buy human lives. I am well aware that however much I begrudge spending my money, however much I hoard it, all that will be left me when I am dead is a single hempen shroud. But until I die I am bound to respect my gold and silver like the gods or Buddha himself—that is the way prescribed by Heaven for merchants. Supposing I gave still more money to that rogue, lavished it on him, even after he's been punished for his wicked extravagance. What dreadful punishment, what disasters would he then encounter! The more affectionately I think of him, the harder I find it to give him the money. I have the reputation of being a miser. Money is not the only thing I prize. I am loath to part even with dust and ashes. How could I not be reluctant to lose the life of my only son?

NARRATOR: He leans his shaven head over the chessboard and weeps.

JŌKAN: I realize, Jibu, that your affection for Yojibei has made you bitter. But if you are so fond of him, why didn't you invite him to see you regularly and give him your advice? This sort of thing would never have happened.—But here I am forgetting that the foolishness was my son's, not yours. Next I may be saying something quite uncalled for. I'm going inside, Jibu.—Ah, my wife is lucky to be dead!

NARRATOR: He rises, choking with tears, and Jibuemon, unable to speak a word of reproach, goes outside weeping. Okiku, left behind, stands there helplessly, wondering what to do with the chessboard or herself.

OKIKU: There's something in what Jōkan says, but the fact remains that without money Yojibei's life is doomed. What good are money boxes in the safe if they're not put to use? They're worthless as these chess pieces here. What a heartless father to have!

NARRATOR: Her eyes dim with tears at this realization of the uncertainty of the world; a sense of the impermanence of things steals over her as the evening bell tolls its doleful message and the darkness spreads.

Under a misty moon across whose face the flying geese might be counted, helpless, like a lone rook seeking its nest, Azuma of the Wisteria House hurries to the country, her palanquin freighted with her agitation, her life unstable as the flow of the River Yodo. She follows mist-enshrouded paths through the rice fields "to Yamazaki, going or returning, still in Yamazaki." [30] Seeing the log bridge over the river—frightening to eyes unaccustomed to the sight—she stops her palanquin and descends. She wears the plain robes of a townsman's wife, and the unfeeling midnight winds calling to one another through the pines snap at the hems of her skirts. She asks a passerby for Yamazaki where her lover lives. "Over there, just ahead," he tells her, pointing at a house unusually imposing for the countryside. A glance at the rear gate and walls tells her intuitively that this is his prison.

AZUMA: Bearers, this is where Yojibei lives. That room you can see over the wall must be his. The poor man—I'm sure that's where he's confined. I'll go to him. It may take a little time before I return, but wait for me without fail. I depend on you to take me back. If you're out of tobacco I'll give you some, may I? I'll come back very soon.

NARRATOR: She lifts her kimono and steps lightly towards the wall, but the closer she gets, the higher it seems. She stands on tiptoes, she stretches high as she can, but the house is so carefully guarded that not even a chink of light escapes. A harsh wind rattles the garden door, and her heart dances with expectation as she pounds on it. She presses her ear to the wall and listens, but all is silence.

AZUMA: I might stand here forever, and there'd still be no assurance that he'd discover me. I'll call out that Azuma has come.

NARRATOR: She hesitates, her feet cold as nails or ice, her body chilled by the bitter cold. Okiku, worrying whether Yojibei is asleep or still lies awake in his prison room, which lacks even a foot warmer, goes to visit him. At the sound of her sandals echoing along the steppingstones in the garden, Azuma all but jumps for joy. She thinks, "It is he!"

AZUMA: Yoji, is that you? It's Azuma. I've come to see you. I couldn't stand waiting any longer.

NARRATOR: Okiku is startled by the words.

OKIKU (*to herself*): The brazen hussy! What has she come here for? I'll test her.

NARRATOR: She taps on the wall from inside, gently and somehow affectionately.

AZUMA: He's heard me! (*Calls out.*) I was so sure that the doors

[30] A quotation from a seventeenth-century song about Yamazaki.

would all be locked and I wouldn't be let inside that I wrote everything I've been thinking in this letter. Please read it carefully and
send an answer in your own hand. This is the greatest favor I ask
in this life.

NARRATOR: She throws the letter over the wall.

OKIKU (*to herself*): Such impudence! At the house of a married man,
not knowing who might retrieve it!

NARRATOR: She opens the letter. It is in a woman's hand she well
knows—even by the pale light of the moon there is no mistaking
Azuma's writing. The letter has an impressive, formal look. Okiku
reads, "This razor is a blade sharpened by my love. Should the
necessity arise, I beg you not to allow yourself to die at some base ex-
ecutioner's hands, but to end your life honorably. The hour may differ,
but I shall die that same day and, though apart in death, in the next
world we shall share an everlasting bond on the same lotus. May
all be well."

OKIKU: Imagine putting a razor in a letter! Yojibei's life is so
precious to us that my father and I have been weeping ourselves sick.
We've even quarreled with Yojibei's father. But she, under pretense
of kindness, sends this letter, ordering him in this superior way to
die! What does she mean ending it "May all be well"? Shall I order
my servants to beat her from the door? No, if I do that it'll be all
the worse for my husband's reputation. I'll meet her. I'll put her in
her place.

NARRATOR: She opens the garden door and comes out.

AZUMA: Is that you, Yojibei? I've missed you so.

NARRATOR: Okiku firmly seizes the groping hands.

OKIKU: So you're the Azuma I've heard so much about! I've seen
your letter just now. I am Yojibei's wife, Kiku. It was good of you
to come such a distance. I am sure that you would like to see my
husband, but he has been confined to his quarters for reasons of which
you are no doubt aware, and I do not intend to bring you together.
No, I shall not let you meet.

I ought really to have called on you long ago, Azuma, to express
my gratitude. Thanks to you my husband has neglected the family
business and has shown himself completely indifferent to what happens at home. Day and night he spends in visits to the Quarter, to
the displeasure of his father and the evil gossip of the world. Now,

with his present troubles, people are mocking him more than ever. "Have you ever seen the like?" they ask. Do you suppose that I, as his wife, can help being furious? I've always restrained myself lest people call me a bad wife and a disgrace to my husband, and people have said, "Okiku's an admirable woman, a model wife who's never jealous." I have been flattered into submission. And you, Azuma, have made a fool of me. I thought of you merely as a prostitute, but I wonder now if you're actually not a fiend or some diabolical spirit. What did you mean by sending this razor to another woman's husband with the command that he kill himself? If you think that death is so desirable, you should die by yourself. Whose fault it is that my precious husband's body has been wasted and the secrets of his heart ferreted out, that he's slandered in the public gossip, and now is reduced to such straits that he doesn't know if he'll live or die? It's all because of you, my lady courtesan.—Cursed strumpet! Shameless creature!

NARRATOR: Yojibei, hearing her voice rise with pent-up rage, softly slides open the *shōji*. Each woman has her claims; he alone has no excuse. His heart goes out to both and, though his face is flushed as from a burning brand, cold sweat flows. His only wish is to vanish altogether.

AZUMA: Now that we've met, I have no excuses to offer, however bitterly you may abuse me. Even a prostitute, for all her many customers, knows like another woman what jealousy and envy are. I can well understand that a lady who's had your strict upbringing would consider me a faithless strumpet, a deceiver and betrayer of men, an utterly hateful person. But when I've been with Yojibei neither of us has ever suggested that I become his wife, his kept woman, or even his mistress. At first we met merely on a professional basis but, as we became more intimate, our love grew from one night to the next. Madam, you have a fine husband, a man whose looks make every woman fall in love with him, and you are now the only one who can look after him.

Yojibei's present troubles began when he gallantly accepted blame for another man's crime, but the source of his difficulties goes back much farther, to me. Tonight I heard the other women saying that Hikosuke is on the point of death. I was the only one upset by the news. I sneaked from the Quarter because I wanted to tell Yojibei and to prepare him. I knew that if I were caught outside I'd be punished as a warning to other women. I brought my razors so that if Hikosuke died Yojibei could kill himself and I might join him. My desire was to save your husband from disgrace, and to kill myself afterwards in gratitude for his love. I had no intention of interfering in his relations with you. Please let me see his face just once again. I will then shut my eyes for the last time. Have pity on me.

NARRATOR: She takes out a razor kept hidden at her bosom, and presses it against her throat. Before a grief too intense to yield to tears of regret at leaving this world of dust, Okiku at last feels her heart relent. She stays Azuma's arm.

OKIKU: Azuma! Anyone willing to give up her life, even if it is only a gesture to society, cannot be lying. I am touched by your sincerity. My husband, I am sure, will want to see you. I'll take you to him secretly.

AZUMA: Thank you. How understanding you are, Okiku! Forgive me, please, for having so often held your beloved husband in my arms and slept with him.

OKIKU: You can't change what has happened. Consider you've had that much good fortune.

NARRATOR: As the two of them stand in the lane, their reserve melted, they hear Jōkan's voice calling Okiku. Soon he approaches, a mousetrap in his hand.

JŌKAN (*offstage*): Where is my daughter-in-law?

OKIKU: My father's come. At the worst moment. Wait here a few minutes.

NARRATOR: She hides Azuma in the shadow of the wall.

OKIKU: Haven't you retired yet, Father? What brings you here so late at night?

JŌKAN: Nothing in particular. Look at this, Okiku. It's a mousetrap that the young servants have laid. I heard the noise of the trap springing, and I opened it, but it seems that the mouse has escaped. The trap is empty. This little incident has given me a sudden understanding of the world. If a mouse's greed for the bait makes him careless, he'll fall into the trap and be killed at once. If, however, he resolutely renounces the bait and makes his escape, not only will his own life be saved, but the whole family of mice—there must be a father mouse, a father-in-law mouse, and a wife mouse, too—will all rejoice. You can imagine the special relief and joy of the old father mouse. Perhaps the young mouse imagines in his thoughtlessness that after his escape the father mouse may fall into the same trap. He may entertain foolish notions of that kind, but the father mouse has the cunning of the old. He will never allow himself to be caught in the trap. I'm sure there must be an uncle mouse, too. As long as the young mouse hides in the uncle mouse's nest and does not show himself here, not a sound will be heard from the mousetrap, and everything will quickly blow over. If only his present experience in the mousetrap chastens the young mouse into forsaking his running along the rafters every night, his scampering through the cupboards, chewing on the cups, sneaking off with his father's gold pieces, and all his other wildnesses! Can you imagine how much joy it would bring the father mouse to see his son one day enjoy the prosperity of the white mouse? [31] Of late I've been unable to sleep at night, wondering how that foolish, irresolute mouse can fail to understand what he must do.

NARRATOR: His voice blurs with tears.

OKIKU: Of course, I see now. How kind of you to make such elaborate calculations on behalf of the mouse. I shall certainly persuade him to escape.

JŌKAN: I'm satisfied. I have nothing more to ask. A heavy weight has been lifted from my heart. Lately I have been so obsessed with this worry that even when I stood before the altar I could not see the Buddha's face. I feel infinitely relieved. Tonight I will be able to read the sutras with a mind at peace.

NARRATOR: As she watches him depart, strengthened by his belief in the power of prayer, Okiku is assailed by unshakable melancholy.

Yojibei rushes out and looks in the direction from which his father's voice came. Tears of gratitude start to his eyes. Okiku lifts in her hands the earth trodden by her father-in-law's feet.

OKIKU: Yojibei—did you hear those words of mercy? The sooner you leave, the greater will be your father's relief, and the better son you will show yourself. I shall remain to look after Jōkan. I promise to take better care of him than ever. Don't worry, I beg you, about what may happen once you leave. I wish I could send someone with you. What shall I do?

---

[31] This passage of course describes in thinly veiled terms Jōkan's hope that Yojibei will make his escape. A "white mouse" was considered to be a harbinger of good luck, and a house where white mice dwelt would surely prosper.

NARRATOR: She reflects a moment.

AZUMA: Okiku! I am here. Azuma is here, for just that purpose. I left the Quarter at the risk of my life, and I have no desire to return. I shall be most grateful if you will consent and say, "Go with him." I will never return to the Quarter.

NARRATOR: Okiku catches the note of urgency in her words.

OKIKU: Then everything is arranged. Hurry, before it gets too late.

NARRATOR: She tugs at Yojikei's sleeve, urging him on, but he shakes his arm free.

YOJIBEI: No, that's impossible. They say that a man's highest duty as a father is to show compassion for his child, and as a child to serve his father.[32] I am in my father's custody now. If I escape and Hikosuke dies, they will immediately arrest my father in my place and behead him as the culprit. Even if Hikosuke recovers, my father will be guilty of having allowed his charge to escape, and they will punish him accordingly. My father has fulfilled his duty as a parent by showing a compassion indifferent to danger. But I have disobeyed my father's wishes in everything, to this very day. If I were to crown my sins by running away and saving my life at the expense of his, I could never mingle in human society again, not if I lived a hundred or a thousand years. Life in this world would be intolerable. I don't wish to disobey him again—causing him grief gives me no pleasure—but I ask you to let me die as I am. I would like, by giving up my life, to discharge the filial duties of a lifetime.

NARRATOR: He raises his voice and weeps.

OKIKU *and* AZUMA: Yes, what you say is reasonable too.

NARRATOR: The two women cannot shake his resolve; they can only weep.

Jōkan calls from inside.

JŌKAN: Okiku, Okiku! Do I hear aright? Is that disobedient scoundrel saying that he won't escape? Heartless, inhuman wretch!—I haven't told anyone for fear that people might say that old Jōkan at the age of seventy allowed himself to be blackmailed, but I secretly sent a man to Hikosuke. I tried to settle things privately by offering up to two hundred pieces of gold. Hikosuke took advantage of my position, and said he was unwilling, even for a thousand pieces. I've heard that his wounds are superficial, but he's mortal, after all, and there's no telling when he might die. Can you imagine the agonies

[32] A paraphrase of a passage in the Confucian classic *The Great Learning*.

I've gone through as a father? I have tried to distract myself with chess, only to be harassed. The more I have been reminded of Yojibei's plight, the more painful it has been. All evening long I have racked my mind thinking up that plan of escape from the trap. Try to understand the immeasurable fatherly love that went into it. (*To Yojibei.*) You can't remain a child all your life. Some day you'll be a father yourself. If only I could make you realize how a father feels for his son! Tell me at once—will you or won't you escape?

NARRATOR: His voice is harsh, but the tears on his face may be surmised even by those outside the wall. Yojibei, weeping, prostrates himself.

YOJIBEI: My gratitude makes it all the more impossible to run away. Forgive me, I implore you.

NARRATOR: He bows his head in tears.

JŌKAN: Very well. A man normally hopes to survive an aged father, even by a single day, and he tries to remain in good health so that on the anniversaries of his father's death he may offer prayers for his happiness in the other world. Would you prefer to be mourned by your father and make him suffer? Very well, stay here if you like, but first I will thrust this dagger into my wrinkled belly! *Namu Amida Butsu.*

YOJIBEI: Father! I'll go away! Wait!

NARRATOR: He collapses in tears.

JŌKAN: Do you swear it?

YOJIBEI: How could I lie to you?

JŌKAN: I'm happy. My mind is at rest. I forgive you all your disobedience of the past. I accept this one act as the equivalent of thirty years of dutiful service as a son. Your dead mother must also be rejoicing. Okiku has a father, and I have Okiku. Don't worry about us here.—I see that you'll have a lady to go with you. Madam, please make sure that Yojibei takes moxa treatment [33] however much he objects, and don't let him drink any saké. Always travel in a sedan chair, even if it's expensive—people may recognize you on horseback. Please do as I ask.

NARRATOR: His words are brief, but his agitated heart is torn in ways numberless as the stripes of the purse he tosses to Yojibei. "Farewell" is his only word; the rest is choked by tears.

[33] In this treatment, still practiced today, pellets of medicinal herbs are burned at various places on the patient's skin. It is believed to be effective for many ailments.

Yojibei, overwhelmed by his father's kindness and his wife's love, seems numbed by the grief of parting. He staggers forward as in a trance, unaware of what happens.

AZUMA: I'm Azuma—don't you recognize me? And that is your wife, Okiku. At least say good-by to her. How fainthearted you are!

NARRATOR: She tries to lend him strength, but tonight she too must hide.

AZUMA: Come, let us climb into this sedan chair for two. No one can see us there.

NARRATOR: She whispers to him and, brushing away the spring frost that lies on her sleeve, she calls to her bearers. Okiku's voice is hoarse with tears.

OKIKU: When you find a haven, wherever it may be, write me that you are safe. I'll be waiting for your letter. Please be careful not to catch a chill on cold mornings and evenings at the inns where you stay. I have so many things to tell you, but they're in my heart and don't come to my lips. All I can say is, keep safe and well.

NARRATOR: These are her only words—the rest is tears.

OKIKU (to herself): I should be the one going off with my husband —that's the proper way. Why has such a thing happened to me? Here I am sending him off in a chair for two with that woman I've envied and detested so. I feel only jealousy and utter misery.

NARRATOR: Many are the reasons for her tears, but all are joined in the single thread of love for her husband. As she watches the chair disappear into the distance, the late night bell tolls, drowning the voices calling last farewells. The clouds seem to retreat across the sky, but the palanquin hurries relentlessly forward, not pausing even to give the bearers a momentary rest. To the heavy burden of love borne in the chair is added the sorrow of father and son at parting as Yojibei leaves, bound for no one knows where.

ACT THREE

Scene One: The journey of Azuma and Yojibei from Yamazaki to Nara.

NARRATOR:

The butterfly that tempts the cherry to blossom
Will not know the taste of the rapeseed;

The butterfly dancing over the rapeseed,
Though hatched the same spring,
Will not have known the cherry blossoms.
Each unknown to the other,
Each unaware the other exists,
They will never know love's first delights,
Nor the madness of passion.
What a sad contrast to Yojibei! Azuma draws closer to him.

AZUMA: I am so happy! Do you feel calmer now? Look—see how even butterflies, the swallowtails, fly close to their mates! We two are together, a couple well-versed in love, yet how timorous you are!

NARRATOR: She tries to encourage him.

YOJIBEI (*sings*):
Ransom Azuma, Yojibei!
Ransom her, ransom her, Yojibei!
When was it the pangs of love were first assuaged,
Loosened with the strings of your lady's underclothes?
Now when you think of the past,
How sad, how bitter it seems!
How sad, how bitter, the past you remember,
How sad and how bitter!

AZUMA: Alas, who might you be if not Yojibei of Yamazaki, a man never outdone by others, who never had a hair out of place? But now your senses are disordered. You have even forgotten Azuma's face, you have lost your mind.

NARRATOR: She places a staying hand on him.

YOJIBEI: Are you Azuma of the Wisteria House? You've been cruelly treated by Yojibei—how poor your coloring is, unhappy woman! I thought I would surely ransom you soon and enable you to live in comfort. We would have a house and a child and, when we proudly walked together through the streets of Yamazaki, a nurse would carry our child on her shoulders, and her husband would hold a parasol. But I have rejected the kindness of my father in Yamazaki, and now I am dependent on you, in appearance no longer the man I was. From Otokoyama we go to Akishino.[34] Now I have wearied of people. O pines of Toyama, I would ask you something—which is more painful, to wait or to part? The wife my father bestowed on me, so that

---

[34] Places between Kyoto and Nara; the name Akishino contains the word *aki*, meaning "weariness [of people]".

I would have neither to wait nor to part, I thought of with respect and affection, but in vain, for we could not remain together. I am now an untethered steed roaming the ends of the moors. Yesterday I carried my love to Azuma; [35] today as I weep in longing I am drawn to my home. I am an autumn leaf careening madly of itself, too unsettled to alight; for me there is no waking and no sleeping; only tears of waiting wet my sleeve. "Even if by chance you're waited for, never become the one who waits," they say. The mountains between my father and me block all news from Yamazaki, where my wife must be distraught with waiting, her disheveled hair unbound. Her last words to me will be my strength.

AZUMA: My love, a threefold sash, [36] has bound you close during the long nights we have slept together. I felt no jealousy nor envy, but one is half owner of an object given in trust, they say. [37] Have you forgotten our last moon-viewing at the Izutsu House? In the moonlight that filled every corner, completely given to each other that night, we danced till the dawn. How wonderful it was! I shan't forget it, not if I live to be a hundred years.

YOJIBEI: It's something I'll never forget. I couldn't get my fill of you as you walked along, your toes pointed out, [38] lovely enough to kill a man with a glance, to steal his senses away. A courtesan's basin is her faithful companion, her wife, and she may herself seem desirable enough for you to make her your wife, but once you ransom her the bottom of the basin drops away, it holds no more moonlight. [39] After spending the night with you, I weep for the father I have lost, I long for my wife. My heart is one but torn in two, like the notes of the cuckoo which passes us now, telling its name. [40] "You resemble your

---

[35] Azuma means at once his sweetheart and the direction East; the eastern part of Japan is sometimes called Azuma.

[36] The phrase possibly suggests that Azuma is so wasted with love that her sash, which normally goes twice around the body, can be wrapped three times around her.

[37] A proverb, which here refers to Yojibei's being left by Okiku in Azuma's care.

[38] Japanese women normally walk with toes pointed inwards; in this more seductive walk the toes are first pointed outwards, then turned in.

[39] This line may also mean that the bottom fell out of Yojibei's plans to ransom Azuma. The effect of the whole (rather obscure) passage is to show that running away with the great courtesan, Yojibei's dream for so long, does not actually bring him happiness; he needs his wife and father too.

[40] The cuckoo's call is in two notes. The following line alludes to the cuckoo's habit of leaving its eggs in another bird's nest.

father, but your song's not like his." The son's first song brought him fame in the gay quarters. . . . I wore no cap of office, but they called me "minister of state." [41] I passed through the gate where the procuresses examine the customers; I saw the Chasers slap the dozing harlots' maids. All was a world within a dream and, when I awoke, elegance and vulgarity seemed much the same. These things I knew, but when I was caught like a tangle of willow branches in a sudden mountain wind, how my father's harsh words of reproof, my wife's single word of farewell filled me with longing and love!

NARRATOR: They take each other's hands and weep, giving voice to their grief.

The setting sun approaches the mountain crest. In the northwest a wind rises, and the feet of the clouds scurry to the southeast sky. The bough tips and the branches rustle; water murmurs in a little stream; clouds spread their feather sleeves, inclining them now this way, now that, round and round as they circle. The moon follows its appointed course, but Yojibei's suffering has no limits. His father's wrath has struck him now, and he rushes ahead, oblivious to his fate. He runs; his reflection in the stream runs too. He stops; it stops. Azuma's sleeves were unruffled, but now they are twisted too, and her mind seems about to snap—a courtesan's fate is beyond her control. They search in their misery for a humble farmer's cottage, a place to pause for a while in their flight through the world.

Scene Two: The Izutsu House in Shimmachi.
Time: Late summer of the same year.

NARRATOR: The shores of Naniwa Bay are famous for Plum blossoms; the Pines grow thick, and even by day the Maple leaves form a bright brocade. [42] Nocturnal brothels have recently been permitted, [43] and men eagerly throng to the Quarter to see Shimmachi at night. Lanterns gleam like stars deep under the eaves along the four streets, more brilliant than the face of the full Moon. [44] The swelling Tides, the

[41] *Daijin*, meaning "a minister of state", is the homophone of *daijin*, meaning "a great patron [of the gay quarter]".
[42] "Maple leaves" were courtesans of the third rank.
[43] The brothels had formerly been allowed to operate only during the day, but in 1675 nocturnal visits were permitted. It is not clear why Chikamatsu says "recently."
[44] The Shimmachi Quarter had four streets. Moons, Tides, Reflections, and Half-prices

shining Reflections, the experienced Half-prices, all bespeak good service to customers: the towels in the chambers have no time to dry. No one has beaten the drum, but at the Great Gate resounds a horse's loud neighing; the guest riding up to the Izutsu House is Hard-luck Yohei of Yawata. He leaps from his mount, high-spirited and handsome, to be greeted by the master of the house with exaggerated bows.

YOHEI: You needn't get so excited, Kurozaemon. Have you forgotten me? I'm Yohei. Last New Year I was hospitably received here, and you were personally very kind. Then I was a minister without portfolio or money, but I come to you today a minister of the treasury, with ready cash in my wallet and something to discuss in private. I'll go in now.

NARRATOR: He steps confidently inside.

KUROZAEMON: Yes, indeed, I remember now. What a surprise to see you again! But first, please have a cup of tea and a smoke.

NARRATOR: He speaks in obsequious tones. The oil lamp is immediately replaced with candles:[45] life in this Quarter is dedicated to pleasure.

YOHEI: Come closer, Kuroza. As you know, I accepted money from Azuma of the Wisteria House at the New Year. I took it to Edo, where it soon began to sprout, and I made a quick fortune without harming anyone. My backbreaking toil was worth it—I've come back now with a well-laden horse. I learned on the road that Azuma's escaped and that she's being sought on charges of having illegally left the Quarter. I'd be disgraced as a man if I abandoned her now, after having accepted her generosity and sworn I would help her. I will ransom Azuma and enable her to go where she pleases. I'm sure that you have the documents for her contract. I want them. Please arrange everything so that I can redeem them for cash and settle matters this evening. I'm counting on you, Kuroza.

KUROZAEMON: Splendid! My congratulations! I need say no more about Azuma since you have already heard the rumors. But the most curious thing has happened. This evening a rustic-looking old samurai appeared. He wishes to buy up the contract even though Azuma

---

were ranks of courtesans, named (in the first three instances) after a passage in the Nō play *Matsukaze:* "The moon is one, the reflections two, the three-fold tide swelling in . . ." (Sanari, *Yōkyoku Taikan,* v, 2829). Thus, a prostitute who received a one-*momme* fee was called a "Moon", etc.

[45] Candles were more extravagant than oil lamps and were therefore put out for customers.

herself is not here. He hasn't any money, but he will offer in exchange a two-foot broadsword authenticated as a genuine Kuniyuki. The old gentleman is waiting inside. I haven't informed the owner of the contract yet, but I'll go at once and report on both the offers.

NARRATOR: He starts to leave. A clamor at the gate announces Hikosuke.

KUROZAEMON: You're quite a stranger, sir.

HIKOSUKE: How's business these days? You're a lucky fellow, Kuroza —if you're trying to make money, I'm your man. This is a casual visit, merely to discuss a ransom.—Impressed with me, aren't you? Early this spring, as you remember, I had my hair trimmed a bit by that scoundrel Yojibei of Yamazaki. I complained to the police, absolutely determined, as the god Hachiman is my witness, that I would not endure such an affront. Yojibei was left in his father's custody. Ever since then Jōkan has secretly been sending people with apologies. I told him that I wouldn't call off the suit, not for a million pieces of gold—that's the kind of man I am. However, as you can see, my wounds are completely healed, and though I detest that villain Yojibei, I feel sorry for his father, and I've forgiven him. Jōkan, as a token of his thanks, sent me a pittance to buy myself some drinks. They say it brings bad luck if you return saké when it's offered as a present, so I decided to accept. Then Azuma, at Yojibei's instigation, ran away from the Quarter, and Yojibei broke his confinement to escape with her. Jōkan has paid for this. All his possessions have been impounded, and he himself has been placed under house arrest until Azuma and Yojibei are discovered. I'm told that Yojibei dropped dead on the road somewhere. Lucky for him, isn't it, considering that he was sure to be beheaded the moment he showed himself. But to get back to our business. I came to talk about Azuma. She's guilty of having left the Quarter illegally, and there's not much chance of saving her life. But I was born with a heart warm as Buddha's—it's my great weakness—and I'd like to rescue her. I'll redeem Azuma's contract first and look for her later, at my leisure. When I find her I'll use her as my cook or my washerwoman, or perhaps I'll let her massage my hands and feet. I'm resolved to kill her with kindness for the rest of her life. Only a man of my stature would make such a proposal. Discuss it with the owner and reach a settlement. Here's the ready cash.

NARRATOR: He throws a bag of fifty pieces of gold before the master.

Yohei, who has heard everything, slides open the partition with an "Excuse me."

YOHEI: Master! My request to redeem Azuma came first! Here is the money.

NARRATOR: He sets down a plain wooden stand laden with a packet of a thousand pieces of gold. A voice calls from the next room.

JIBUEMON: If you are disputing who came first, I claim that honor!

NARRATOR: A samurai enters.

JIBUEMON: I offer as the price of the ransom this sword with an attested value of three thousand *kan*.

NARRATOR: He throws down sword and certificate both. Yohei does not recognize the sword, but he is certain from the man's appearance that this must be the Jibuemon of whom Yojibei had spoken. He gazes at the man in silence. Kuroza is at a loss to decide among the three contenders.

KUROZAEMON: In any case, it's up to the owner to decide. Shall I send for him? No, I'll go myself. Alas for poor Kuroza!

NARRATOR: He rushes off talking to himself. The three men left behind glance at one another. Hikosuke is ill at ease before Yohei, recalling his terrible beating. His nerves are on edge, but true son of Hattori that he is, he looks strong as the local tobacco;[46] pulling over the tobacco tray, he begins with a sour expression to smoke. His pipe is a good distraction, and he keeps knocking out the ashes as he waits for an answer.

The owner of Azuma's contract, Kan'emon, enters accompanied by the master of the house.

KAN'EMON: I've gathered what's happened from Kuroza's description. Ransoming Azuma under these circumstances would be quite unprecedented in the Quarter. It's difficult for me to answer one way or the other. If I surrender her contract—it doesn't matter to whom— word of this will get around. People will form the unfortunate impression that they can get away with anything, even absconding with a woman from the Quarter, provided they give enough money. The Quarter will be in an uproar with elopements and runaways on all sides and constant violations of our code. This represents a difficult problem for owners of contracts. It is pointless to discuss the matter further. I'll do what I can when once I've seen Azuma.

46 Hattori was a famous tobacco-growing region.

NARRATOR: Hikosuke interrupts.

HIKOSUKE: I see. I don't know what anybody else plans to do, but I'm going at once to search for Azuma. Ransoming her will be my privilege—I've sworn as much. I'm leaving.

NARRATOR: He springs to his feet.

YOHEI: I won't let you!

NARRATOR: Yohei grabs Hikosuke's wrist and, raising him over his shoulder, flings him violently to the floor. He firmly straddles Hikosuke's back.

YOHEI: You're a born racer—a fast man on your feet when it comes to running from me. If you make a move, I'll smash your head in. Do you understand? (*To owner.*) I find your arguments entirely reasonable, sir. Are you quite certain that you will allow Azuma to be ransomed on the spot, providing you see her face?

KAN'EMON: Why should I lie to you? Azuma's contract hasn't much longer to run, and she's made a good deal of money for me in the past. I certainly wouldn't deceive you.

YOHEI: Excellent! And I take it that there'll be no trouble with the police?

KAN'EMON: I'm sure that everything will be settled quite simply if I ask them to withdraw the complaint.

YOHEI: Splendid! Servants, bring those two leather trunks over here. Master, would you open them, please?

NARRATOR: The master quickly unfastens the straps and from inside the trunks emerge Azuma and Yojibei, restored to his senses. Hikosuke is astonished, and the owner and master look dumfounded. Jibuemon, overjoyed, can no longer conceal his identity.

JIBUEMON: Yojibei! It's Jibu! I'm delighted that you're safe.

NARRATOR: The rest is speechless tears of joy. Yojibei bows his head.

YOJIBEI: Please forgive me for everything and offer my apologies to my father.

JIBUEMON: There is no need to ask that. He's told me his feelings and I know that he understands. Azuma, you've had a harrowing ordeal. Here, Kan'emon, please take this sword in exchange for the contract and surrender Azuma to me.

NARRATOR: He bows humbly.

AZUMA (*to master*): I've been away a long time, Kuroza. Please offer the owner my apologies.

NARRATOR: She weeps. Yohei vigorously jerks Hikosuke to his feet.

YOHEI: Listen carefully. My reason for going to Edo was to raise money so that I could ransom Azuma and rescue her from the hardships of the Quarter. I was so determined to succeed that I easily managed to make close to 500 *kamme* in one transaction. On my way back I met Yojibei, and learned from him the exact situation. I, Yohei, was the man who stabbed you. You falsely accused Yojibei and extorted a great deal of money, didn't you? I could thrash you all day and still not feel satisfied. But since this is a festive occasion—leave at once!

NARRATOR: He pushes him away.

HIKOSUKE: Thank you. At New Year you threw me to the floor of this very room, and later you stabbed me. Today I rather expected to get killed, and I'm grateful to be spared. The third time is the lucky time for me.

NARRATOR: As Hikosuke makes his escape Jibuemon twists his arm and wrenches him down.

JIBUEMON: I won't let you leave. You must inform the police of Jōkan's innocence, and secure his release from confinement.

NARRATOR: He quickly ties Hikosuke.

JIBUEMON: Is the ransom completed, Yohei?

YOHEI: No, not yet. Here are one thousand pieces of gold. I offer them in exchange for the contract.

NARRATOR: Yohei places the money before the owner. Kan'emon shakes his head.

KAN'EMON: Azuma's term expires next March. She'll become a free woman. What would people think if I accepted your thousand pieces of gold? I'd be disgraced. I'd prefer not to take any money at all, but I'm sure you wouldn't agree. I'll accept three hundred pieces for the six months remaining in her contract. The rest I don't need.

NARRATOR: He pushes the money away. Yohei, by nature a lighthearted fellow, shouts:

YOHEI: It's all over! I've got the contract. He's taken the money. Azuma's ransom's completed!

Here are the three hundred pieces to ransom her, clap hands on that.[47]

NARRATOR: Clap, clap, once again, clap, clap.

[47] The 300-*ryō* ransom paid by one Sakanoue Yojiemon for the courtesan Azuma about 1670 occasioned a famous ballad, and probably was one of the origins of this play.

YOHEI: Clap hands once again. Master, I put aside these thousand pieces of gold for the ransom. I won't feel right if even one copper coin remains. Three hundred pieces are my present for you.

KUROZAEMON: I'm deeply obliged.

YOHEI: Put them together and they make six hundred. Clap hands once again! Clap, clap! Four hundred pieces still remain, four hundred pieces weigh on my brain. Come close and celebrate.

NARRATOR: He scatters pieces of gold all over the floor, till you can't see its color any more. Men and maidservants, each for himself, jostle and shove to pick up the pelf.

YOHEI: Have you taken them all? Hurrah, hurrah! Celebrate with three rounds more. Clap, clap!

NARRATOR: With a clapping of hands and a rhythmical song, to a joyous beat they drink three and three and nine times long. They pledge that through a thousand years, ten thousand years of life, they'll remain to the end a loving husband and wife.[48]

---

[48] Apparently Yojibei and Azuma will be joined happily; it is not clear what will happen to Okiku.

THE LOVE SUICIDES AT AMIJIMA

First performed on January 3, 1721. No source for this play, often acclaimed as Chikamatsu's masterpiece, has been determined, but traditional (though unreliable) accounts state that the suicides at Amijima occurred on November 13, 1720, one day earlier than in the drama. Takano Masami, a recent Japanese critic, has suggested that *The Love Suicides at Amijima* was a reworking of *The Love Suicides at Umeda* (1706) by Chikamatsu's rival, Ki no Kaion. There are striking points of resemblance between the two plays, and it may be that Chikamatsu, when shaping into dramatic form the events which took place at Amijima, borrowed from the earlier work. Chikamatsu's play has in turn been many times revised. The version most commonly performed today dates from the early nineteenth century.

Cast of Characters

KAMIYA JIHEI, aged 28, a paper merchant
KONAYA MAGOEMON, his brother, a flour merchant
GOZAEMON, Jihei's father-in-law
TAHEI, a rival for Koharu
DEMBEI, proprietor of the Yamato House
SANGORŌ, Jihei's servant
KANTARŌ, aged 6, Jihei's son
A MINSTREL PRIEST
PORTERS, FISHERMEN, PERSONS OF THE QUARTER
KOHARU, aged 19, a courtesan at the Kinokuni House in Sonezaki
OSAN, Jihei's wife
OSAN'S MOTHER (who is also Jihei's aunt), aged 56
OSUE, aged 4, Jihei's daughter
PROPRIETRESS at Kawachi House
KIYO, a receptionist
TAMA, Osan's servant
SUGI, Koharu's maid
MAIDS, PROSTITUTES, SERVANTS

ACT ONE

Scene One: A street in Sonezaki New Quarter, Osaka.
Time: November 4, 1720.

NARRATOR:

Sanjō bakkara fungoro nokkoro
Chokkoro fungoro de
Mate tokkoro wakkara yukkuru
Wakkara yukkuru ta ga
Kasa wo wanga ranga ra su
Sora ga kunguru kunguru mo
Renge rengere bakkara fungoro.[1]
The love of a prostitute is deep beyond measure; it's a bottomless sea of affection that cannot be emptied or dried. By Shell River,[2] love songs in every mood fill the air, and hearts stop short at the barrier[3] of doorway lanterns. Men roam the streets in high spirits, humming snatches of puppet plays, mimicking the actors, or singing bawdy ballads as they pass; others are drawn into the houses by samisens played in upstairs rooms. But here is a visitor who hides his face, avoiding the gift day.[4] See how he creeps along, afraid to be forced into spending too much!

Kiyo, the receptionist, notices him.[5]

KIYO: Who's this trying to avoid me?

NARRATOR: She snatches again and again at his hood-flap; he dodges

---

[1] Japanese scholars have puzzled over these curious syllables for years, and many explanations of them have been offered. Their meaning, if any, is less important than the lively rhythm, which evokes the atmosphere of the Sonezaki Quarter.

[2] Shijimi River, frequently mentioned in the course of the play, flowed along the border of the Sonezaki Quarter. Its name *shijimi* means the *corbicula*, a small mollusc related to the clam. There is a play on words here: the sea cannot be emptied by ladling it with tiny clam shells.

[3] A play on words: *moji ga seki* (the barrier of Chinese characters) suggests that customers stop short when they read on doorway lanterns the names in characters of their favorite teahouses; *Moji ga seki* (the Barrier of Moji) refers to the Straits of Shimonoseki.

[4] Festive days in the gay quarter on which customers were required to make presents to the teahouses. For a detailed description, see Shively, *The Love Suicide at Amijima*, p. 100.

[5] The following few lines are based on a passage in the Nō play *Kagekiyo*. See Waley, *The Nō Plays of Japan*, p. 98. The maid's name Kiyo suggests that of Kagekiyo, and the effect is one of burlesque.

her twice or thrice, but this is a valuable customer, and she refuses to let him escape. At last she pounces on him with the cry:

KIYO: No more of your nonsense! Come along!

NARRATOR: And the customer, caught flap and cap, is trapped into folly by this female Kagekiyo.

Among the flowers on display—even the bridges are called Plum and Cherry Blossom—[6] here is Koharu of the Kinokuni House, now graduated from the smock of a bath attendant in the South[7] to the garments of love in the New Quarter. Is her name "Second Spring"[8] a sign that she is fated to leave behind a fleeting name in November?

"Who has sent for me tonight?" she wonders, uncertain as a dove in the uncertain light of a standing lantern. A prostitute passes her, then turns back.

PROSTITUTE: Is that you, Koharu? Where have you been keeping yourself? We don't get invited to the same parties any more, and I never see you or hear a word from you. Have you been sick? Your face looks thinner. Somebody was telling me that the master at your place now gives all your customers a thorough examination and hardly lets you out of the house, all on account of your Kamiji.[9] But I've also heard that you're to be ransomed by Tahei and go live with him in the country—in Itami, was it? Is it true?

KOHARU: I'd be much obliged if you'd please stop talking about Itami! The relations between Jihei and myself, I'm sorry to say, are not as close as people suppose. It's that loud-mouthed Tahei who's started the rumors and spread them everywhere, until every last customer has deserted me. The master blames Kamiya Jihei, and he's done everything to keep us from meeting. Why, I'm not even allowed to receive letters from Jihei. Tonight, strangely enough, I've been sent to Kawashō.[10] My customer's a samurai, I'm told. But I keep worrying that I might meet that dreadful Tahei on the way. I feel exactly as if I had some mortal enemy. Do you suppose he might be over there?

---

[6] References to Umeda Bridge and Sakura Bridge over the Shijimi River.

[7] The "south" refers to the Shimanouchi Quarter, a section of low-class brothels which originally had been bathhouses. Sonezaki Quarter was north of this section.

[8] The name Koharu, literally "little spring", means Indian summer.

[9] A familiar contraction for Kamiya Jihei.

[10] A contraction of Kawachi House and the owner's name, which began with the syllable "Shō".

PROSTITUTE: If you feel that way about Tahei, you'd better hide quickly. Look—coming out of the first block—there's one of those street minstrels, singing his nonsense hymns.[11] I can see in the crowd round him a dissolute-looking fellow with his hair tricked up in some funny style—the stuck-up swell! I'm sure it's Tahei. Oh—they're heading this way!

NARRATOR: A moment later the defrocked priest, in a flat cap and ink-black robes with the sleeves tucked back, comes bumbling along, surrounded by a crowd of idlers. He bangs at random on his bell, mixing his nonsense with the burden of a hymn.

MINSTREL:

"Fan Kuai's style was no great shakes—
See how Asahina of Japan used to break down gates!"
He rips through the gate bars and tangle of felled trees,
Slays Uryōko and Saryōko and passes the barrier,
As time passes by.[12]
Namamida Namaida Namamida Namaida.
Ei Ei Ei Ei Ei.
"Though I wander all over,
The sad world holds no one
Who looks like my dear Matsuyama!" [13]
—He weeps, he howls, only to burst into laughs.
"How wretched that I must end my life in madness!"
He falls prostrate, the grass for his pallet,
A sight too sad for the eyes to behold.
Namamida Namaida Namamida Namaida.
Ei Ei Ei Ei Ei.
Tokubei of the dyer's shop,
Since he first fell in love with Fusa,
Has yielded to passion that absorbs his fortune,
A love stained so deep lye itself cannot cleanse it.[14]
Namamida Namaida Namamida Namaida
Namamida Namaida.

SUGI: Excuse me, priest.

[11] Sections from popular puppet dramas with a quasi-religious refrain.
[12] Adapted from *The Battles of Coxinga.* See above, p. 118.
[13] From the play *Wankyū Sue no Matsuyama* (1707). See Shively, p. 104.
[14] From the festive epilogue to "Yosaku from Tamba," in Keene, *Major Plays of Chikamatsu,* and see also Shively, pp. 104-5.

MINSTREL: What is it?

SUGI: It's bad luck to sing those songs, just when stories about love suicides in the Quarter have at last quieted down. Why don't you give us instead a *nembutsu* song on the journey from *The Battles of Coxinga?*

NARRATOR: Sugi offers him some coins from her sleeve.

MINSTREL:

> For a mere one or two coppers
> You can't expect to travel all the way,
> Three thousand leagues to the Land of Great Ming!
> It doesn't pay, it doesn't pray Amida Buddha.

NARRATOR: Grumbling in this strain, he moves on.

Scene Two: The Kawachi House, a Sonezaki teahouse.

NARRATOR: Koharu slips away, under cover of the crowd, and hurries into the Kawachi House.

PROPRIETRESS: Well, well, I hadn't expected you so soon.—It's been ages even since I've heard your name mentioned. What a rare visitor you are, Koharu! And what a long time it's been!

NARRATOR: The proprietress greets Koharu cheerfully.

KOHARU: Oh—you can be heard as far as the gate. Please don't call me Koharu in such a loud voice. That horrible Ri Tōten [15] is out there. I beg you, keep your voice down.

NARRATOR: Were her words overheard? In bursts a party of three men.

TAHEI: I must thank you first of all, dear Koharu, for bestowing a new name on me, Ri Tōten. I never was called *that* before. Well, friends, this is the Koharu I've confided to you about—the good-hearted, good-natured, good-in-bed Koharu. Step up and meet the whore who's started all the rivalry! Will I soon be the lucky man and get Koharu for my wife? Or will Kamiya Jihei ransom her?

NARRATOR: He swaggers up.

KOHARU: I don't want to hear another word. If you think it's such an achievement to start unfounded rumors about someone you don't even know, throw yourself into it, say what you please. But I don't want to hear.

NARRATOR: She steps away suddenly, but he sidles up again.

[15] The villain of the play *The Battles of Coxinga*. See above, pp. 60 ff.

TAHEI: You may not want to hear me, but the clink of my gold coins will make you listen! What a lucky girl you are! Just think—of all the many men in Temma and the rest of Osaka, you chose Jihei the paper dealer, the father of two children, with his cousin for his wife and his uncle for his father-in-law! A man whose business is so tight he's at his wits' ends every sixty days merely to pay the wholesalers' bills! Do you think he'll be able to fork over nearly ten *kamme* [16] to ransom you? That reminds me of the mantis who picked a fight with an oncoming vehicle! [17] But look at me—I haven't a wife, a father-in-law, a father, or even an uncle, for that matter. Tahei the Lone Wolf— that's the name I'm known by. I admit that I'm no match for Jihei when it comes to bragging about myself in the Quarter, but when it comes to money, I'm an easy winner. If I pushed with all the strength of my money, who knows what I might conquer?—How about it, men?—Your customer tonight, I'm sure, is none other than Jihei, but I'm taking over. The Lone Wolf's taking over. Hostess! Bring on the saké! On with the saké!

PROPRIETRESS: What are you saying? Her customer tonight is a samurai, and he'll be here any moment. Please amuse yourself elsewhere.

NARRATOR: But Tahei's look is playful.

TAHEI: A customer's a customer, whether he's a samurai or a townsman. The only difference is that one wears swords and the other doesn't. But even if this samurai wears his swords he won't have five or six—there'll only be two, the broadsword and dirk. I'll take care of the samurai and borrow Koharu afterwards. (*To Koharu.*) You may try to avoid me all you please, but some special connection from a former life must have brought us together. I owe everything to that ballad-singing priest—what a wonderful thing the power of prayer is! I think I'll recite a prayer of my own. Here, this ashtray will be my bell, and my pipe the hammer. This is fun.

Chan Chan Cha Chan Chan.
Ei Ei Ei Ei Ei.
Jihei the paper dealer—
Too much love for Koharu

---

[16] This would amount to over $5,000 in current purchasing power. The price is unusually high; no doubt Tahei is exaggerating.

[17] A simile, derived ultimately from ancient Chinese texts, for someone who does not know his own limitations. See Shively, p. 107.

Has made him a foolscap,
He wastepapers sheets of gold
Till his fortune's shredded to confetti
And Jihei himself is like scrap paper
You can't even blow your nose on!
Hail, Hail Amida Buddha!
Namaida Namaida Namaida.

NARRATOR: As he prances wildly, roaring his song, a man appears at the gate, so anxious not to be recognized that he wears, even at night, a wicker hat.[18]

TAHEI:Well, Toilet paper's showed up! That's quite a disguise! Why don't you come in, Toilet paper? If my prayer's frightened you, say a Hail Amida! [19] Here, I'll take off your hat!

NARRATOR: He drags the man in and examines him: it is the genuine article, a two-sworded samurai, somber in dress and expression, who glares at Tahei through his woven hat, his eyeballs round as gongs. Tahei, unable to utter either a Hail or an Amida, gasps "Haaa!" in dismay, but his face is unflinching.

TAHEI: Koharu, I'm a townsman. I've never worn a sword, but I've lots of New Silver [20] at my place, and I think that the glint could twist a mere couple of swords out of joint. Imagine that wretch from the toilet paper shop, with a capital as thin as tissue, trying to compete with the Lone Wolf! That's the height of impertinence! I'll wander down now from Sakura Bridge to Middle Street, and if I meet that Wastepaper along the way, I'll trample him under foot. Come on, men.

NARRATOR: Their gestures, at least, have a cavalier assurance as they swagger off, taking up the whole street.

The samurai customer patiently endures the fool, indifferent to his remarks because of the surroundings, but every word of gossip about Jihei, whether for good or ill, affects Koharu. She is so depressed that she stands there blankly, unable even to greet her guest. Sugi, the maid from the Kinokuni House, runs up from home, looking annoyed.

---

[18] Customers visiting the Quarter by day wear these deep wicker hats (which virtually conceal the face) in order to preserve the secrecy of their visits; but this customer wears a hat even at night, when the darkness normally is sufficient protection.

[19] A play on words devolving on the syllables *ami*, part of the name Amida and on *amigasa*, meaning "woven hat".

[20] Good-quality coinage of about 1720. It was necessary to specify the kind of silver one meant because devaluations and revaluations altered the value of coins of nominally the same denomination.

SUGI: When I left you here a while ago, Miss Koharu, your guest hadn't appeared yet, and they gave me a terrible scolding when I got back for not having checked on him. I'm very sorry, sir, but please excuse me a minute.

NARRATOR: She lifts the woven hat and examines the face.

SUGI: Oh—it's not him! There's nothing to worry about, Koharu. Ask your guest to keep you for the whole night, and show him how sweet you can be. Give him a barrelful of nectar! [21] Good-by, madam, I'll see you later, honey.

NARRATOR: She takes her leave with a cloying stream of puns. The extremely hard-baked [22] samurai is furious.

SAMURAI: What's the meaning of this? You'd think from the way she appraised my face that I was a tea canister or a porcelain cup! I didn't come here to be trifled with. It's difficult enough for me to leave the Residence even by day, and in order to spend the night away I had to ask the senior officer's permission and sign the register. You can see how complicated the regulations make things. But I'm in love, miss, just from hearing about you, and I wanted very badly to spend a night with you. I came here a while ago without an escort and made the arrangements with the teahouse. I had been looking forward to your kind reception, a memory to last me a lifetime, but you haven't so much as smiled at me or said a word of greeting. You keep your head down, as if you were counting money in your lap. Aren't you afraid of getting a stiff neck? Madam—I've never heard the like. Here I come to a teahouse, and I must play the part of night nurse in a maternity room!

PROPRIETRESS: You're quite right, sir. Your surprise is entirely justified, considering that you don't know the reasons. This girl is deeply in love with a customer named Kamiji. It's been Kamiji today and Kamiji tomorrow, with nobody else allowed a chance at her. Her other customers have scattered in every direction, like leaves in a storm. When two people get so carried away with each other, it often leads to trouble, for both the customer and the girl. In the first place, it inteferes with business, and the owner, whoever he may be, is bound to prevent it. That's why all her guests are examined. Koharu is nat-

[21] I have altered the imagery used by the maid from puns on saltiness (soy sauce, green vegetables, etc.) to puns on sweetness, somewhat easier to manage in English.

[22] A technical term of pottery making, meaning "hard-fired". Here used to introduce the mention of "tea canister" and "porcelain cup".

urally depressed—it's only to be expected. You are annoyed, which is equally to be expected. But, speaking as the proprietress here, it seems to me that the essential thing is for you to meet each other halfway and cheer up. Come, have a drink.—Act a little more lively, Koharu.

NARRATOR: Koharu, without answering, lifts her tear-stained face.

KOHARU: Tell me, samurai, they say that, if you're going to kill yourself anyway, people who die during the Ten Nights [23] are sure to become Buddhas. Is that really true?

SAMURAI: How should I know? Ask the priest at your family temple.

KOHARU: Yes, that's right. But there's something I'd like to ask a samurai. If you're committing suicide, it'd be a lot more painful, wouldn't it, to cut your throat rather than hang yourself?

SAMURAI: I've never tried cutting my throat to see whether or not it hurt. Please ask more sensible questions.—What an unpleasant girl!

NARRATOR: Samurai though he is, he looks nonplussed.

PROPRIETRESS: Koharu, that's a shocking way to treat a guest the first time you meet him. I'll go and get my husband. We'll have some saké together. That ought to liven things a bit.

NARRATOR: The gate she leaves is illumined by the evening moon low in the sky; the clouds and the passers in the street have thinned.

For long years there has lived in Temma, the seat of the mighty god,[24] though not a god himself, Kamiji,[25] a name often bruited by the gongs of worldly gossip, so deeply, hopelessly, is he tied to Koharu by the ropes [26] of an ill-starred love. Now is the tenth moon, the month when no gods will unite them; [27] they are thwarted in their love, unable to meet. They swore in the last letters they exchanged that if only they could meet, that day would be their last. Night after night Jihei, ready for death, trudges to the Quarter, distractedly, as though his soul had left a body consumed by the fires of love.

[23] A period from the sixth to the sixteenth nights of the tenth moon when special Buddhist services were conducted in temples of the Pure Land (Jōdo) Sect. It was believed that persons who died during this period immediately became Buddhas.

[24] Temma, one of the principal districts of Osaka, was the site of the Tenjin Shrine, to the memory of the deified Sugawara no Michizane (845–903).

[25] The word kami for "paper" is the homophone of kami, "god". We have thus "Kami who is not a kami"—the paper dealer who is not a god.

[26] The sacred ropes (mishimenawa) at a Shinto shrine. Here mentioned (like the gongs) as a word related to the imagery of Shinto.

[27] The tenth month, called kannazuki (literally "month of no gods") was a time when the gods were believed to gather at Izumo; they were thus absent from the rest of Japan.

At a roadside eating stand he hears people gossiping about Koharu. "She's at Kawashō with a samurai customer," someone says, and immediately Jihei decides, "It will be tonight!"

He peers through the latticework window and sees a guest in the inside room, his face obscured by a hood. Only the moving chin is visible, and Jihei cannot hear what is said.

JIHEI: Poor Koharu! How thin her face is! She keeps it averted from the lamp. In her heart she's thinking only of me. I'll signal her that I'm here, and we'll run off together. Then which will it be— Umeda or Kitano? [28] Oh—I want to tell her I'm here. I want to call her.

NARRATOR: He beckons with his heart, his spirit flies to her, but his body, like a cicada's cast-off shell, clings to the latticework. He weeps with impatience.

The guest in the inside room gives a great yawn.

SAMURAI: What a bore, playing nursemaid to a prostitute with worries on her mind!—The street seems quiet now. Let's go to the end room. We can at least distract ourselves by looking at the lanterns. Come with me.

NARRATOR: They go together to the outer room. Jihei, alarmed, squeezes into the patch of shadow under the lattice window. Inside they do not realize that anyone eavesdrops.

SAMURAI: I've been noticing your behavior and the little things you've said this evening. It's plain to me that you intend a love suicide with Kamiji, or whatever his name is—the man the hostess mentioned. I'm sure I'm right. I realize that no amount of advice or reasoning is likely to penetrate the ears of somebody bewitched by the god of death, but I must say that you're exceedingly foolish. The boy's family won't blame him for his recklessness, but they will blame and hate you. You'll be shamed by the public exposure of your body. Your parents may be dead, for all I know, but if they're alive, you'll be punished in hell as a wicked daughter. Do you suppose that you'll become a Buddha? You and your lover won't even be able to fall smoothly into hell together! What a pity—and what a tragedy! This is only our first meeting but, as a samurai, I can't let you die without trying to save you. No doubt money's the problem. I'd like to help, if five or ten *ryō* would be of service. I swear by the god Hachiman

[28] Both places had well-known cemeteries.

and by my good fortune as a samurai that I will never reveal to anyone
what you tell me. Open your heart without fear.

NARRATOR: He whispers these words. She joins her hands and bows.

KOHARU: I'm extremely grateful. Thank you for your kind words
and for swearing an oath to me, someone you've never had for a lover
or even a friend. I'm so grateful that I'm crying.—Yes, it's as they
say, when you've something on your mind it shows on your face. You
were right. I have promised Kamiji to die with him. But we've been
completely prevented from meeting by my master, and Jihei, for various
reasons, can't ransom me at once. My contracts with my former master [29] and my present one still have five years to run. If somebody
else claimed me during that time, it would be a blow to me, of course,
but a worse disgrace to Jihei's honor. He suggested that it would be
better if we killed ourselves, and I agreed. I was caught by obligations
from which I could not withdraw, and I promised him before I knew
what I was doing. I said, "We'll watch for a chance, and I'll slip out
when you give the signal." "Yes," he said, "slip out somehow." Ever
since then I've been leading a life of uncertainty, never knowing from
one day to the next when my last hour will come.

I have a mother living in a back alley south of here. She has no one
but me to depend on, and she does piecework to eke out a living. I
keep thinking that after I'm dead she'll become a beggar or an outcast, and maybe she'll die of starvation. That's the only sad part about
dying. I have just this one life. I'm ashamed that you may think me
a coldhearted woman, but I must endure the shame. The most important thing is that I don't want to die. I beg you, please help me to
stay alive.

NARRATOR: As she speaks the samurai nods thoughtfully. Jihei,
crouching outside, hears her words with astonishment; they are so
unexpected to his manly heart that he feels like a monkey who has
tumbled from a tree. He is frantic with agitation.

JIHEI (*to himself*): Then was everything a lie? Ahhh—I'm furious!
For two whole years I've been bewitched by that rotten she-fox! Shall
I break in and kill her with one blow of my sword? Or shall I
satisfy my anger by shaming her to her face?

NARRATOR: He gnashes his teeth and weeps in chagrin. Inside the
house Koharu speaks through her tears.

---

[29] The master at the bathhouse where Koharu formerly worked.

KOHARU: It's a curious thing to ask, but would you please show the kindness of a samurai and become my customer for the rest of this year and into next spring? Whenever Jihei comes, intent on death, please interfere and force him to postpone and postpone his plan. In this way our relations can be broken quite naturally. He won't have to kill himself, and my life will also be saved.—What evil connection from a former existence made us promise to die? How I regret it now!

NARRATOR: She weeps, leaning on the samurai's knee.

SAMURAI: Very well, I'll do as you ask. I think I can help you.—But there's a draft blowing. Somebody may be watching.

NARRATOR: He slams shut the latticework *shōji*. Jihei, listening outside, is in a frenzy.

JIHEI: Exactly what you'd expect from a whore, a cheap whore! I misjudged her foul nature. She robbed the soul from my body, the thieving harlot! Shall I slash her down or run her through? What am I to do?

NARRATOR: The shadows of two profiles fall on the *shōji*.

JIHEI: I'd like to give her a taste of my fist and trample her.—What are they chattering about? See how they nod to each other! Now she's bowing to him, whispering and sniveling. I've tried to control myself —I've pressed my chest, I've stroked it—but I can't stand any more. This is too much to endure!

NARRATOR: His heart pounds wildly as he unsheathes his dirk, a Magoroku of Seki. "Koharu's side must be here," he judges, and stabs through an opening in the latticework. But Koharu is too far away for his thrust, and though she cries out in terror, she remains unharmed. Her guest instantly leaps at Jihei, grabs his hands, and jerks them through the latticework. With his sword knot he quickly and securely fastens Jihei's hands to the window upright.

SAMURAI: Don't make any outcry, Koharu. You are not to look at him.

NARRATOR: At this moment the proprietor and his wife return. They exclaim in alarm.

SAMURAI: This needn't concern you. Some ruffian ran his sword through the *shōji*, and I've tied his arms to the latticework. I have my own way of dealing with him. Don't untie the cord. If you attract a crowd, the place is sure to be thrown in an uproar. Let's all go inside. Come with me, Koharu. We'll go to bed.

NARRATOR: Koharu answers, "Yes," but she recognizes the handle of the dirk, and the memory—if not the blade—transfixes her breast.

KOHARU: There're always people doing crazy things in the Quarter when they've had too much to drink. Why don't you let him go without making any trouble? I think that's best, don't you, Kawashō?

SAMURAI: Out of the question. Do as I say—inside, all of you. Koharu, come along.

NARRATOR: Jihei can still see their shadows even after they enter the inner room, but he is bound to the spot, his hands held in fetters which grip him the tighter as he struggles, his body beset by suffering as he tastes a living shame worse than a dog's.[30] More determined than ever to die, he sheds tears of blood, a pitiful sight.

Tahei the Lone Wolf returns from his carousing.

TAHEI: That's Jihei standing by Kawashō's window. I'll give him a tossing.

NARRATOR: He catches Jihei by the collar and starts to lift him over his back.

JIHEI: Owww!

TAHEI: Owww? What kind of weakling are you? Oh, I see—you're tied here. You must've been pulling off a robbery. You dirty pickpocket! You rotten pickpocket!

NARRATOR: He drubs Jihei mercilessly.

TAHEI: You burglar! You convict!

NARRATOR: He kicks him wildly.

TAHEI: Kamiya Jihei's been caught burgling, and they've tied him up!

NARRATOR: Passersby and people of the neighborhood, attracted by his shouts, quickly gather. The samurai rushes from the house.

SAMURAI: Who's calling him a burglar? You? Tell what Jihei's stolen! Out with it!

NARRATOR: He seizes Tahei and forces him into the dirt. Tahei rises to his feet only for the samurai to kick him down again and again. He grips Tahei.

SAMURAI: Jihei! Trample him to your heart's content!

NARRATOR: He pushes Tahei under Jihei's feet. Bound though he is, Jihei stamps furiously over Tahei's face. Tahei, thoroughly trampled and covered with mire, gets to his feet and glares around him.

[30] A proverb of Buddhist origin, "Suffering follows one like a dog," is imbedded in the text.

TAHEI (*to bystander*): How could you fools stand there calmly and let him step on me? I've memorized every one of your faces, and I intend to pay you back. Remember that!

NARRATOR: He makes his escape, still determined to have the last word. The spectators burst out laughing.

VOICES: Listen to him brag, even after he's been trampled on! Let's throw him from the bridge and give him a drink of water! Don't let him get away!

NARRATOR: They chase after him. When the crowd has dispersed, the samurai approaches Jihei and unfastens the knots. He shows his face with his hood removed.

JIHEI: Magoemon! My brother! How shaming!

NARRATOR: He sinks to the ground and weeps, prostrating himself in the dirt.

KOHARU: Are you his brother, sir?

NARRATOR: Koharu runs to them. Jihei, catching her by the front of the kimono, forces her to the ground.

JIHEI: Beast! She-fox! I'd sooner trample on you than on Tahei!

NARRATOR: He raises his foot, but Magoemon calls out.

MAGOEMON: That's the kind of foolishness responsible for all your trouble. A prostitute's business is to deceive men. Have you just now waked up to that? I've seen to the bottom of her heart the very first time I met her, but you're so scatter-brained that in over two years of intimacy with the woman you never discovered what she was thinking. Instead of stamping on Koharu, why don't you use your feet on your own misguided disposition?—It's deplorable. You're my younger brother, but you're almost thirty, and you've got a six-year-old boy and a four-year-old girl, Kantarō and Osue. You run a shop with a thirty-six foot frontage,[31] but you don't seem to realize that your whole fortune's collapsing. You shouldn't have to be lectured to by your brother. Your father-in-law is your aunt's husband, and your mother-in-law is your aunt. They've always been like real parents to you. Your wife Osan is my cousin too. The ties of marriage are multiplied by those of blood. But when the family has a reunion the only subject of discussion is our mortification over your incessant visits to Sonezaki. I feel sorry for our poor aunt. You know what a stiff-necked gentleman of

---

[31] It was customary to refer to the size of shops by giving their frontage on the street.

the old school her husband Gozaemon is. He's forever flying into a rage and saying, "We've been tricked by your nephew. He's deserted our daughter. I'll take Osan back and ruin Jihei's reputation throughout Temma." Our aunt, with all the heartache to bear herself, sometimes sides with him and sometimes with you. She's worried herself sick. What an ingrate, not to appreciate how she's defended you in your shame! This one offense is enough to make you the target for Heaven's future punishment!

I realized that your marriage couldn't last much longer at this rate. I decided, in the hopes of relieving our aunt's worries, that I'd see with my own eyes what kind of woman Koharu was, and work out some sort of solution afterwards. I consulted the proprietor here, then came myself to investigate the cause of your sickness. I see now how natural it was that you should desert your wife and children. What a faithful prostitute you discovered! I congratulate you!

And here I am, Magoemon the Miller,[32] known far and wide for my paragon of a brother, dressed up like a masquerader at a festival or maybe a lunatic! I put on swords for the first time in my life, and announced myself, like a bit player in a costume piece, as an officer at a residence. I feel like an absolute idiot with these swords, but there's nowhere I can dispose of them now.—It's so infuriating—and ridiculous—that it's given me a pain in the chest.

NARRATOR: He gnashes his teeth and grimaces, attempting to hide his tears. Koharu, choking the while with emotion, can only say:

KOHARU: Yes, you're entirely right.

NARRATOR: The rest is lost in tears. Jihei pounds the earth with his fist.

JIHEI: I was wrong. Forgive me, Magoemon. For three years I've been possessed by that witch. I've neglected my parents, relatives—even my wife and children—and wrecked my fortune, all because I was deceived by Koharu, that sneak thief! I'm utterly mortified. But I'm through with her now, and I'll never set foot here again. Weasel! Vixen! Sneak thief! Here's proof that I've broken with her!

NARRATOR: He pulls out the amulet bag which has rested next to his skin.

[32] Magoemon is a dealer in flour (for noodles). His shop name Konaya—"the flour merchant"—is used almost as a surname, in the manner that Jihei is known as Kamiya Jihei.

JIHEI: Here are the written oaths we've exchanged, one at the beginning of each month, twenty-nine in all. I return them. This means our love and affection are over. Take them.

NARRATOR: He flings the notes at her.

JIHEI: Magoemon, collect from her my pledges. Please make sure you get them all. Then burn them with your own hands. (*To Koharu.*) Hand them to my brother.

KOHARU: As you wish.

NARRATOR: In tears, she surrenders the amulet bag. Magoemon opens it.

MAGOEMON: One, two, three, four . . . ten . . . twenty-nine. They're all here. There's also a letter from a woman. What's this?

NARRATOR: He starts to unfold it.

KOHARU: That's an important letter. I can't let you see it.

NARRATOR: She clings to Magoemon's arm, but he pushes her away. He holds the letter to the lamplight and examines the address, "To Miss Koharu from Kamiya Osan." As soon as he reads the words, he casually thrusts the letter into his kimono.

MAGOEMON: Koharu. A while ago I swore by my good fortune as a samurai, but now Magoemon the Miller swears by his good fortune as a businessman that he will show this letter to no one, not even his wife. I alone will read it, then burn it with the oaths. You can trust me. I will not break this oath.

KOHARU: Thank you. You save my honor.

NARRATOR: She bursts into tears again.

JIHEI (*laughs contemptuously*): Save your honor! You talk like a human being! (*To Magoemon.*) I don't want to see her cursed face another minute. Let's go. No—I can't hold so much resentment and bitterness! I'll kick her one in the face, a memory to treasure for the rest of my life. Excuse me, please.

NARRATOR: He strides up to Koharu and stamps on the ground.

JIHEI: For three years I've loved you, delighted in you, longed for you, adored you, but today my foot will say my only farewells.

NARRATOR: He kicks her sharply on the forehead and bursts into tears. The brothers leave, forlorn figures. Koharu, unhappy woman, raises her voice in lament as she watches them go. Is she faithful or unfaithful? Her true feelings are hidden in the words penned by Jihei's

wife, a letter no one has seen. Jihei goes his separate way without
learning the truth.[33]

ACT TWO

Scene: The house and shop of Kamiya Jihei.
Time: Ten days later.

NARRATOR: The busy street that runs straight to Tenjin Bridge[34]
named for the god of Temma, bringer of good fortune, is known as
the Street Before the Kami,[35] and here a paper shop does business under
the name Kamiya Jihei. The paper is honestly sold, the shop well
situated; it is a long-established firm, and customers come thick as
raindrops.

Outside crowds pass in the street, on their way to the Ten Nights
service, while inside the husband dozes in the *kotatsu*,[36] shielded from
draughts by a screen at his pillow. His wife Osan keeps solitary, anxious watch over shop and house.

OSAN: The days are so short—it's dinnertime already, but Tama still
hasn't returned from her errand to Ichinokawa.[37] I wonder what can
be keeping her. That scamp Sangorō isn't back either. The wind is
freezing. I'm sure the children will both be cold. He doesn't even
realize that it's time for Osue to be nursed. Heaven preserve me from
ever becoming such a fool! What an infuriating creature!

NARRATOR: She speaks to herself.

KANTARŌ: Mama, I've come back all by myself.

NARRATOR: Her son, the older child, runs up to the house.

OSAN: Kantarō—is that you? What's happened to Osue and Sangorō?

KANTARŌ: They're playing by the shrine. Osue wanted her milk and
she was bawling her head off.

---

[33] An extremely complicated set of word plays runs through the last two sentences. See
Shively, p. 113.

[34] The reference is to Temma Tenjin, the name as a deity of Sugawara no Michizane.

[35] Again a play on the words *kami* (god) and *kami* (paper).

[36] A source of heat in which a charcoal burner is placed under a low, quilt-covered
table.

[37] Ichinokawa was the site of a large vegetable market near the north end of Tenjin
Bridge.

OSAN: I was sure she would. Oh—your hands and feet are frozen stiff as nails! Go and warm yourself at the *kotatsu.* Your father's sleeping there.—What am I to do with that idiot?

NARRATOR: She runs out impatiently to the shop just as Sangorō shuffles back, alone.

OSAN: Come here, you fool! Where have you left Osue?

SANGORŌ: You know, I must've lost her somewhere. Maybe somebody's picked her up. Should I go back for her?

OSAN: How could you? If any harm has come to my precious child, I'll beat you to death!

NARRATOR: But even as she screams at him, the maid Tama returns with Osue on her back.

TAMA: The poor child—I found her in tears at the corner. Sangorō, when you're supposed to look after the child, do it properly.

OSAN: You poor dear. You must want your milk.

NARRATOR: She joins the others by the *kotatsu* and suckles the child.

OSAN: Tama—give that fool a taste of something that he'll remember! [38]

NARRATOR: Sangorō shakes his head.

SANGORŌ: No, thanks. I gave each of the children two tangerines just a while ago at the shrine, and I tasted five myself.

NARRATOR: Fool though he is, bad puns come from him nimbly enough, and the others can only smile despite themselves.

TAMA: Oh—I've become so involved with this half-wit that I almost forgot to tell you, ma'am, that Mr. Magoemon and his aunt [39] are on their way here from the west.

OSAN: Oh dear! I'll have to wake Jihei in that case. (*To Jihei.*) Please get up. Mother and Magoemon are coming. They'll be upset again if you let them see you, a businessman, sleeping in the afternoon, with the day so short as it is.

JIHEI: All right.

NARRATOR: He struggles to a sitting position and, with his abacus in one hand, pulls his account book to him with the other.

JIHEI: Two into ten goes five, three into nine goes three, three into six goes two, seven times eight is fifty-six.

NARRATOR: His fifty-six-year old aunt enters with Magoemon.

[38] A pun on the two meanings of *kurawasu:* "to cause to eat" and "to beat".

[39] Magoemon's (and Jihei's) aunt, but Osan's mother.

JIHEI: Magoemon, aunt. How good of you. Please come in. I was in the midst of some urgent calculations. Four nines makes thirty-six *momme*. Three sixes make eighteen *fun*. That's two *momme* less two *fun*.[40] Kantarō! Osue! Granny and Uncle have come! Bring the tobacco tray! One times three makes three. Osan, serve the tea![41]

NARRATOR: He jabbers away.

AUNT: We haven't come for tea or tobacco. Osan, you're young I know, but you're the mother of two children, and your excessive forbearance does you no credit. A man's dissipation can always be traced to his wife's carelessness. Remember, it's not only the man who's disgraced when he goes bankrupt and his marriage breaks up. You'd do well to take notice of what's going on and assert yourself a bit more.

MAGOEMON: It's foolish to hope for any results, aunt. The scoundrel even deceives me, his elder brother. Why should he take to heart criticism from his wife? Jihei—you played me for a fool. After showing me how you returned Koharu's pledges, here you are, not ten days later, redeeming her! What does this mean? I suppose your urgent calculations are of Koharu's debts! I've had enough!

NARRATOR: He snatches away the abacus and flings it clattering into the hallway.

JIHEI: You're making an enormous fuss without any cause. I haven't crossed the threshold since the last time I saw you except to go twice to the wholesalers in Imabashi and once to the Tenjin Shrine. I haven't even thought of Koharu, much less redeemed her.

AUNT: None of your evasions! Last evening at the Ten Nights service I heard the people in the congregation gossiping. Everybody was talking about the great patron from Temma who'd fallen in love with a prostitute named Koharu from the Kinokuni House in Sonezaki. They said he'd driven away her other guests and was going to ransom her in the next couple of days. There was all kinds of gossip about the abundance of money and fools even in these days of high prices.

My husband Gozaemon has been hearing about Koharu constantly, and he's sure that her great patron from Temma must be you, Jihei. He told me, "He's your nephew, but for me he's a stranger, and my daughter's happiness is my chief concern. Once he ransoms the prosti-

[40] Meaningless calculations. Twenty *fun* made two *momme*.
[41] The name Osan echoes the word *san* (three).

tute he'll no doubt sell his wife to a brothel. I intend to take her back before he starts selling her clothes." He was halfway out of the house before I could restrain him. "Don't get so excited. We can settle this calmly. First we must make sure whether or not the rumors are true." That's why Magoemon and I are here now. He was telling me a while ago that the Jihei of today was not the Jihei of yesterday—that you'd broken all connections with Sonezaki and completely reformed. But now I hear that you've had a relapse. What disease can this be? Your father was my brother. When the poor man was on his deathbed, he lifted his head from the pillow and begged me to look after you, as my son-in-law and nephew. I've never forgotten those last words, but your perversity has made a mockery of his request!

NARRATOR: She collapses in tears of resentment. Jihei claps his hands in sudden recognition.

JIHEI: I have it! The Koharu everybody's gossiping about is the same Koharu, but the great patron who's to redeem her is a different man. The other day, as my brother can tell you, Tahei—they call him the Lone Wolf because he hasn't any family or relations—started a fight and was trampled on. He gets all the money he needs from his home town, and he's been trying for a long time to redeem Koharu. I've always prevented him, but I'm sure he's decided that now is his chance. I have nothing to do with it.

NARRATOR: Osan brightens at his words.

OSAN: No matter how forbearing I might be—even if I were an angel —you don't suppose I'd encourage my husband to redeem a prostitute! In this instance at any rate there's not a word of untruth in what my husband has said. I'll be a witness to that, Mother.

NARRATOR: Husband's and wife's words tally perfectly.

AUNT: Then it's true?

NARRATOR: The aunt and nephew clap their hands with relief.

MAGOEMON: Well, I'm happy it's over, anyway. To make us feel doubly reassured, will you write an affidavit which will dispel any doubts your stubborn uncle may have?

JIHEI: Certainly. I'll write a thousand if you like.

MAGOEMON: Splendid! I happen to have bought this on the way here.

NARRATOR: Magoemon takes from the fold of his kimono a sheet of oath-paper from Kumano, the sacred characters formed by flocks of crows.[42] Instead of vows of eternal love, Jihei now signs under penalty of Heaven's wrath an oath that he will sever all ties and affections with Koharu. "If I should lie, may Bonten and Taishaku above, and the Four Great Kings below afflict me!"[43] So the text runs, and to it is appended the names of many Buddhas and gods. He signs his name, Kamiya Jihei, in bold characters, imprints the oath with a seal of blood, and proffers it.

OSAN: It's a great relief to me too. Mother, I have you and Magoemon to thank. Jihei and I have had two children, but this is his firmest pledge of affection. I hope you share my joy.

AUNT: Indeed we do. I'm sure that Jihei will settle down and his business will improve, now that he's in this frame of mind. It's been entirely for his sake and for love of the grandchildren that we've intervened. Come, Magoemon, let's be on our way. I'm anxious to set my husband's mind at ease.—It's become chilly here. See that the children don't catch cold.—This too we owe to the Buddha of the Ten Nights. I'll say a prayer of thanks before I go. Hail, Amida Buddha!

NARRATOR: She leaves, her heart innocent as Buddha's. Jihei is perfunctory even about seeing them to the door. Hardly have they crossed the threshold than he slumps down again at the *kotatsu*. He pulls the checked quilting over his head.

OSAN: You still haven't forgotten Sonezaki, have you?

NARRATOR: She goes up to him in disgust and tears away the quilting. He is weeping; a waterfall of tears streams along the pillow, deep enough to bear him afloat. She tugs him upright and props his body against the *kotatsu* frame. She stares into his face.

OSAN: You're acting outrageously, Jihei. You shouldn't have signed that oath if you felt so reluctant to leave her. The year before last, on the middle day of the Boar of the tenth moon,[44] we lit the first fire in the *kotatsu* and celebrated by sleeping here together, pillow to pillow. Ever since then—did some demon or snake creep into my

---

[42] The charms issued by the Shinto shrine at Kumano were printed on the face with six Chinese characters, the strokes of which were in the shape of crows. The reverse side of these charms was used for writing oaths. See Shively, p. 116, for a fuller description.

[43] A formal oath. Bonten (Brahma) and Taishaku (Sakra), though Hindu gods, were considered to be protective deities of the Buddhist law. The four Deva kings served under Sakra and were also protectors of Buddhism.

[44] It was customary to light the first fire of the winter on this day, which would generally be towards the end of November in the Western calendar.

bosom that night?—for two whole years I've been condemned to keep watch over an empty nest. I thought that tonight at least, thanks to Mother and Magoemon, we'd share sweet words in bed as husbands and wives do, but my pleasure didn't last long. How cruel of you, how utterly heartless! Go ahead, cry your eyes out, if you're so attached to her. Your tears will flow into Shijimi River and Koharu, no doubt, will ladle them out and drink them! You're ignoble, inhuman.

NARRATOR: She embraces his knees and throws herself over him, moaning in supplication. Jihei wipes his eyes.

JIHEI: If tears of grief flowed from the eyes and tears of anger from the ears, I could show my heart without saying a word. But my tears all pour in the same way from my eyes, and there's no difference in their color. It's not surprising that you can't tell what's in my heart. I have not a shred of attachment left for that vampire in human skin, but I bear a grudge against Tahei. He has all the money he wants, no wife or children. He's schemed again and again to redeem her, but Koharu refused to give in, at least until I broke with her. She told me time and again, "You have nothing to worry about. I'll never let myself be redeemed by Tahei, not even if my ties with you are ended and I can no longer stay by your side. If my master is induced by Tahei's money to deliver me to him, I'll kill myself in a way that'll do you credit!" But think—not ten days have passed since I broke with her, and she's to be redeemed by Tahei! That rotten whore! That animal! No, I haven't a trace of affection left for her, but I can just hear how Tahei will be boasting. He'll spread the word around Osaka that my business has come to a standstill and I'm hard pressed for money. I'll meet with contemptuous stares from the wholesalers. I'll be dishonored. My heart is broken and my body burns with shame. What a disgrace! How maddening! I've passed the stage of shedding hot tears, tears of blood, sticky tears—my tears now are of molten iron!

NARRATOR: He collapses with weeping. Osan pales with alarm.

OSAN: If that's the situation, poor Koharu will surely kill herself.

JIHEI: You're too well bred, despite your intelligence, to understand her likes! What makes you suppose that faithless creature would kill herself? Far from it—she's probably taking moxa treatments and medicine to prolong her life!

OSAN: No, that's not true. I was determined never to tell you so long as I lived, but I'm afraid of the crime I'd be committing if I concealed the facts and let her die with my knowledge. I will reveal my great secret. There is not a grain of deceit in Koharu. It was I who schemed to end the relations between you. I could see signs that you were drifting towards suicide. I felt so unhappy that I wrote a letter, begging her as one woman to another to break with you, though I knew how painful it would be. I asked her to save your life. The letter must have moved her. She answered that she would give you up, though you were more precious than life itself, because she could not shirk her duty to me. I've kept her letter with me ever since—it's been like a protective charm. Could such a noble-hearted woman violate her promise and brazenly marry Tahei? When a woman—I no less than another—has given herself completely to a man, she does not change. I'm sure she'll kill herself. I'm sure of it. Ahhh—what a dreadful thing to have happened! Save her, please.

NARRATOR: Her voice rises in agitation. Her husband is thrown into a turmoil.

JIHEI: There was a letter in an unknown woman's hand among the written oaths she surrendered to my brother. It must have been from you. If that's the case, Koharu will surely commit suicide.

OSAN: Alas! I'd be failing in the obligations I owe her as another woman if I allowed her to die. Please go to her at once. Don't let her kill herself.

NARRATOR: Clinging to her husband, she melts in tears.

JIHEI: But what can I possibly do? It'd take half the amount of her ransom in earnest money merely to keep her out of Tahei's clutches. I can't save Koharu's life without administering a dose of 750 *momme* in New Silver.[45] How could I raise that much money in my present financial straits? Even if I crush my body to powder, where will the money come from?

OSAN: Don't exaggerate the difficulties. If that's all you need, it's simple enough.

NARRATOR: She goes to the wardrobe, and opening a small drawer takes out a bag fastened with cords of twisted silk. She unhesitantly tears it open and throws down a packet which Jihei retrieves.

JIHEI: What's this? Money? Four hundred *momme* in New Silver? How in the world—

NARRATOR: He stares astonished at this money he never put there.

---

[45] The medical images are occasioned by considering Koharu's plight as a sickness. If 750 *me* is half the sum needed to redeem Koharu, the total of 1,500 *me* (or 6,000 *me* in Old Silver) is considerably less than the 10 *kamme*, or 10,000 *me* in Old Silver, mentioned by Tahei. See above, p. 175

osan: I'll tell you later where this money came from. I've scraped it together to pay the bill for Iwakuni paper that falls due the day after tomorrow. We'll have to ask Magoemon to help us keep the business from betraying its insolvency. But Koharu comes first. The packet contains 400 *momme*. That leaves 350 *momme* to raise.

narrator: She unlocks a large drawer. From the wardrobe lightly fly kite-colored Hachijō silks; [46] a Kyoto crepe kimono lined in pale brown, insubstantial as her husband's life which flickers today and may vanish tomorrow; a padded kimono of Osue's, a flaming scarlet inside and out—Osan flushes with pain to part with it; Kantarō's sleeveless, unlined jacket—if she pawns this, he'll be cold this winter. Next comes a garment of striped Gunnai silk lined in pale blue and never worn, and then her best formal costume—heavy black silk dyed with her family crest, an ivy leaf in a ring. They say that those joined by marriage ties can even go naked at home, though outside the house clothes make the man: she snatches up even her husband's finery, a silken cloak, making fifteen articles in all.

osan: The very least the pawnshop can offer is 350 *momme* in New Silver.

narrator: Her face glows as though she already held the money she needs; she hides in the one bundle her husband's shame and her own obligation, and puts her love in besides.

osan: It doesn't matter if the children and I have nothing to wear. My husband's reputation concerns me more. Ransom Koharu. Save her. Assert your honor before Tahei.

narrator: But Jihei's eyes remain downcast all the while, and he is silently weeping.

jihei: Yes, I can pay the earnest money and keep her out of Tahei's hands. But once I've redeemed her, I'll either have to maintain her in a separate establishment or bring her here. Then what will become of you?

narrator: Osan is at a loss to answer.

osan: Yes, what shall I do? Shall I become your children's nurse or the cook? Or perhaps the retired mistress of the house?

narrator: She falls to the floor with a cry of woe.

jihei: That would be too selfish. I'd be afraid to accept such gen-

[46] Hachijō silks were woven with a warp of brown and a woof of yellow thread to give a color like that of the bird called the kite. "Kite" also suggests that the material flies out of the cupboard.

erosity. Even if the punishment for my crimes against my parents, against Heaven, against the gods and the Buddhas fails to strike me, the punishment for my crimes against my wife alone will be sufficient to destroy all hope for the future life. Forgive me, I beg you.

NARRATOR: He joins his hands in tearful entreaty.

OSAN: Why should you bow before me? I don't deserve it. I'd be glad to rip the nails from my fingers and toes, to do anything which might serve my husband. I've been pawning my clothes for some time in order to scrape together the money for the paper wholesalers' bills. My wardrobe is empty, but I don't regret it in the least. But it's too late now to talk of such things. Hurry, change your cloak and go to her with a smile.

NARRATOR: He puts on an under kimono of Gunnai silk, a robe of heavy black silk, and a striped cloak. His sash of figured damask holds a dirk of middle length worked in gold: Buddha surely knows that tonight it will be stained with Koharu's blood.

JIHEI: Sangorō! Come here!

NARRATOR: Jihei loads the bundle on the servant's back, intending to take him along. Then he firmly thrusts the wallet next to his skin and starts towards the gate.

VOICE: Is Jihei at home?

NARRATOR: A man enters, removing his fur cap. They see—good heavens!—that it is Gozaemon.

OSAN *and* JIHEI: Ahhh—how fortunate that you should come at this moment!

NARRATOR: Husband and wife are upset and confused. Gozaemon snatches away Sangorō's bundle and sits heavily. His voice is sharp.

GOZAEMON: Stay where you are, harlot!—My esteemed son-in-law, what a rare pleasure to see you dressed in your finest attire, with a dirk and a silken cloak! Ahhh—that's how a gentleman of means spends his money! No one would take you for a paper dealer. Are you perchance on your way to the New Quarter? What commendable perseverance! You have no need for your wife, I take it.—Give her a divorce. I've come to take her home with me.

NARRATOR: He speaks needles and his voice is bitter. Jihei has not a word to reply.

OSAN: How kind of you, Father, to walk here on such a cold day. Do have a cup of tea.

NARRATOR: Offering the teacup serves as an excuse for edging closer.

osan: Mother and Magoemon came here a while ago, and they told my husband how much they disapproved of his visits to the New Quarter. Jihei was in tears and he wrote out an oath swearing he had reformed. He gave it to Mother. Haven't you seen it yet?

gozaemon: His written oath? Do you mean this?

narrator: He takes the paper from his kimono.

gozaemon: Libertines scatter vows and oaths wherever they go, as if they were monthly statements of accounts. I thought there was something peculiar about this oath, and now that I am here I can see I was right. Do you still swear to Bonten and Taishaku? Instead of such nonsense, write out a bill of divorcement!

narrator: He rips the oath to shreds and throws down the pieces. Husband and wife exchange looks of alarm, stunned into silence. Jihei touches his hands to the floor and bows his head.

jihei: Your anger is justified. If I were still my former self, I would try to offer explanations, but today I appeal entirely to your generosity. Please let me stay with Osan. I promise that even if I become a beggar or an outcast and must sustain life with the scraps that fall from other people's chopsticks, I will hold Osan in high honor and protect her from every harsh and bitter experience. I feel so deeply indebted to Osan that I cannot divorce her. You will understand that this is true as time passes and I show you how I apply myself to my work and restore my fortune. Until then please shut your eyes and allow us to remain together.

narrator: Tears of blood stream from his eyes and his face is pressed to the matting in contrition.

gozaemon: The wife of an outcast! That's all the worse. Write the bill of divorcement at once! I will verify and seal the furniture and clothes Osan brought in her dowry.

narrator: He goes to the wardrobe. Osan is alarmed.

osan: My clothes are all here. There's no need to examine them.

narrator: She runs up to forestall him, but Gozaemon pushes her aside and jerks open a drawer.

gozaemon: What does this mean?

narrator: He opens another drawer: it too is empty. He pulls out every last drawer, but not so much as a foot of patchwork cloth is to be seen. He tears open the wicker hampers, long boxes, and clothes chests.

GOZAEMON: Stripped bare, are they?

NARRATOR: His eyes set in fury. Jihei and Osan huddle under the striped *kotatsu* quilts, ready to sink into the fire with humiliation.[47]

GOZAEMON: This bundle looks suspicious.

NARRATOR: He unties the knots and dumps out the contents.

GOZAEMON: As I thought! You were sending these to the pawnshop, I take it. Jihei—you'd strip the skin from your wife's and your children's bodies to squander the money on your whore! Dirty thief! You're my wife's nephew, but an utter stranger to me, and I'm under no obligation to suffer for your sake. I'll explain to Magoemon what has happened and ask him to make good whatever inroads you've already made on Osan's belongings. But first, the bill of divorcement!

NARRATOR: Even if Jihei could escape through seven padlocked doors, eight thicknesses of chains, and a hundred girdling walls, he could not evade so stringent a demand.

JIHEI: I won't use a brush to write the bill of divorcement. Here's what I'll do instead! Good-by, Osan.

NARRATOR: He lays his hand on his dirk, but Osan clings to him.

OSAN: Father—Jihei admits that he's done wrong and he's apologized in every way. You press your advantage too hard. Jihei may be a stranger, but his children are your grandchildren. Have you no affection for them? I will not accept a bill of divorcement.

NARRATOR: She embraces her husband and raises her voice in tears.

GOZAEMON: Very well. I won't insist on it. Come with me, woman.

NARRATOR: He pulls her to her feet.

OSAN: No, I won't go. What bitterness makes you expose to such shame a man and wife who still love each other? I will not suffer it.

NARRATOR: She pleads with him, weeping, but he pays her no heed.

GOZAEMON: Is there some greater shame? I'll shout it through the town!

NARRATOR: He pulls her up, but she shakes free. Caught by the wrist she totters forward when—alas!—her toes brush against her sleeping children. They open their eyes.

CHILDREN: Mother dear, why is Grandfather, the bad man, taking you away? Whom will we sleep beside now?

NARRATOR: They call out after her.

OSAN: My poor dears! You've never spent a night away from Mother's

[47] I have omitted here an irrelevant allusion to Urashima Tarō. See Shively, p. 85.

side since you were born. Sleep tonight beside your father. (*To Jihei.*) Please don't forget to give the children their tonic before breakfast. —Oh, my heart is broken!

NARRATOR: These are her parting words. She leaves her children behind, abandoned as in the woods; the twin-trunked bamboo of conjugal love is sundered forever.

ACT THREE

Scene One: Sonezaki New Quarter, in front of the Yamato House.

Time: That night.

NARRATOR: This is Shijimi River, the haunt of love and affection. Its flowing water and the feet of passersby are stilled now at two in the morning, and the full moon shines clear in the sky. Here in the street a dim doorway lantern is marked "Yamatoya Dembei" in a single scrawl. The night watchman's clappers take on a sleepy cadence as he totters by on uncertain legs. The very thickness of his voice crying, "Beware of fire! Beware of fire!" tells how far advanced the night is. A serving woman from the upper town comes along, followed by a palanquin. "It's terribly late," she remarks to the bearers as she clatters open the side door of the Yamato House and steps inside.

SERVANT: I've come to take back Koharu of the Kinokuni House.

NARRATOR: Her voice is faintly heard outside. A few moments later, after hardly time enough to exchange three or four words of greeting, she emerges.

SERVANT: Koharu is spending the night. Bearers, you may leave now and get some rest. (*To proprietress, inside the doorway.*) Oh, I forgot to tell you, madam. Please keep an eye on Koharu. Now that the ransom to Tahei has been arranged and the money's been accepted, we're merely her custodians. Please don't let her drink too much saké.

NARRATOR: She leaves, having scattered at the doorway the seeds that before morning will turn Jihei and Koharu to dust.

At night between two and four even the teahouse kettle rests; the flame flickering in the low candle stand narrows; and the frost spreads in the cold river-wind of the deepening night. The master's voice breaks the stillness.

DEMBEI (*to Jihei*): It's still the middle of the night. I'll send somebody with you. (*To servants.*) Mr. Jihei is leaving. Wake Koharu. Call her here.

NARRATOR: Jihei slides open the side door.

JIHEI: No, Dembei, not a word to Koharu. I'll be trapped here till dawn if she hears I'm leaving. That's why I'm letting her sleep and slipping off this way. Wake her up after sunrise and send her back then. I'm returning home now and will leave for Kyoto immediately on business. I have so many engagements that I may not be able to return in time for the interim payment.[48] Please use the money I gave you earlier this evening to clear my account. I'd like you also to send 150 *me* of Old Silver to Kawashō for the moon-viewing party last month. Please get a receipt. Give Saietsubō [49] from Fukushima one piece of silver as a contribution to the Buddhist altar he's bought, and tell him to use it for a memorial service. Wasn't there something else? Oh yes—give Isoichi a tip of four silver coins. That's the lot. Now you can close up and get to bed. Good-by. I'll see you when I return from Kyoto.

NARRATOR: Hardly has he taken two or three steps than he turns back.

JIHEI: I forgot my dirk. Fetch it for me, won't you?—Yes, Dembei, this is one respect in which it's easier being a townsman. If I were a samurai and forgot my sword, I'd probably commit suicide on the spot!

DEMBEI: I completely forgot that I was keeping it for you. Yes, here's the knife with it.

NARRATOR: He gives the dirk to Jihei, who fastens it firmly into his sash.

JIHEI: I feel secure as long as I have this. Good night!

NARRATOR: He goes off.

DEMBEI: Please come back to Osaka soon! Thank you for your patronage!

NARRATOR: With this hasty farewell Dembei rattles the door bolt shut; then not another sound is heard as the silence deepens. Jihei pretends to leave, only to creep back again with stealthy steps. He

---

[48] On the last day of the tenth moon (November 29, 1720). This day was one of the times established during the course of the year for making payments.

[49] The name of a male entertainer in the Quarter. Fukushima was west of Sonezaki.

clings to the door of the Yamato House. As he peeps within he is
startled by shadows moving towards him. He takes cover at the house
across the way until the figures pass.

Magoemon the Miller, his heart pulverized with anxiety over his
younger brother, comes first, followed by the apprentice Sangorō
with Jihei's son Kantarō on his back. They hurry along until they
spy the lantern of the Yamato House. Magoemon pounds on the door.

MAGOEMON: Excuse me. Kamiya Jihei's here, isn't he? I'd like to
see him a moment.

NARRATOR: Jihei thinks, "It's my brother!" but dares not stir from his
place of concealment. From inside a man's sleep-laden voice is heard.

DEMBEI: Jihei left a while ago saying he was going up to Kyoto. He's
not here.

NARRATOR: Not another sound is heard. Magoemon's tears fall unchecked.

MAGOEMON (*to himself*): I ought to have met him on the way if
he'd been going home. I can't understand what takes him to Kyoto.
Ahhh—I'm trembling all over with worry. I wonder if he didn't take
Koharu with him.

NARRATOR: The thought pierces his heart; unable to bear the pain, he
pounds again on the door.

DEMBEI: Who is it, so late at night? We've gone to bed.

MAGOEMON: I'm sorry to disturb you, but I'd like to ask one more
thing. Has Koharu of the Kinokuni House left? I was wondering if she
mightn't have gone with Jihei.

DEMBEI: What's that? Koharu's upstairs, fast asleep.

MAGOEMON: That's a relief, anyway. There's no fear of a lovers' suicide. But where is he hiding himself causing me all this anxiety? He
can't imagine the agony of suspense that the whole family is going
through on his account. I'm afraid that bitterness towards his father-
in-law may make him forget himself and do something rash. I brought
Kantarō along, hoping he would help to dissuade Jihei, but the gesture
was in vain. I wonder why I failed to meet him?

NARRATOR: He murmurs to himself, his eyes moist with tears. Jihei's
hiding place is close enough for him to hear every word. He chokes
with emotion, but can only swallow his tears.

MAGOEMON: Sangorō! Where does the fool go night after night?
Don't you know anywhere else?

NARRATOR: Sangorō imagines that he himself is the fool referred to.

SANGORŌ: I know a couple of places, but I'm too embarrassed to mention them.

MAGOEMON: You know them? Where are they? Tell me.

SANGORŌ: Please don't scold me when you've heard. Every night I wander down below the warehouses by the market.

MAGOEMON: Imbecile! Who's asking about that? Come on, let's search the back streets. Don't let Kantarō catch a chill. The poor kid's having a cold time of it, thanks to that useless father of his. Still, if the worst the boy experiences is the cold I won't complain. I'm afraid that Jihei may cause him much greater pain. The scoundrel!

NARRATOR: But beneath the rancor in his heart of hearts is profound pity.

MAGOEMON: Let's look at the back street!

NARRATOR: They pass on. As soon as their figures have gone off a distance Jihei runs from his hiding place. Standing on tiptoes he gazes with yearning after them and cries out in his heart.

JIHEI: He cannot leave me to my death, though I am the worst of sinners! I remain to the last a burden to him! I'm unworthy of such kindness!

NARRATOR: He joins his hands and kneels in prayer.

JIHEI: If I may make one further request of your mercy, look after my children!

NARRATOR: These are his only words; for a while he chokes with tears.

JIHEI: At any rate, our decision's been made. Koharu must be waiting.

NARRATOR: He peers through a crack in the side door of the Yamato House and glimpses a figure.

JIHEI: That's Koharu, isn't it? I'll let her know I'm here.

NARRATOR: He clears his throat, their signal. "Ahem, ahem"—the sound blends with the clack of wooden clappers as the watchman comes from the upper street, coughing in the night wind. He hurries on his round of fire warning, "Take care! Beware!" Even this cry has a dismal sound to one in hiding. Jihei, concealing himself like the god of Katsuragi,[50] lets the watchman pass. He sees his chance and rushes to the side door, which softly opens from within.

[50] The god was so ashamed of his ugliness that he ventured forth only at night.

JIHEI: Koharu?

KOHARU: Were you waiting? Jihei—I want to leave quickly.

NARRATOR: She is all impatience, but the more hastily they open the door, the more likely people will be to hear the casters turning. They lift the door; it gives a moaning that thunders in their ears and in their hearts. Jihei lends a hand from the outside, but his fingertips tremble with the trembling of his heart. The door opens a quarter of an inch, a half, an inch—an inch ahead are the tortures of hell, but more than hell itself they fear the guardian-demon's eyes. At last the door opens, and with the joy of New Year's morn [51] Koharu slips out. They catch each other's hands. Shall they go north or south, west or east? Their pounding hearts urge them on, though they know not to what destination: turning their backs on the moon reflected in Shijimi River, they hurry eastward as fast as their legs will carry them.

Scene Two: The farewell journey of many bridges.

NARRATOR:

The running hand in texts of Nō is always Konoe style;
An actor in a woman's part is sure to wear a purple hat.[52]
Does some teaching of the Buddha as rigidly decree
That men who spend their days in evil haunts must end like
    this?

Poor creatures, though they would discover today their destiny in the Sutra of Cause and Effect,[53] tomorrow the gossip of the world will scatter like blossoms the scandal of Kamiya Jihei's love suicide, and, carved in cherry wood,[54] his story to the last detail will be printed in illustrated sheets.

Jihei, led on by the spirit of death—if such there be among the

[51] Mention of New Year is connected with Koharu's name, in which *haru* means "spring."
[52] The Konoe style of calligraphy, originated by Konoe Nobutada (1565–1614), was invariably used in books of Nō texts. Custom also decreed that young actors playing the parts of women cover their foreheads with a square of purple cloth to disguise the fact that they were shaven.
[53] A sacred text of Buddhism (Karma Sūtra); Chikamatsu here alludes to the line from that text: "If you wish to know the past cause, look at the present effect; if you wish to know the future effect, look at the present cause." See Shively, p. 125.
[54] The blocks from which illustrated books were printed were frequently of cherry wood. The illustrated sheets mentioned here featured current scandals, such as lovers' suicides.

gods—is resigned to this punishment for neglect of his trade. But at times—who could blame him?—his heart is drawn to those he has left behind, and it is hard to keep walking on. Even in the full moon's light, this fifteenth night of the tenth moon,[55] he cannot see his way ahead—a sign perhaps of the darkness in his heart? The frost now falling will melt by dawn but, even more quickly than this symbol of human frailty, the lovers themselves will melt away. What will become of the fragrance that lingered when he held her tenderly at night in their bedchamber?

This bridge, Tenjin Bridge, he has crossed every day, morning and night, gazing at Shijimi River to the west. Long ago, when Tenjin, then called Michizane,[56] was exiled to Tsukushi, his plum tree, following its master, flew in one bound to Dazaifu, and here is Plum-field Bridge.[57] Green Bridge recalls the aged pine that followed later, and Cherry Bridge the tree that withered away in grief over parting. Such are the tales still told, bespeaking the power of a single poem.[58]

JIHEI: Though born the parishioner of so holy and mighty a god, I shall kill you and then myself. If you ask the cause, it was that I lacked even the wisdom that might fill a tiny Shell Bridge.[59] Our stay in this world has been short as an autumn day. This evening will be the last of your nineteen, of my twenty-eight years. The time has come to cast away our lives. We promised we'd remain together faithfully, till you were an old woman and I an old man, but before we knew each other three full years, we have met this disaster. Look,

---

[55] November 14, 1720. In the lunar calendar the full moon occurs on the fifteenth of the month.

[56] Sugawara no Michizane, unfairly abused at court, was exiled to Dazaifu in Kyushu. When he was about to depart he composed a poem of farewell to his favorite plum tree. The tree, moved by this honor, flew after him to Kyushu. The cherry tree in his garden withered away in grief. Only the pine seemed indifferent, as Michizane complained in another poem. The pine thereupon also flew to Kyushu. See also n. 24, above.

[57] Umeda Bridge. "Green Bridge" is Midori-bashi.

[58] The poem by Michizane bewailing the inconstancy of his pine tree.

[59] Shijimi Bridge. Twelve bridges are mentioned in the *michiyuki*. The lovers' journey takes them along the north bank of Shijimi River to Shijimi Bridge, where they cross to Dōjima. At Little Naniwa Bridge they cross back again to Sonezaki. Continuing eastward, they cross Horikawa, then cross the Temma Bridge over the Ōkawa. At "Eight Houses" (Hakkenya) they journey eastward along the south bank of the river as far as Kyō Bridge. They cross this bridge to the tip of land at Katamachi, and then take the Onari Bridge to Amijima.

there is Ōe Bridge. We follow the river from Little Naniwa Bridge to Funairi Bridge. The farther we journey, the closer we approach the road to death.

NARRATOR: He laments. She clings to him.

KOHARU: Is this already the road to death?

NARRATOR: Falling tears obscure from each the other's face and threaten to immerse even the Horikawa bridges.

JIHEI: A few steps north and I could glimpse my house, but I will not turn back. I will bury in my breast all thoughts of my children's future, all pity for my wife. We cross southward over the river. Why did they call a place with as many buildings as a bridge has piers "Eight Houses"? Hurry, we want to arrive before the down-river boat from Fushimi comes—with what happy couples sleeping aboard!

Next is Temma Bridge, a frightening name [60] for us about to depart this world. Here the two streams Yodo and Yamato join in one great river, as fish with water, and as Koharu and I, dying on one blade will cross together the River of Three Fords.[61] I would like this water for our tomb offering!

KOHARU: What have we to grieve about? Though in this world we could not stay together, in the next and through each successive world to come until the end of time we shall be husband and wife. Every summer for my devotions [62] I have copied the All Compassionate and All Merciful Chapter of the Lotus Sutra, in the hope that we may be reborn on one lotus.

NARRATOR: They cross over Kyō Bridge and reach the opposite shore.[63]

KOHARU: If I can save living creatures at will when once I mount a lotus calyx in Paradise and become a Buddha, I want to protect women of my profession, so that never again will there be love suicides.

NARRATOR: This unattainable prayer stems from worldly attachment, but it touchingly reveals her heart.

[60] The characters used for Temma mean literally "demon".

[61] A river in the Buddhist underworld which had to be crossed to reach the world of the dead. Mention here is induced arithmetically: one blade plus two people equal three fords.

[62] It was customary for Buddhist monks and some of the laity in Japan to observe a summer retreat from the sixteenth day of the fourth moon to the fifteenth day of the seventh moon, a period of ninety days. During this time they practiced various austerities and copied out the holy books or wrote the Buddha's name over and over.

[63] "Opposite shore" suggests the Buddhist term *higan* (nirvana).

They cross Onari Bridge.[64] The waters of Noda Creek are shrouded with morning haze; the mountain tips show faintly white.

JIHEI: Listen—the voices of the temple bells begin to boom. How much farther can we go on this way? We are not fated to live any longer—let us make an end quickly. Come this way.

NARRATOR: Tears are strung with the 108 beads of the rosaries in their hands. They have come now to Amijima, to the Daichō Temple; the overflowing sluice gate of a little stream beside a bamboo thicket will be their place of death.

Scene Three: Amijima.

JIHEI: No matter how far we walk, there'll never be a spot marked "For Suicides." Let us kill ourselves here.

NARRATOR: He takes her hand and sits on the ground.

KOHARU: Yes, that's true. One place is as good as another to die. But I've been thinking on the way that if they find our dead bodies together people will say that Koharu and Jihei committed a lovers' suicide. Osan will think then that I treated as mere scrap paper the letter I sent promising her, when she asked me not to kill you, that I would not, and vowing to break all relations. She will be sure that I lured her precious husband into a lovers' suicide. She will despise me as a one-night prostitute, a false woman with no sense of decency. I fear her contempt more than the slander of a thousand or ten thousand strangers. I can imagine how she will resent and envy me. That is the greatest obstacle to my salvation. Kill me here, then choose another spot, far away, for yourself.

NARRATOR: She leans against him. Jihei joins in her tears of pleading.

JIHEI: What foolish worries! Osan has been taken back by my father-in-law. I've divorced her. She and I are strangers now. Why should you feel obliged to a divorced woman? You were saying on the way that you and I will be husband and wife through each successive world until the end of time. Who can criticize us, who can be jealous if we die side by side?

KOHARU: But who is responsible for your divorce? You're even less reasonable than I. Do you suppose that our bodies will accompany

[64] The name Onari is used here for the bridge more properly called Bizenjima because of a play on words meaning "to become a Buddha".

us to the afterworld? We may die in different places, our bodies may be pecked by kites and crows, but what does it matter as long as our souls are twined together? Take me with you to heaven or to hell!

NARRATOR: She sinks again in tears.

JIHEI: You're right. Our bodies are made of earth, water, fire, and wind, and when we die they revert to emptiness. But our souls will not decay, no matter how often reborn. And here's a guarantee that our souls will be married and never part!

NARRATOR: He whips out his dirk and slashes off his black locks at the base of the top knot.

JIHEI: Look, Koharu. As long as I had this hair I was Kamiya Jihei, Osan's husband, but cutting it has made me a monk. I have fled the burning house of the three worlds of delusion; I am a priest, unencumbered by wife, children, or worldly possessions. Now that I no longer have a wife named Osan, you owe her no obligations either.

NARRATOR: In tears he flings away the hair.

KOHARU: I am happy.

NARRATOR: Koharu takes up the dirk and ruthlessly, unhesitantly, slices through her flowing Shimada coiffure. She casts aside the tresses she has so often washed and combed and stroked. How heartbreaking to see their locks tangled with the weeds and midnight frost of this desolate field!

JIHEI: We have escaped the inconstant world, a nun and a priest. Our duties as husband and wife belong to our profane past. It would be best to choose quite separate places for our deaths, a mountain for one, the river for the other. We will pretend that the ground above this sluice gate is a mountain. You will die there. I shall hang myself by this stream. The time of our deaths will be the same, but the method and place will differ. In this way we can honor to the end our duty to Osan. Give me your under sash.

NARRATOR: Its fresh violet color and fragrance will be lost in the winds of impermanence; the crinkled silk long enough to wind twice round her body will bind two worlds, this and the next. He firmly fastens one end to the crosspiece of the sluice, then twists the other into a noose for his neck. He will hang for love of his wife like the "pheasant in the hunting grounds." [65]

[65] A reference to a poem by Ōtomo no Yakamochi (718–85): "The pheasant foraging in the fields of spring reveals his whereabouts to man as he cries for his mate" (*Shūishū*, no. 21).

Koharu watches Jihei prepare for his death. Her eyes swim with tears, her mind is distraught.

KOHARU: Is that how you're going to kill yourself?—If we are to die apart, I have only a little while longer by your side. Come near me.

NARRATOR: They take each other's hands.

KOHARU: It's over in a moment with a sword, but I'm sure you'll suffer. My poor darling!

NARRATOR: She cannot stop the silent tears.

JIHEI: Can suicide ever be pleasant, whether by hanging or cutting the throat? You mustn't let worries over trifles disturb the prayers of your last moments. Keep your eyes on the westward-moving moon, and worship it as Amida himself.[66] Concentrate your thoughts on the Western Paradise. If you have any regrets about leaving the world, tell me now, then die.

KOHARU: I have none at all, none at all. But I'm sure you must be worried about your children.

JIHEI: You make me cry all over again by mentioning them. I can almost see their faces, sleeping peacefully, unaware, poor dears, that their father is about to kill himself. They're the one thing I can't forget.

NARRATOR: He droops to the ground with weeping. The voices of the crows leaving their nests at dawn rival his sobs. Are the crows mourning his fate? The thought brings more tears.

JIHEI: Listen to them. The crows have come to guide us to the world of the dead. There's an old saying that every time somebody writes an oath on the back of a Kumano charm, three crows of Kumano die on the holy mountain. The first words we've written each New Year have been vows of love, and how often we've inscribed oaths at the beginning of the month! If each oath has killed three crows, what a multitude must have perished! Their cries have always sounded like "beloved, beloved," but hatred for our crime of taking life makes their voices ring tonight "revenge, revenge!"[67] Whose fault is it they demand revenge? Because of me you will die a painful death. Forgive me!

[66] Amida's paradise lies in the west. The moon is also frequently used as a symbol of Buddhist enlightenment.

[67] The cries have always sounded like *kawai, kawai,* but now they sound like *mukui, mukui.* These Japanese sounds seem more within the range of a crow's articulatory powers than "beloved" and "revenge".

NARRATOR: He takes her in his arms.

KOHARU: No, it's my fault!

NARRATOR: They cling to each other, face pressed to face; their side-locks, drenched with tears, freeze in the winds blowing over the fields. Behind them echoes the voice of the Daichō Temple.

JIHEI: Even the long winter night seems short as our lives.

NARRATOR: Dawn is already breaking, and matins can be heard. He draws her to him.

JIHEI: The moment has come for our glorious end. Let there be no tears on your face when they find you later.

KOHARU: There won't be any.

NARRATOR: She smiles. His hands, numbed by the frost, tremble before the pale vision of her face, and his eyes are first to cloud. He is weeping so profusely that he cannot control the blade.

KOHARU: Compose yourself—but be quick!

NARRATOR: Her encouragement lends him strength; the invocations to Amida carried by the wind urge a final prayer. *Namu Amida Butsu.* He thrusts in the saving sword.[68] Stabbed, she falls backwards, despite his staying hand, and struggles in terrible pain. The point of the blade has missed her windpipe, and these are the final tortures before she can die. He writhes with her in agony, then painfully summons his strength again. He draws her to him, and plunges his dirk to the hilt. He twists the blade in the wound, and her life fades away like an unfinished dream at dawning.

He arranges her corpse head to the north, face to the west, lying on her right side,[69] and throws his cloak over her. He turns away at last, unable to exhaust with tears his grief over parting. He pulls the sash to him and fastens the noose around his neck. The service in the temple has reached the closing section, the prayers for the dead. "Believers and unbelievers will equally share in the divine grace," the voices proclaim, and at the final words Jihei jumps from the sluice gate.

JIHEI: May we be reborn on one lotus! Hail Amida Buddha!

NARRATOR: For a few moments he writhes like a gourd swinging in the wind, but gradually the passage of his breath is blocked as the

[68] The invocation of Amida's name freed one from spiritual obstacles, just as a sword freed one from physical obstacles. Here the two images are blended.

[69] The dead were arranged in this manner because Shakyamuni Buddha chose this position when he died.

stream is dammed by the sluice gate, where his ties with this life are snapped.

Fishermen out for the morning catch find the body in their net.[70]

FISHERMEN: A dead man! Look, a dead man! Come here, everybody!

NARRATOR: The tale is spread from mouth to mouth. People say that they who were caught in the net of Buddha's vow immediately gained salvation and deliverance, and all who hear the tale of the Love Suicides at Amijima are moved to tears.

[70] "Net" (*ami*) is mentioned because of the connection with fishermen. It is echoed a few lines later in the mention of the name *Ami*jima. The vow of the Buddha to save all living creatures is likened to a net which catches people in its meshes. For a further explanation of this image (and of the title of the play), see Shively, p. 41.

APPENDIX I

A NOTE ON PROSTITUTION
IN CHIKAMATSU'S PLAYS

Most of Chikamatsu's domestic plays are directly connected with the activities of the gay quarters, and scenes or whole acts of some of the history plays are also set in this world. The prominence of prostitution in the plays of course reflects conditions in society. In the major cities of Chikamatsu's day the licensed quarters were a center of urban life. It was no disgrace for townsmen to visit the quarters, and their affairs with prostitutes were matters of common gossip. Samurai also frequently visited the quarters, though they might feel obliged to conceal their faces beneath broad wicker hats.

Townsmen and samurai alike went to the quarters for an escape from the tensions and obligations of the feudalistic society in which they lived. They were also likely to be bored with married life. The long-suffering, obedient Japanese wife, for all her virtues, was not an especially interesting partner in conversation, and married men (as well as young blades) found female companionship in the quarters.[1]

In 1679 there were over one hundred licensed quarters in Japan.[1] The courtesans were divided into two classes, the *age-jorō* and the *mise-jorō*. The *age-jorō* was often women of considerable culture whose skill in the arts or conversation won them renown. Though prostitutes, they were privileged to refuse would-be customers. Azuma in *The Uprooted Pine* is a *tayū*, the highest rank of *age-jorō*, and she is represented as refusing her favors to all men except her sweetheart Yojibei. The *mise-jorō*, on the other hand, were common prostitutes, obliged to sleep with any man who paid their fees. Most of the courtesans in Chikamatsu's plays are of this class. He is frequently at pains

[1] See the illuminating article by Ivan Morris, "Hierarchy of Lust in 17th Century Japan" (*Today's Japan*, August, 1960).

to show that, although these women are reputed to be cold-hearted and calculating, they actually possess the deepest affections. Ohatsu in *The Love Suicides at Sonezaki* and Koharu in *The Love Suicides at Amijima* are among the *mise-jorō* who join the men they love in death. Both *age-jorō* and *mise-jorō* were ranked in an elaborate hierarchy. The three top classes of *age-jorō* were the *tayū, tenjin,* and *kakoi,* known also as Pines, Plum-blossoms, and Maple-leaves because of complicated literary allusions. Below these lofty ranks came the Tides, Reflections, and Moons, names derived from a passage in the Nō play *Matsukaze,* "The moon is one, the reflections two, the swelling tides. . .". "Swelling" is the homonym for "three" (*mitsu*), and the passage, as applied to courtesans, came to mean that a Tide received three pieces of silver for her services, a Reflection two pieces, and a Moon only one piece. There were even poorer paid *mise-jorō* in houses (*mise*), as well as streetwalkers. The prices for courtesans ranged from about $350 for a single night with a *tayū* down to about fifty cents for a night with a common *mise-jorō*. Only a "great spender" (*daijin,* a homonym for a word meaning "minister of state") could afford the pleasures of a *tayū*'s company. One reason why her services came so high was that she was invariably accompanied by a Towboat (*hikifune*) of the *kakoi* rank and a courtesan's maid (*kamuro*), both of whom had to be paid for, though they did not sleep with the customer. A steady patron of a courtesan also had to reckon on innumerable tips to her house. On gift days (*mombi*) throughout the year, and especially at the New Year, costly presents had to be offered persons at the courtesan's house, including the proprietress (*kasha*) and the Chaser (*yarite*). The latter apparently served both as a procuress and guardian of the courtesans, but in Chikamatsu's plays she usually figures in the latter function, warding off unwanted guests.

Courtesans of the *mise-jorō* class were generally driven into prostitution by poverty. In many of the plays a *mise-jorō* is portrayed as supporting indigent parents or even working to keep her father out of a debtor's prison. The *age-jorō*, on the other hand, was normally a woman long trained for her calling. At first she served as a *kamuro*, waiting on some great courtesan. Later she graduated to Launch (*shinzō*), or fledgling courtesan, and finally took her place in the hierarchy. An *age-jorō* who had not previously served as a *kamuro* was known as a Debutante (*tsukidashi*).

The pleasures of the quarter frequently ruined the guests. The worst danger to a man's finances was that he might fall deeply in love with a prostitute and decide to buy her freedom. Ransom (*miuke*) involved negotiations with the proprietor of the courtesan's house and then with the owner of her contract. It was an unbelievably expensive process, judging by the figures given in the plays, for it entailed numerous tips and presents. Chūbei (in *The Courier for Hell*) scatters close to ten thousand dollars in gold (using a rough approximation of what the money would buy today) when ransoming Umegawa, a courtesan of low rank. Chikamatsu undoubtedly exaggerated the ransom for theatrical effect, but the cost by any standards was enormous.

APPENDIX II

PUPPET PERFORMANCES OF

CHIKAMATSU'S PLAYS

Chikamatsu's major works were written for the puppet theater. Many later came to be performed also by Kabuki actors, but puppet performances are still considered more authentic than those by actors. Yet the puppet theater itself has changed considerably over the years, and contemporary performances are thus only relatively more faithful than Kabuki to the works as presented in Chikamatsu's day.

The puppet theater was an invention of the late sixteenth century. At this time the three main elements were joined—the puppets (known at least five centuries earlier in Japan), the texts of the plays (derived from historical romances and other narratives), and the musical accompaniment (the samisen, a three-stringed musical instrument introduced from the Ryukyu Islands about 1570). Puppet performances in the seventeenth century, judging from surviving accounts and drawings, were extremely crude. The theaters were at first small, unroofed areas fenced in only by rough bamboo stockades, and without even a rudimentary flooring. Not until 1670 or thereabouts were performances on rainy days made possible by overhead protection. The stage was about thirty feet across, and equipped with both a curtain and a backdrop. The operators in the seventeenth century (as now) stood in trenches several feet below the level of the stage as they moved the puppets.

The puppets in use during Chikamatsu's lifetime were large hand puppets, about two and one half feet tall, operated by one man who held the puppet over his head by inserting both arms inside the skirts of the figure. The operators were at first concealed from the spectators, but the opaque curtain shielding them gave way to one of a gauzy material in 1699, and in 1703, for the final scene of *The Love Suicides at Sonezaki,* the curtain was removed altogether, permitting the operators to be seen plainly.[1]

The chanters, who sang and recited both the narration and the parts of the different characters, until the end of the seventeenth century remained out of the sight of the audience, seated behind the playing stage. But from the time of *The Love Suicides at Sonezaki,* the chanter at times appeared before the public, sitting to stage left with the samisen player who accompanied him. In 1728 the Takemoto Theater installed as a regular part of the theater a dais to stage left for the chanter and musician, and this has remained their place.

Thus, the Japanese puppet theater which originally (like Western counterparts) sought to achieve an illusion of reality by concealing both operator and narrator, in order that the audience might imagine that the puppets moved independently and spoke their lines, gradually turned its back on such realism. This may explain why the puppet theater in Japan attained a higher artistic level than similar entertainments elsewhere.

By renouncing the illusion of reality, the puppet theater was able to develop many refinements. The three-man puppet, the most notable feature of performances today, was evolved after experiments with several different types of puppets. String-operated marionettes were known in the seventeenth century, but were superseded by the puppets most common in Chikamatsu's day (operated from below, in the manner already described). Puppets which could be operated with one arm (and were thus more mobile than the two-arm variety) were tried in the early eighteenth century in an attempt to enhance the spectacular effects. A start was made on three-man puppets in 1728, and they came into general use in 1734.[2] The chief operator of the three men moves the head, body, and right arm; the second operator moves the left arm; and the third operator the feet. Coordination of the movements is extremely difficult, but the three-man puppet is capable of extraordinary subtlety of portrayal. Indeed, the puppets at times surpass actors in ther ability to suggest states of emotional agitation or exaltation; in some plays even today the Kabuki actors deliberately imitate the movements of puppets. The obvious presence of the three

---

[1] See Mori Shū, *Chikamatsu Monzaemon,* pp. 64–66.
[2] Utsumi Shigetarō, *Ningyō Jōruri to Bunraku,* p. 340.

operators, the chief of them attired in formal costume and unmasked (the two assistants usually wear black hoods), never permits the reverse to happen—an attempt by the puppets to imitate Kabuki actors. Despite the demands made on the audience to blot out mentally the presence of the human intruders in the world of the puppets, a powerful dramatic effect is obtained, and the spectators enjoy seeing their favorite operators lovingly follow the puppets around the stage.

Of the three elements which make up puppet performances—the puppets, the texts, and the music—the texts are traditionally considered to be of the greatest importance. The chanters lift the texts reverently before a performance, to express their intent of interpreting them faithfully. The chanter's part is the hardest: he must be expert in speaking with the voices of men and women, old and young, often in rapid succession. The gruff muttering of a warrior is followed by a woman's gentle protestations, and then by a child's plaintive piping, all delivered with intense conviction. The chanter must also possess the vocal beauty necessary for such lyrical passages as the *michiyuki*. Sometimes several chanters divide the parts of a single scene, a young chanter taking the part of the child, an old chanter the part of an old woman, and so on, but more commonly one chanter takes all the parts of a given scene. Each chanter generally works in partnership with his favorite samisen player. In a few plays an accompaniment on an instrument other than the samisen is required, including the *koto* (a zither-like instrument) and the *kokyū* (a doleful-sounding instrument played with a bow).

For most spectators, however, the *jōruri* is above all a theater of puppets. The puppets today stand about three and one half to four feet tall (male puppets are larger and have feet). The costuming is colorful, and the sets, stylized representations of familiar scenes, are at once attractive and designed to permit maximum freedom of movement for the puppet operators. The puppets must be manipulated in exact time with the chanter's words, and he in turn is guided by the samisen.

Chikamatsu's puppet plays have no stage directions in the texts, but various traditions (some perhaps dating back to the eighteenth century) are observed in the stage business (*kata*). The following passage from *Yosaku from Tamba* illustrates how the puppet for the character Shigenoi is operated by Kiritake Monjūrō, an outstanding contemporary performer.

SHIGENOI: Now here you are. You're only a child, I know, but you're the heir of a disgraced father, and I'm worried what may happen if they find you out. (*She strokes Sankichi's right shoulder.*) Never tell anyone that you're Yosaku's child. (*Her voice suggests that she is whispering the words into Sankichi's ear; all the while, however, she is looking from right to left, from one end of the stage to the other, as if to make sure that no one can hear them. She looks into Sankichi's face. Suddenly her emotions overpower her, and she draws him to her lap. She weeps, only to push him away and rise.*) Hurry outside now. (*Sankichi remains crouching helplessly on the floor in tears. She takes his hands and lifts him in her arms, only again to reject him, this time resolutely. She stands and moves stage left.*) Ahhh— (*she glances towards the rear, the quarters of her mistress*) what did I ever do to deserve such a fate? (*She turns stage right towards her child.*) To have my own child (*points with her left hand at Sankichi*) become a horse driver, and not to know where my husband is. (*Points into the distance.*) What use is it to wear fine clothes (*lifts her right and then her left sleeve, and looks at each; then she rearranges the hanging part of the sleeves, as if to assert her dignity*), to be addressed respectfully as madam governess, milady in waiting (*moves her head by degrees from stage left to stage right*), or to ride in a splendid palanquin? (*She swings her sleeves from right to left in irritation; but, suddenly remembering that the robe was a present from her ladyship and should not be treated so roughly, she lifts the right sleeve of the garment reverently over her head for a moment, only to lower it. Fearful that the sound of her weeping may be overheard, she stuffs the sleeve into her mouth and lowers her gaze in grief.*)[3]

This climactic moment, when Shigenoi bites her sleeve to stifle her sobs, is heightened by the prolonged notes of the chanter's voice and the sharp accents of the samisen. The elaborate stage business suggests how much is lost when we read, rather than see, Chikamatsu's plays. We can only hope that the puppet theater, faced by public indifference and financial problems, will somehow survive, so that one of the world's great dramatists may continue to be seen under the circumstances which do him the most justice.

[3] These stage directions are derived from the article by Yoshinaga Takao, "Ningyō no Enshutsu ni tsuite," in *Kaishaku to Kanshō*, XXII (no. 1), 45.

BIBLIOGRAPHY

I have appended brief comments to the Japanese books listed, in the hope that they may be helpful to Western scholars intending to consult them.

TEXTS

Fujii Otoo. *Chikamatsu Zenshū.* 12 vols. 1925–28. A great piece of scholarship and the standard text of Chikamatsu's complete works, but of limited use to Western readers because of the paucity of notes.

Higuchi Yoshichiyo. *Kessaku Jōruri Shū: Chikamatsu Jidai* (in *Hyōshaku Edo Bungaku Sōsho* series). 1935. Helpful and fairly detailed comments on twelve plays given in full or in part.

Itō Masao. *Shinjū Ten no Amijima Shōkai.* 1935. The best commentary and modern Japanese translation of a single play by Chikamatsu.

Kawatake Shigetoshi. *Gendaigoyaku Chikamatsu Meisaku Shū.* 2 vols. 1938. Translations into modern Japanese of fourteen plays. Often helpful, but the *michiyuki* and other complex passages are not translated.

Kuroba Hideo. *Chikamatsu Meisaku Shinkō.* 1957. Detailed commentaries and translations into modern Japanese of five plays. The translations are sometimes mistaken and often misleading.

Shigetomo Ki. *Chikamatsu Jōruri Shū,* I (in *Nihon Koten Bungaku Taikei* series). 1958. Admirable texts and good (though somewhat skimpy) notes on fourteen domestic plays. Now the standard texts for the plays included.

Shuzui Kenji, and Ōkubo Tadakuni. *Chikamatsu Jōruri Shū,* II (in *Nihon Koten Bungaku Taikei series*). 1959. Admirable texts but inadequate notes on six history plays and the preface to *Naniwa Miyage.*

————, and Urayama Masao. *Chikamatsu Meisaku Hyōkai.* 1949. Useful notes and translations into modern Japanese of *Sonezaki Shinjū* and *Nebiki no Kadomatsu.*

Tadami Keizō. *Chikamatsu Jōruri Shū* (in *Yūhōdō Bunko* series). 3 vols. 1926. Texts are punctuated and the speakers indicated, but the notes on these forty-two plays are grossly inadequate. Useful now mainly for plays not found in editions with commentaries.

Takano Masami. *Chikamatsu Monzaemon Shū* (in *Nihon Koten Zensho* series). 3 vols. 1950–52. Texts of nineteen plays with fairly detailed notes.

—— *Chikamatsu Monzaemon Shū* (in *Koten Nihon Bungaku Zenshū* series). 1959. Translations into modern Japanese of thirteen plays. The translations are generally free.

Wakatsuki Yasuji. *Zen'yaku Chikamatsu Kessaku Shū*. 3 vols. 1928–30. Extremely helpful and honest translations into modern Japanese plus useful notes on twenty-four domestic plays. Still indispensable, despite more recent commentaries.

SECONDARY WORKS

Barth, Johannes. "Kagekiyo. Eine Betrachtung zum japanischen historischen Schauspiel." Deutschen Gesellschaft für Natur- und Völkerkunde Ostasiens, *Jubiläumsband,* I (1933), 299–329.

Brenan, Gerald. *The Literature of the Spanish People.* New York, Meridian Books, 1957.

Chikamatsu Kenkyūkai, ed. *Chikamatsu Monzaemon.* 1956. Essays, mainly introductory, plus some bibliographical information.

Engeki Kenkyūkai, ed. *Chikamatsu no Kenkyū to Shiryō.* 1959. A small but valuable collection of essays and source materials.

Fergusson, Francis. *The Idea of a Theater.* Garden City, N.Y., Doubleday, 1949.

Harvey, Paul, ed. *The Oxford Companion to English Literature,* Oxford, Clarendon Press, 1946.

Hibbett, Howard. *The Floating World in Japanese Fiction.* New York, Oxford University Press, 1959.

Higuchi Yoshichiyo. *Chikamatsu Kō.* 1955. Themes in Chikamatsu's writings illustrated by excerpts from the plays. Somewhat old-fashioned in approach, but unquestionably the product of a profound knowledge of the texts.

Hirosue Tamotsu. *Chikamatsu Josetsu.* 1957. A stimulating but sometimes doctrinaire left-wing approach.

Katō Junzō. *Chikamatsu Shishō no Kenkyū.* 1926. Still the best work on Chikamatsu's style.

Kawatake Shigetoshi. *Chikamatsu Monzaemon.* 1958. A popular introduction to Chikamatsu's life and views.

—— *Nihon Engeki Zenshi.* 1959. A mine of information on all aspects of the Japanese theater.

Keene, Donald, ed. *Anthology of Japanese Literature.* New York, Grove Press, 1955.

—— *The Battles of Coxinga.* London, Taylor's Foreign Press, 1951.

—— trans. *Major Plays of Chikamatsu.* New York, Columbia University Press, 1961.

Kitani Hōgin. *Chikamatsu no Tennō Geki.* 1947. Chikamatsu's "emperor plays" classified and described; a product of the postwar "humanization."

Kuroki Kanzō. *Chikamatsu Monzaemon.* 1942. Mainly devoted to summaries of the chief plays, but contains some valuable essays.

McCullough, H. C., trans. *The Taiheiki.* New York, Columbia University Press, 1959.

Maejima Shunzō. *Chikamatsu Kenkyū no Johen.* 1925. Advanced for its time, but now largely superseded.

Mashimo Saburō. "Chikamatsu no Sakuhin ni mirareru Joseigo," *Kokugo to Kokubungaku,* October, 1959. An important study of women's language in Chikamatsu.

Minamoto Ryōen. "Chikamatsu ni okeru Ai to Shi," *Kokoro,* June, 1960. A student of philosophy examines themes in Chikamatsu.

Miyamori, Asataro. *Masterpieces of Chikamatsu.* London, Kegan Paul, 1926.

Mori Shū. *Chikamatsu Monzaemon.* 1959. The best book on Chikamatsu; unqualifiedly recommended.

Morris, Ivan. "Hierarchy of Lust in 17th Century Japan," *Today's Japan,* August, 1960.

Nakada Yasunao. "Chikamatsu to Chōnin no Sekai," *Kokugo to Kokubungaku,* January, 1955. An interesting study of the background of the plays.

Nakamura Kichizō. *Nihon Gikyoku Gikō Ron.* 1942. Analysis by a student of Western drama of the structures and techniques of plays by Chikamatsu and later men.

Ōkubo Tadakuni. *Chikamatsu* (in *Nihon Koten Kanshō Kōza* series). 1957. Extracts with notes from six plays, plus a number of good essays.

Sanari Kentarō. *Yōkyoku Taikan.* 7 vols. 1931. The standard work.

Sansom, G. B. "The *Tsuredzuregusa* of Yoshida no Kaneyoshi," Asiatic Society of Japan, *Transactions,* XXXIX, 1911.

Seo Fukiko. "Chikamatsu ni okeru Nōminteki naru mono," *Bungaku,* July, 1951. Stiffly written but well documented study of the "peasant mentality" in Chikamatsu's plays.

Sheldon, Charles David. *Rise of the Merchant Class in Tokugawa Japan.* Locust Valley, N.Y., J. J. Augustin, 1958.

Shigetomo Ki, ed. *Chikamatsu no Hitobito.* 1950. Essays of uneven interest, the best being one by Tanabe Yukio on the character of Chūbei.

Shinoda Jun'ichi. "Shusse Kagekiyo no Seiritsu ni tsuite," *Kokugo Kokubun,* June, 1959. Brilliant analysis of the background and structure of Chikamatsu's important early play.

Shively, Donald H. "Chikamatsu's Satire on the Dog Shogun," *Harvard Journal of Asiatic Studies,* XXVIII (1955), 159–80.

—— *The Love Suicide at Amijima.* Cambridge, Harvard University Press, 1953.

Shuzui Kenji. *Chikamatsu Monzaemon.* 1949. A general introduction.

—— *Giri.* 1941. An interesting essay on the manner in which *giri* is treated by Chikamatsu and later playwrights.

Statler, Oliver. *Japanese Inn.* New York, Random House, 1961.

Takano Masami. "Chikamatsu Sakuhin no Bunruihō," *Kokugo to Kokubungaku,* March, 1948. A useful guide to the classification of Chikamatsu's plays.

Takano Tatsuyuki. *Nihon Engeki no Kenkyū.* 1921. Valuable essays by a great scholar.

—— *Nihon Engeki Shi,* III. 1949. Unexciting but thorough.

Tanamachi Tomomi. "Chikamatsu Kenkyū Bunken Mokuroku," *Kaishaku to Kanshō,* January, 1957. The best bibliography of Chikamatsu studies. Particularly useful because of its evaluations.

Tjikamats, Monzâemon. *Dramatische Verhalen,* translated into Dutch by S. van Praag. Santpoort, C. A. Mees, 1927.

Tsunoda, Ryusaku, *et al. Sources of the Japanese Tradition.* New York, Columbia University Press, 1958.

Ueda Mannen, and Higuchi Yoshichiyo. *Chikamatsu Go-i.* 1930. Universally praised but maddening work. One loses so much time consulting it that the information gained seldom seems worth the trouble. Mercifully now largely superseded.

Utsumi Shigetarō. *Ningyō Jōruri to Bunraku.* 1958. Emphasizes the importance of puppets in *jōruri.* Long and diffuse.

—— *Ningyō Shibai to Chikamatsu no Jōruri.* 1940. Much in the same vein as the preceding, but more engrossing.

Wakatsuki Yasuji. *Chikamatsu Ningyō Jōruri no Kenkyū.* 1936. A massive study, full of useful information.

—— *Ningyō Jōruri Shi Kenkyū.* 1942. Probably the best history of the *jōruri.*

Waley, Arthur. *The Nō Plays of Japan.* New York, Knopf, 1922.

Watsuji Tetsurō. *Nihon Geijutsu Shi Kenkyū,* I. 1955. A scholarly work by an outstanding authority.

Yokoyama Tadashi. "Chikamatsu Michiyuki Zakkō," *Kokugo Kokubun,* September, 1940. This and the following three articles are careful studies of specific features of Chikamatsu's writings.

—— "Chikamatsu no Maruhon," *Kaishaku to Kanshō,* January, 1957.

—— "Chikamatsu Shinjū Jōruri no Tenkai," *Kokugo to Kokubungaku,* May, 1958.

—— "Chikamatsu Shoki Shinjū Jōruri ni okeru Bōto Hyōgen," *Kokugo to Kokubungaku,* October, 1958.

Yoshinaga Takao. "Ningyō no Enshutsu ni tsuite," *Kaishaku to Kanshō,* January, 1957. Valuable especially for the detailed account of a present-day production of a scene from *Tamba Yosaku.*

Yuda Yoshio. "Chikamatsu Nempyō," *Kaishaku to Kanshō,* January, 1957. The best chronology of Chikamatsu.

—— "Sonezaki Shinjū no Kabukiteki Kiban" (in Kansai Daigaku Kokubungakkai: *Shimada Kyōju Koki Kinen Kokubungaku Ronshū,* ed. by Iida Shōichi and others, 1960). Excellent account of Kabuki precedents for Chikamatsu's famous play.